D1547161

Black Politics in New York City

Black Politics

in

New York City

Edwin R. Lewinson

Seton Hall University

Twayne Publishers, Inc.   ::   New York

Library of Congress Cataloging in Publication Data

Lewinson, Edwin R
    Black politics in New York city.

    Bibliography: p. 221.
    1. Negroes—New York (City)—Politics and suffrage.
I. Title.
F128.9.N3L48   320.9'747'104   73-1744
ISBN 0-8057-5326-5

MANUFACTURED IN THE UNITED STATES OF AMERICA

To my favorite restaurateur
Dick Edwards
and his staff

Acknowledgments

I began the research which resulted in this book when I was searching for a topic for a doctoral dissertation in history at Columbia University in 1953. Many people have helped me through the years. Mrs. Jean Blackwell Hudson and her staff at the Schomberg Collection have been of invaluable aid. I have also received help from the main branch of the New York Public Library and the Manuscripts Division of the Library of Congress. When the New York *Herald-Tribune* ceased publication, its morgue was given to the New York University Library. Mrs. May Bowler not only made her knowledge of the arrangement of the clippings available to me and allowed me to use them, but gave me special permission to take batches of clippings out of the building for more convenient research.

Being totally blind, I accumulated material by having people read to me and taking notes in Braille. Most of my readers have been volunteers at the New York Association for the Blind, generally known as the Lighthouse. Through the years literally hundreds of people have read to me. My heartfelt thanks go both to the volunteers and to the Lighthouse staff members who have obtained and scheduled readers for me and for other blind people.

The list of those whom I have interviewed as part of this project is found in the bibliography. I owe them a deep debt of gratitude for their helpfulness and co-operation. My special thanks go to Julian Garfield and Arthur Williams, who have made available written material concerning the organizations of black transit employees and firemen respectively. My friend Collis Crocker not only furnished me with valuable reminiscences of the years when he was one of J. Raymond Jones's principal assistants, but read and criticized portions of the manuscript. Other friends who have read and criticized portions of the manuscript include Dr. John Duff, Provost of Seton Hall University, Professor August Meier of Kent State University, Professor George Furniss of Grinnell College in Iowa, and Dr. Jacob Freid of the Jewish Braille Institute of America. Professor Furniss, who wrote his doctoral dissertation on the political assimilation of Negroes in New York, not only made helpful suggestions for the manuscript, but made his notes and the results of his personal interviews available to me.

The research for this book was facilitated by a summer grant in 1966 from the American Philosophical Society.

In 1967 Richard Natole, who was then an undergraduate student at Seton Hall, worked as my research assistant under a work-study grant. His pleasantness and helpfulness greatly eased my tasks.

Miss Alice M. Johnson, a volunteer at the Lighthouse and head proofreader at Price Waterhouse Co., donated her services in reading the proofs.

When it is too late, I will probably remember people whom I have forgotten to thank. I hope that they will not confuse my forgetfulness with an intentional slight. Needless to say, I assume the sole responsibility for errors and misinterpretations.

EDWIN R. LEWINSON

Introduction

New York is probably the only city in the United States where the development of Blacks in politics could have occurred as it did. Professor Edwin R. Lewinson's book, *Black Politics in New York City*, pulls together, in a straightforward manner, the elements which contributed to this development. His study of Blacks in politics in New York City covers a period of over one hundred and fifty years. Woven throughout Professor Lewinson's account of the Black man's struggle for political respect and power is the optimistic hope that the progress that has been made in the past is somewhat of an indication of hope for more meaningful advancements in the future. The author seems to concur with a statement by the late U.S. Congressman Adam Clayton Powell which he quotes in his book, "I'm always optimistic. To be pessimistic is to die."

Nonetheless, the author is not so optimistic as not to openly present the variables which must be made constant in order that his closing lines can come true: "Even in the cosmopolitan atmosphere of New York, prejudice and poverty have hobbled the Black struggle to gain political recognition to a slower pace than the progress of earlier groups. But recognition has come, and it will increasingly come in the future. For New York Negroes [Blacks] as for other groups, political participation has constituted one means of attempting to make the American dream a reality."

In reading *Black Politics in New York City,* giving all due deference to the size and relative political sophistication of this City, and because of Prof. Lewinson's thoroughness and honesty with the subject matter, I was left with the question, "how long?"

Since I have been Mayor of Newark, New Jersey, I have stated and restated that I am testing the system. Considering the fact that the United States of America is an experiment, and as nations go, not a particularly old experiment, the author's desire for Blacks to remain in the laboratory of social, economic and political experimentation has merit.

Black Politics in New York City demonstrates that there is much to be learned from the successes and failures of the people and the processes which have taken place in our nation's largest city. It requires that we go from the specific to the general and apply that which is applicable—deductive politics. The less than 1% of elected public officials who are Black can only be seen as the foundation of a four-sided pyramid on which to build social equality, political power, economic inclusion, and ideological purpose. When this pyramid reaches its pinnacle, it will probably be the most meaningful place on which to raise our national flag. Prof. Lewinson's book relates those examples of progress which could lead to this accomplishment.

Professor Lewinson's study would be a learning experience for most people, even the scholarly. Within the context of New York politics, the author takes the pieces of the puzzle from the time when Black people were virtually excluded from politics, even the "privilege" of voting for politicians from other ethnic groups, to the time of Black political influence and the advent of political leaders such as Adam Clayton Powell, J. Raymond Jones and Shirley Chisholm, and puts them in place. Thus, one sees a picture rather than pieces. Irrespective of one's political analysis, or whether or not one agrees with the import placed on certain people and events by the author, the organization of events is extremely valuable.

How and why did Black people change from strongly supporting the Republican party and move slowly and steadily into the Democratic column? What influenced the first major appointments of Black people to high level political positions? Who were the key people in bringing about these appointments? What was there in the Caribbean Blacks' background that made them proportionately outdistance Afro-Americans in the political race? Why did Black migrant southerners excel politically over northern Blacks? What were the cross-currents which confounded solidarity between Black people in politics and impeded Black political progress? *Black Politics in New York City* delves into these and other pertinent questions.

Professor Lewinson examines, to a large extent, the desire of Black politicians to receive political patronage as opposed to concentrating on profound social change. Although this was one of the few avenues open to Black people to enter the "middle class," in the long run it has proven to be the "Achilles' heel" of general upward mobility for the Black masses. When the author discusses

Introduction

Dr. Kenneth Clark's *Youth in the Ghetto*, it is implicit in the examples of social conditions selected by the author that the poor remained poor, for the most part, throughout the period of time covered by the book.

The author does not indulge often in direct criticism of the political system of the United States. Most of the faults to be found are implicit in Lewinson's account of the facts. Perhaps his most direct criticism is to be found in his closing words of the chapter on the late Congressman Adam Clayton Powell: The author wrote: "Yet, Adam Clayton Powell has undoubtedly enshrined himself as a permanent Black hero. His greatest contribution is in giving Black Americans a sense of self and self-esteem, of full manhood, of having wombs to give birth to fully male humans. Powell himself was the creature of the Black ghetto and of a manner designed, enforced, and perpetuated by White men. The fatal dualism in him is, in fact, a symptom of the double moral standard, and ultimately, of the hypocrisy of White America."

If one just glances at the hope the author has for greater inclusion of Black people in the social, political and economic life of the United States, then one will not see that the author understands the "hypocrisy" which must change. Implicit in Prof. Lewinson's desire for more meaningful participation by Blacks is not the current political notions of "a piece of the action" or "a bigger slice of the pie," but the total social, political and economic telescopic evolution which must take place before this participation is possible.

Also, implicit in his writing are the changes caused by racism, in the rules of the social, political, economic process when Black people become involved. The normal economic growth pattern can be disrupted by irate immigrant Whites. The voting patterns can change when a Black candidate is seeking elected office. Political boundaries are gerrymandered to contain Black political power. The political trade-offs come to Black people at much greater expense. The power of an office, or political "tradition," does not remain constant. Yes, the rules generally change; and the implications of these changes fill the book. Therefore, the reader is forced to go below the surface of that which is written, but the guidelines are crystal clear. Perhaps, this is what drove Adam Clayton Powell to say: "As a member of Congress, I have done nothing more than any other member and by the grace of God, I intend to do not one bit less."

BLACK POLITICS IN NEW YORK CITY

For me, the most valuable chapter, in terms of knowledge which I was lacking, was some insight into the life, growth and style of "The Fox," J. Raymond Jones. Professor Lewinson explains in some detail how Jones defied the "rule changes" by shrewdly outguessing his political colleagues. This is an unusual account of a great political leader. It is necessary because his style was to avoid publicity and maintain a low public profile while wielding power the likes of which no other Black had within his grasp prior to his time.

Professor Lewinson's book must be read, particularly at this point in time when the whole proposition of whether or not this system is worth saving is being asked from all corners of our country. Moreover, the entire world is taking a serious look at the viability of the political system under which we live, seriously questioning our stability in light of some rather bizarre political and economic practices to reach questionable goals. Again, Prof. Lewinson leaves us with the positive prospect of hope for the future. Many Blacks are still willing to share that hope and continue the experiment, which is the United States. Yet, using *Black Politics in New York City* to go from the specific to the general, it is the system which will be questioned and not hope. Historically, people have strived for a better tomorrow, which is synonymous with hope. Sooner or later, racism will no longer blind us to or confuse our mutual desire to have our basic need fulfilled, irrespective of race. At this point "hope" will be required to become a reality. . . . Or this newly organized mass will demand viable alternatives.

KENNETH A. GIBSON
Mayor

Newark, New Jersey

Contents

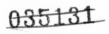

CHAPTER 1

Overview

In their efforts to combat racial discrimination, Negroes have sometimes regarded political activity with cynicism and suspicion. Black distrust of politics has partially resulted from a feeling of powerlessness. A related factor has been the years of disfranchisement in the South after temporarily successful efforts to enter the political arena during Reconstruction. Blacks have frequently felt that political candidates and issues were irrelevant to their particular needs. This feeling has often resulted in a lower rate of political participation than among whites. Black suspicions about politics have been directed at political leaders of both races. Whites have been accused of being unresponsive to black needs and demands, while blacks have been charged with subservience to white domination and susceptibility to opportunism. Sometimes these accusations have been justified; at other times they have not.

Despite such misgivings politics is a major road to the achievement of power and leverage in American society for blacks, as it has been for ethnic groups in the past and continues to be for Latin Americans in various parts of the United States today. Both the importance of Negroes as a political factor and the importance of political activity to the black community are increasing and will continue to increase in the foreseeable future. The importance of blacks as a political factor stems not only from their being 10 percent of the population and the nation's largest minority, but from their concentration in the cities of the North and their inextricable involvement with the fate of the United States as an urban society. Political activity is of continued and increasing importance to the black community because it provides potentially the most effective vehicle for the expression of grievances and the most effective form of pressure to bring about their remedy. In striving for political power, Negroes have resembled other groups and yet have faced problems peculiar to their situation and experience. Like members of ethnic groups, they have received recognition as their numbers have increased. But recognition has frequently come more slowly and hesitantly because of race prejudice, because of a feeling of powerlessness which has sometimes made black people reluctant to register and vote, and because the majority of Negroes have been poor and therefore have had only votes and not money to contribute to the coffers of political parties. To a considerable degree Negroes are still in the position occupied by immigrant groups several decades ago before they moved into the middle class in large numbers. Although politics has been altered by the fact that since the New Deal the federal government has exercised many of the functions formerly performed by political clubs, Negroes are still largely preoccupied with using politics to gain recognition and personal security. To blacks more than to ethnic groups which have moved into the middle class in large numbers, issues such as fair treatment by the police and by landlords and adequate welfare payments are more meaningful than democratic political organizations, economy and efficiency in government, and lower taxes.

As yet, the process by which Negroes have gained political power has been thoroughly studied only in Chicago, probably because they gained recognition earlier in Chicago than in other cities.[1] As has frequently been the case with other groups, more blacks live in New York City than in any other city in the world. Nevertheless the Negro percentage is small compared to the percentage in some other cities. According to the 1970 census 19 percent of New York's population is Negro, compared with more than 50 percent in Newark and Washington and more than one third in Cleveland and Detroit. Portions of each of New York's five boroughs are predominantly black. Negroes are concentrated in sufficiently large numbers in all but Staten Island to enable them to elect at least one member of the race to the State Assembly, the lower house of the state legislature, and one to be a district leader and thus have a voice in party councils. Every court but the Court of Appeals has at least one black judge. At this writing other elected black New York City officeholders include two members of Congress, two members of the City Council, the borough president of Manhattan, and state senators from Manhattan, Brooklyn, and the Bronx.

Black involvement in New York City politics goes back at least to the early nineteenth century. Negroes were disfranchised in most Northern states in the years before the Civil War. Most New York

Negroes were disfranchised by the Constitutional Convention of 1821, and remained unable to vote until the adoption of the Fifteenth Amendment to the Federal Constitution in 1870. In the intervening years the political activities of blacks were largely confined to efforts to get the right to vote on an equal basis.

Between 1870 and the turn of the century Negroes voted and participated in politics in New York City, but they received little recognition, even when compared with members of the race in other cities. The first black member of the Illinois legislature took his seat in Springfield in 1876, and by the turn of the century Negroes had been elected to state legislatures and boards of aldermen from predominantly black constituencies in several cities and states. None were elected in New York at this time because they were not concentrated in sufficiently large numbers in any one district and because the vast majority of Negroes were Republican and the city government was normally Democratic.

The first permanent organization of black Democrats was founded at the time of the formation of greater New York in 1898. Its existence meant more jobs for blacks, the beginning of a division of the black vote, and majorities for mayoral and gubernatorial candidates in the early 1920's, a decade before Negroes began voting Democratic in most other parts of the country. "In most Northern cities," wrote Samuel Lubell, "the Democrats have actually developed a ladder-like succession of posts, where the political progress of various minority elements is recognized. . . . The earliest stirrings of any group usually are appeased by an appointment as assistant district attorney, which entails little more than that some members of the group be educated as Lawyers." [2]

Negroes attained this rung of the ladder at the turn of the century. Before a minority ethnic or racial group is able to achieve elective office, its political leadership is selected by party leaders. Because their power emanates from the party leadership and not from the minority group, their ability to articulate and advance the aims of their group is often limited. Elected officials whose power is derived from the votes of minority group members can show more independence.

For New York Negroes elective office had to await the migration of large numbers to Harlem during World War I. Early Harlem residents included a group of middle-class blacks who were independent of the political power structure and who possessed the money and know-how necessary to make demands for civic improvements and to conduct independent political campaigns.

After several unsuccessful attempts the independent candidates for the State Assembly and for the Board of Aldermen in the districts with the largest number of Negroes defeated the organization candidates in the Republican primaries and went on to win the general election. The first member of the race was elected to the State Assembly in 1917, and the first black alderman was chosen two years later.

Between 1929 and 1939 Negroes defeated and took over Republican and Democratic party organizations in Harlem. They won the leadership of the organizations of each party while that party was in a weakened condition. Blacks obtained leadership posts in the Republican Party while the Democrats were in control both of the city and state. They won Tammany leadership while La-Guardia and the Fusionists were in control of City Hall and the local Democratic organization was feuding intermittently with the state and national organizations.

In an effort to increase their share of the vote, third or minor parties have frequently run black candidates in districts with some Negroes, but with too few to attain major party recognition at the time. Comparing gains made by Negroes politically in Chicago and New York, James Q. Wilson concludes that blacks have made more gains in New York because of frequent divisions within the ranks of the Democratic Party of the city and state. For example, such divisions were responsible for the election of the first state supreme court justice, member of the state senate, and borough president of Manhattan.

Thirty years passed between the election of the first black officeholder from Manhattan and his counterpart from Brooklyn, the first from one of the other boroughs. Negroes began to move into the Bedford-Stuyvesant area of Brooklyn and to integrate the St. Albans section of Queens in the 1930's. Yet the settlement of blacks in large numbers in parts of the city outside Manhattan has largely been a post–World War II occurrence. The sections of Brooklyn, Bronx, and Queens occupied predominantly by Negroes have all been on direct subway routes from Harlem, and have offered the possibility of escape from overcrowded Harlem living conditions, and have contained low-cost housing. The years which elapsed between the election of the first black officeholders in Manhattan and Brooklyn and the increasing numbers and power of the city's black community meant that Negroes were increasingly visible politically as well as in other ways. Although blacks have had to struggle for political recognition both in Brooklyn and in Queens, their struggle was more purely a power struggle and less a combination of a power struggle with race prejudice than had been the efforts of Manhattan Negroes. "Members of the New group serve sometimes as intermediaries between the group and the older leaders," wrote Robert Dahl, "acquiring in the process moderate influence and experience as subleaders. Some of these ethnic subleaders eventually receive nominations for minor offices . . . where the constituency is drawn primarily from the subleader's ethnic group."[3] In three boroughs outside Manhattan, blacks took this route to elective office and district leadership, rather than defeating the party candidates in a primary as they had done in Manhattan. The Democratic organization in the Bronx anticipated the demands of blacks and Puerto Ricans for recognition and chose them to run for elective office and as district leaders before they could challenge the party leadership.

The careers of two New York Negro political leaders, Adam Clayton Powell and J. Raymond Jones, require special study and analysis because they enjoyed more than purely local power, because of their contrasting leadership styles, and the contrasting roles which the question of race played in their careers. Throughout his career Powell was relatively independent of the New York Democratic Party organization. His power was largely personal, based on his church, the force of his personality, and his ability to make black people identify with him. Because of his flamboyance and his concentration upon the civil rights issue, he became undoubtedly the best-known black political leader in American history and to many people the symbol of black political leadership and participation. Perhaps his greatest source of strength while at the same time his greatest shortcoming was his embodiment of the aspirations and the limitations of the average black man. In a sense, he was the average Negro writ large.

On the other hand Jones rose to power and prominence because of his skill as a political strategist. A native of the Virgin Islands, his career resembled the careers of generations of white immigrants who, possessing ambition and ability but lacking money and education, employed politics as a ladder to wealth, power, and social mobility. Although Jones was keenly interested in promoting racial progress and he never forgot that the source of his power rested upon the black vote, he conceived of his role as that of a political leader rather than a race leader.

For Negroes as for ethnic groups, increased political recognition has resulted in more group members holding city and state civil service jobs. The presence of civil service jobs has helped all groups move into the middle class, though it has been more important for some than for others. It has been especially helpful to Negroes because prejudice has often barred them from jobs in the private sector. Like members of other groups, blacks have formed organizations of employees working in the same department which combine social and political functions. In the mid-1950's black civil service groups were strong and numerous enough to form a citywide federation. A large proportion of black civil servants either hold high-level positions dependent upon political influence or low-level unskilled jobs. Comparatively few hold middle-level jobs because questions on examinations have frequently been geared to white middle-class backgrounds and because promotion ladders beyond a certain point have frequently required formal training which was available to comparatively few blacks. Black groups, organizations of public employees such as the State, County, and Municipal Workers, and the City Department of Personnel, are making efforts to remedy this situation.

The future role of the black community in the political life of the city depends upon a number of factors. These include the party alignments within the city and state and which groups appeal most strongly for black votes, the caliber of black leadership and the personalities of individual leaders, the rate of increase of the black middle class and how large a segment of the black middle class remains in the city, and the availability of funds and programs to fight poverty and to raise the economic level of low-income neighborhoods. The black percentage in the city will probably continue to rise in the foreseeable future, though at a slower rate than in many other cities. From time to time Negroes will undoubtedly be elected to city- and statewide office. Black demands for political recognition and for the satisfaction of their needs by the power structure will increase. Study and analysis of the past will most certainly shed light on what is to be.

CHAPTER 2

Slavery and Disfranchisement

New Yorkers owned slaves for almost two centuries. With the coming of abolition, Negroes were accused of political subservience to their former masters. Therefore, the framers of a new state constitution removed them from the political arena by requiring them to own such a large amount of property in order to vote that all but a few were disfranchised. For fifty years Negroes tried unsuccessfully to obtain equal suffrage. But no political party needed their votes, and they remained disfranchised until after the Civil War, when the Republicans required the votes of the race in the South.

I

Among the earliest inhabitants of the Dutch colony of New Amsterdam were Negro slaves. The Dutch made the first settlement on what is now Governor's Island in 1624. By 1626, the year in which Manhattan Island was purchased from the Indians, eleven Negroes were in the colony. Although the Dutch West India Company tried to encourage the importation of Negro slaves, this type of servitude did not flourish under the Dutch. During these years Negroes could obtain their freedom by working for a specified number of years. Some Negroes owned land, and a member of the race held the office of hangman. It was his duty "to lay the latch on the back of all offenders, white or black, male or female, and to pierce their ears and their tongues with hot skewers." [1]

Slavery did take root when the English captured the colony from the Dutch in 1664. That it could be rigorous even in a Northern colony is shown by the slave insurrection of 1712 and the real or imagined Negro plot of 1741. Both events occurred in New York City. About midnight of April 6, 1712, twenty-four slaves gathered in an apple orchard on the outskirts of the town. Some were armed with firearms, some with swords, and some with knives and hatchets.

21

The slaves set fire to an outhouse and then waited in the orchard, expecting to ambush the townspeople who were attracted to the vicinity by the blaze. The first group of whites were surprised, and nine were killed and six wounded. But those who managed to escape spread the alarm, and the next group of whites came armed. After a short struggle all the slaves were killed, captured, or forced to flee to the woods. Eventually, those in the woods were killed or captured. As a result of this riot, a slave code was enacted which made it necessary for a master to post bond before freeing a slave, and forbade free Negroes to own property. This code existed with some modifications as late as 1776. Historians disagree as to whether there actually was a Negro plot in 1741 but, plot or no plot, the fear of one caused as great a panic as had the riot thirty years before. On March 18, 1741, the fort where the Battery now stands was burned. Other fires followed in quick succession. About a month after the fires began, a white indentured servant girl was called before a grand jury to give evidence about a robbery planned at her master's tavern. Under pressure the girl told a story which involved an attempt by Negroes to burn the town, kill the whites, and set themselves up as rulers. In addition to the Negroes, she implicated her master, his wife and daughter, and a prostitute who lived with the family. The tension was heightened because at this time the lieutenant-governor of the province received a letter from the governor of Georgia saying that the Spanish were sending Negroes and Indians to attack all the English colonies. After a series of trials, a number of Negroes and whites, including a newly arrived Episcopal minister who was charged with secretly being a Catholic priest, were killed or forced to leave the colony.[2]

New York, like other Northern states, abolished slavery in the generation following the American Revolution. But as early as 1718 John Burling was writing pamphlets and tracts against Negro servitude. Although many New York Quakers themselves owned slaves, they were the earliest abolitionists. In 1767 the Quakers of Flushing adopted a resolution condemning slavery as inconsistent with the spirit of Christianity. At a provincial meeting in 1771 they agreed not to sell slaves to non-Quakers. The same gathering resulted in the appointment of committees to visit slaveholders and urge them to free their slaves. The Quakers were soon joined by other groups. For years liquor from New York had gone to Africa, where it had been given to natives in return for slaves. The distillers of New York

City resolved to distill no more molasses or syrup for the purpose of carrying on the slave trade. Many slaveholders freed their slaves voluntarily, and some were among the strongest advocates of abolition. They were influenced by the same doctrines of natural law and human rights which served as the philosophic basis of the Declaration of Independence and the American Revolution. Yet, slaveholders did not make a great personal sacrifice when they freed their bondsmen. Slavery was never as important in the North as in the South. As the eighteenth century progressed, it grew increasingly unimportant in the economic life of New York. At the time that New York abolitionists were becoming vocal, most slaves worked for the wealthy as house servants and farm hands, and white labor was becoming increasingly more plentiful.

Opponents of slavery usually expressed their views in moral terms. Edgar J. McManus, the historian of slavery in New York, found that on many manumission certificates the master had written that he was freeing his slaves in order to serve the cause of humanity. Many of the leaders of the New York abolition movement were believers in the rule of the upper class, a fact which later affected Negro political participation. In a state constitutional convention in 1777 Gouverneur Morris, always an opponent of democracy, introduced a resolution urging future legislatures "to take the most effective measures consistent with public safety for abolishing domestic slavery." The resolution looked forward to a day when "every human being who breathes the air of this state shall enjoy the privileges of a free man." John Jay, an aristocrat who was later to become governor of New York and Chief Justice of the United States Supreme Court, wrote in 1780: "Til America comes to this measure, our prayers to Heaven for liberty will be impious.... Were I in your legislature I would prepare a bill [for abolishing slavery] with great care, and I would never cease moving it until it became a law or I ceased to be a member." [3] In 1785 a group of leading citizens of New York City formed the Society for Promoting the Manumission of Slaves and Protecting Them as Have Been or May Be Liberated. John Jay was the first president and Alexander Hamilton the first secretary of the organization, which became popularly known as the Manumission Society. The preamble of the Society's constitution declared, "It is our duty to endeavor, by lawful ways and means to enable them [the slaves] to share equally with us in ... civil and religious liberty ... to which our brethren are, by nature, as much entitled as ourselves." In the range of its activities the Manumission Society resembled a modern civil rights group. It not only lobbied for legislation restricting and abolishing slavery, but it conducted investigations and legal proceedings leading to the freedom of individual slaves. A committee of the Society guarded against efforts to sell free Negroes back into slavery. The Society compiled a list of vessels engaged in the slave trade, as well as lists of their owners and captains. The list was made available to the public so that people could boycott such firms. The abolitionist group employed such familiar methods of publicity as articles in newspapers, printed literature, inviting prominent citizens to serve as honorary members, and awarding medals for special work on behalf of Negroes. The efforts of the Manumission Society went beyond the mere abolition of slavery; its members were equally concerned with the welfare of free Negroes. Even at this time some white women gave birth to mulatto children out of wedlock. Members of the Manumission Society protected these children from social ostracism by providing for their care. Moreover, the Society helped free Negroes secure employment and founded the first colored schools in New York City.

By the 1780's most New Yorkers agreed upon the desirability of abolition, but they disagreed widely as to the status of the free Negroes. An abolition law did not pass the State Legislature in 1785 because members of the two houses could not decide whether Negroes should have the same legal rights as other citizens and whether they should be allowed to vote. Such considerations delayed abolition for over a decade. Nevertheless, the State Legislature hacked away at slavery and at the rights of slaveholders bit by bit. During the American Revolution slaves who served in the army for three years were given their freedom. A law of 1785 freed any slave who was brought into the state to be sold, and fined the seller £100. The next year the legislature freed "all Negro slaves becoming the property of this State, by attainder or by conviction of any person whomsoever, and now in the possession of the Commissioners of Forfeitures." In 1788 all slaves purchased for resale were declared free, and their purchasers were fined £100, and in 1798 all legally defective manumissions were validated. The legislature finally insured complete abolition in 1799 when it passed a law freeing all slave children born after July 4 of that year. According to this law, males were to be servants of their mother's proprietor until the age of twenty-eight and females until twenty-five. Two years later, the legislature restricted importation of slaves so drastically as to amount to prohibition. In the next few years masters were compelled to teach slaves to read the Scriptures, and slaves were permitted to own real and personal property, to marry, and to obtain their freedom by serving in the Army or Navy during the War of 1812. The legislature struck the final blow for abolition on March 31, 1817, when it decreed that all slaves born before 1799 should be free on July 4, 1827.[4]

II

In New York freedom did not result in antagonism between the ex-master and his one-time servant. On the contrary, many Negroes undoubtedly retained close relationships with their former owners. Moreover, ex-slaveholders led the Manumission Society, which worked for abolition and showed concern for the welfare of free Negroes. The majority of members of the Manumission Society as well as most ex-slaveholders were believers in government by an elite, and Negroes voted with them.

In the years following the ratification of the Federal Constitution, the Federalist Party advocated government by the few, while the Republicans believed in greater democracy. A popular Republican campaign song of the day began, "Federalists with blacks unite." The Republicans of New York City formed the Tammany Society. This group, begun for social purposes and to celebrate patriotic holidays such as the Fourth of July, soon became political. In opposition, the Federalists organized the Washington Benevolent Society, including a Negro auxiliary.[5] In 1809 Joseph Sidney, a colored political orator, told members of his race that the right of suffrage carried with it "the indispensible duty of bestowing our votes on those and on those only, whose talents and whose political, moral, and religious principles will most effectively promote the best interests of America." He went on to urge Negro voters "to unite with our Federal friends to bring about this desirable change, so important to commence, to our best interests and the prosperity and glory of our country."[6] In 1820 DeWitt Clinton, a Republican, accepted the support of the Federalists in his successful campaign for reelection as governor. When he won the election, Negroes joined in offering him their congratulations. "Resolved: that we the People of Color Present Our Humble Congratulations to His Excellency's Veneration on Being Re-elected by our utmost endeavors as our Chief Commander and Governor of the State of New York. With sentiments of gratitude from past favors we humbly hope His Excellency will pardon the Liberty we have taken to Drop him those few lines. But to assure His Excellency on the part which he have triumphed over his opponents Makes Us Rejoice with One Accord." [7]

During this period the political control of New York City and state seesawed back and forth between the Federalists and Republicans, with the large vote of the city sometimes determining the political complexion of the state. In some elections, Negroes, who were one tenth of the population of the city, played a pivotal role, and in one, that of 1812, their votes seem to have been decisive.

The Republicans made every effort to limit the number and effectiveness of Negro voters. Republican election inspectors carefully examined every Negro's certificate of freedom in the hope of finding that some were slaves. The 1811 session of the legislature passed a law requiring Negro voters to obtain special identification certificates. By amendments to the law in 1813 and 1815 the legislature increased the "red tape" involved in getting the certificates.[8]

At a state constitutional convention held in Albany in 1821 the Republicans saw a chance of depriving the Federalists of a block of votes by disfranchising the Negroes. They frankly expressed their feelings. "At present," a delegate from Delaware County told the convention in a typical speech, "the number of blacks is so small that if they were scattered all over the state there would not be much danger to be apprehended; but if we may judge of the future by the past, I should suppose there was some cause for alarm—when a few hundred free Negroes in the city of New York, following the train of those who ride in their coaches and whose shoes and boots they had so often blacked, shall go to the polls of the election, and change the political condition of the entire state." During the convention the New York *Advocate,* a Republican paper, told its readers, "... it is perfectly ridiculous to give them the right of suffrage, a right which they do not appreciate and which they cannot value, and which in this city, particularly in the Federal wards, is a mere vendable article." In response the Federalists resorted to moral arguments. One of their newspapers, the New York *Spectator,* summed up this position: "... how or in what manner the proposition to exclude the people of color from the right to vote can be reconciled with one's professions upon the subject of liberty and equality we cannot determine. While we hold this truth to be self-evident that all men are created equal, we surely cannot disfranchise those whose misfortune it is not to have a white skin." The same convention discussed the elimination of property qualifications for white voters. Paradoxically, those who demanded universal white manhood suffrage wanted the Negroes disfranchised, while the advocates of a restricted white electorate assailed Negro disfranchisement as undemocratic.

The compromise adopted by the convention was, in effect, a Republican victory. While the new constitution established universal white manhood suffrage, it imposed a $250 property qualification on Negroes. The previous constitution had required all voters, regardless of race, to own $200 worth of property. With a larger requirement applied to the poorest segment of the population, the Negroes were virtually disfranchised.[9]

They would not have been subject to a property qualification if they had not voted as a block. The ex-slaves were inexperienced, and they naturally took their political cue from those who had helped them out of bondage and had continued to take an interest in them once they were free. By supporting the Federalists, the Negroes aroused the opposition of the Republicans, who used race prejudice for political purposes. Yet throughout the period of their virtual disfranchisement, New York Negroes were better off politically than members of the race in most Northern states. By 1840 93 percent of the Negroes in the free states had been disfranchised. As late as 1870 they voted only in New England and New York. Freedom from slavery did not mean freedom from prejudice.

III

The property qualification for Negro voters remained on the statute books for fifty years. During this period their leaders, sometimes with the aid of white friends, exerted pressure to get equal suffrage. But their numbers were small, their resources limited, and no political party needed their votes.

Throughout the period in which they were subject to a property qualification, some Negroes possessed the necessary wealth and education to assume the leadership of their group. While 163 possessed enough property to vote in 1821, 1,000 cast their ballots twenty-five years later, and the number had reached several thousand by 1870.[10] In New York before the Civil War Negroes obtained wealth and position in several ways. In the early years of the nineteenth century they owned most of the restaurants, did much of the catering, and held a virtual monopoly on the barbering. Later, whites took over these services, but by this time some Negroes had had the opportunity to accumulate wealth. George T. Downing of Newport, R.I., was a nationally known Negro leader who combined restaurant owning with battling for civil rights. Moreover, Negro communities, then as now, included members who attained comparative affluence by serving the needs of the race. By the 1830's most Northern Negroes attended their own churches and studied at segregated schools. Ministers like Henry Highland Garnett and Charles B. Ray and educators like Charles L. Reason and John J. Zuille became spokesmen for their race. The first Negro newspaper came off the press in 1828. Samuel Cornish and later Frederick Douglass used the columns of their papers to demand rights for Negroes. A few Negroes were beginning to attend colleges both in this country and abroad. John B. Ruswurm, editor of *Freedom's Journal*, the first Negro newspaper in the United States, was a graduate of Bowdoin College in Maine, while James McCune Smith, long a race leader, had obtained a medical education in Scotland.

Negroes were never without white support in their demands for equal suffrage and improved living conditions. Members of the Manumission Society continued to interest themselves in the welfare of free Negroes. Interest heightened in the 1830's and 1840's along with interest in other reforms such as Brooke Farm and similar Socialist Utopian experiments, temperance, woman suffrage, penal reform, education of the deaf and blind, pacifism, and abolition. This reform wave stimulated Negroes to organize and press their demands for rights such as equal suffrage.

Between 1830 and 1860 Negroes throughout the free states held a variety of national, state, and local meetings and conventions which considered questions of interest to the race. Those who attended these meetings demanded equal suffrage and debated whether political action or moral suasion would do most to solve their problems or whether they would be happier leaving the country. Moreover, delegates made surveys on living and working conditions and attempted to devise methods of self-improvement.[11]

From the beginning New York Negroes participated in national conventions, held state and local meetings, and formed self-improvement groups. Equal suffrage continued to be one of their major demands. They played a prominent role in the first Negro national convention held in Philadelphia in 1831, and a similar gathering was held in New York four years later. In 1837 New York Negroes became the first members of their race to send a petition to a state legislature demanding equal suffrage. Their petition, which was twenty feet long, contained the signatures of 660 men. The next year, a group in New York City organized the New York Association for the Political Elevation and Improvement of the People of Color. Members of the group contacted Negroes in other parts of the state, with the result that, in August, 1840, 100 delegates from twenty-three cities convened in Albany for the first convention of Negroes of the state. The address of the convention emphasized the necessity of self-help, agitation, and organization among the colored people, while it appealed to the whites for equality. The delegates formed a state organization to supervise Negro activities on state and county levels. The convention also drew up another equal suffrage petition addressed to the State Legislature. New York Negroes continued to hold annual state conventions until 1845.[12]

At this time colored leaders and their white allies sought ways of getting Negroes to buy property and consequently to meet the suffrage requirement. Gerrit Smith, a wealthy white philanthropist and social reformer, purchased 17,000 acres of land for settlement by 3,000 Negroes. But black people did not occupy the land, probably because no thought was given to the means of establishing them there. The *Colored American,* a New York City newspaper, urged its readers to buy other land and offered to pay half the purchase price.[13]

Yet, political and economic considerations worked against the Negroes. While the number of Negro voters was increasing, their relative economic position weakened. In the years before the Civil War thousands of immigrants settled in New York. Most of them were poor and untrained and therefore took menial and unskilled jobs. After 1830 Irishmen replaced Negroes as hod carriers, porters, and domestic servants. As early as 1834 Negro and white longshoremen rioted over jobs, and a few years later a Negro complained in the columns of a Negro newspaper, "These impoverished and destitute beings—transported from the Trans-Atlantic shores, are crowding themselves into every phase of business and of labor, and driving the poor colored American citizen out. Along the wharves, where the colored man once did the whole business of shipping and unshipping—in stores where his services were once rendered, and in families where the chief places were once filled by him, in all these places there are substituted foreigners and white Americans." Competition for jobs may have been the reason why white workers attacked Negroes with such ferocity at the time of the draft riots during the Civil War. Unskilled white workers feared both the actual competition of Negroes and the loss of status involved in working with them. Professor Leon Litwak, the historian of the free Negro in the North, has found virtually no instances of white and Negro working class solidarity. Too great a distance probably separated Negro leaders from the majority of the members of the race and they were too greatly influenced by middle-class and upper-class white reformers to envision the common interests of white and Negro laborers.[14]

Economic competition was supplemented and aggravated because of the politics of Negro leaders and of those black men who could vote. The forthcoming discussion of politics requires a word about the names of American political parties. Shortly after George Washington became president, two parties were formed, the Federalists and the Republicans. The Federalist Party continued until the 1820's, when it was reorganized under the name of the Whig Party. The Whigs disintegrated in the 1850's, and a new party was formed, the modern Republicans. The original Republicans began calling themselves Democrats in the 1820's and they still call themselves Democrats. This is why the original Republicans are now Democrats, and the Federalists, after doing a stint as Whigs, became Republicans. In the years following the partial disfranchisement of Negroes, Whigs and Democrats vied for votes. White unskilled workers along with most of the less privileged members of the community were Democrats, while all the Negroes who could vote cast their ballots either for the Whigs or for third antislavery parties which were sometimes in the field. In the 1830's an English visitor observed that he had never met a Negro who favored Andrew Jackson, the then Democratic president. Another observer saw Irishmen in New York City go to the polls shouting, "Down with the Nagurs. Let them go back to Africa where they belong." At a meeting of a Negro suffrage group in 1838, the Whig candidate for Lieutenant-Governor appealed for votes. In 1842 a Democratic New York legislature passed a law requiring potential Negro voters to swear that they had not taken bets on the election and that this was the only vote they had cast in the present election. The New York City delegation walked out of the Negro state convention of 1844 because its members objected to the efforts of the upstate people to get the convention to endorse a third antislavery party, the Liberty Party.[15] At a constitutional convention held in Albany in 1846, Negroes tried unsuccessfully to have the property qualification eliminated. The question of equal suffrage was entangled in the strife between Whigs and Democrats. The Whigs favored equal suffrage, while the Democrats opposed it. A few months before the convention, George T. Downing, a wealthy Negro restaurateur who was one of the leaders of the Negro community of New York City, wrote in a public letter: "The Democratic Party of this city, with the loud professions of the largest liberty, is the first and the only one to announce its determination to go for the curtailment of human liberty." In a speech Governor William H. Seward explained that he favored Negro suffrage because Negro votes would be Whig votes: "Give them this right and their influence will be immediately felt in the national council and their votes will be cast in favor of those who uphold the cause of human liberty." A Democratic pamphleteer was equally frank. "In the country," he wrote, "where there are few Negroes, the danger of encouraging them... to interfere in our political affairs, through the aid of a fanatical party of whites, is not so apparent, as in our great cities where they are already numerous."[16] The Whigs urged the inclusion of an equal suffrage provision in the new constitution, while the Democrats successfully advocated the separate submission of equal suffrage to the voters at the fall election.[17] The question was submitted to the voters, and Negro suffrage was decisively defeated both in the city and in the state.[18]

After 1846 New York Negroes continued to hold state conventions and to participate in national gatherings. As the result of a state convention in Troy in 1855, the New York State Suffrage Association was formed, with Frederick Douglass as its head. Under the auspices of the Association, speakers toured the state, campaigning for equal suffrage and at the same time urging support of the new Republican Party which had been formed a few years before.[19]

In March 1857, the legislature passed a resolution calling for a referendum at that year's fall election on the constitutional amendment calling for equal suffrage. Perhaps because the Republicans

feared certain defeat, they did not fulfill the constitutional requirement of publishing the proposed amendment three months before
it was to be voted upon. Therefore, there was no referendum
that year. In 1859 the legislature again passed a resolution calling
for a referendum, this time to be held in 1860. But 1860 was the
year of the election of Abraham Lincoln to the presidency. Slavery
and secession occupied the minds of Americans. Although Frederick Douglass toured the western part of the state distributing 25,000
pieces of literature, and suffrage clubs in New York and Brooklyn
were equally active, the suffrage amendment was overwhelmed
by a six-to-one majority in the city and a three-to-one majority in
the state. The New York *Tribune,* which had been a vigorous
champion of equal suffrage in 1846, did not even print the results
of the referendum. "We were overshadowed and smothered by the
presidential struggle—overlaid by Abraham Lincoln," wrote Frederick Douglass. "The black baby of Negro suffrage was thought
too ugly to exhibit on so grand an occasion."

But the problem lay deeper than mere lack of interest. As the
tension over slavery heightened, the Democrats accused the Republicans of desiring social equality between Negroes and whites, and
the Republicans, fearing a loss of votes, confined their efforts
on behalf of the Negro to the limitation of slavery extension. Thirty
thousand anti-Republicans of New York City staged a torchlight
parade a few days before the election of 1860. One float pictured
Lincoln holding a black flag labeled Discord, and Horace Greeley,
editor of the New York *Tribune,* clutching a tribune, while between them sat a thick-lipped Negro man embracing a white girl.
Under the caption "Republicanism" another float pictured a Negro
leading a white woman into the White House. To counter this,
Republican politicians made every effort to show that they were
personally as anti-Negro as their opponents. William H. Seward,
Senator from New York and leading candidate for the presidency
before Lincoln was nominated, told a political rally that the
American Negro was "a foreign and feeble element like the Indians,
incapable of assimilation . . . a pitiful exotic, unwisely and unneces-
sarily transplanted into our fields, and which it is unprofitable
to cultivate at the cost of the desolation of the native vineyard."
This atmosphere pervaded New York politics on the eve of the
Civil War.[20]

After the war Negroes renewed their efforts to get the ballot.

They continued to face a combination of hostility and apathy. Neither state party platform of 1865 mentioned the subject. Again in 1866 a group of New York City Negroes brought the question to the fore. At a meeting they passed resolutions demanding equal suffrage, and they appointed a committee with power to raise money, send out speakers, enlist the support of the press, and use the courts to eliminate the property qualification. But despite meetings and another constitutional convention, nothing was accomplished during the next four years.[21]

Yet Negro suffrage was on its way. In the years after the Civil War the Republican Party tried to maintain itself in power by means of Negro votes in the South. For this purpose it sponsored the Fifteenth Amendment of the Federal Constitution which said that no person should be deprived of the right to vote because of race, color, or previous condition of servitude. The amendment was adopted in 1870. In this way New York Negroes as well as members of the race in other Northern states were given equal suffrage.

CHAPTER 3

Working Toward Elective Office

Forty-seven years elapsed between the passage of the Fifteenth Amendment and the election of the first New York Negro office-holder, making New York one of the last of the big Northern cities to have elected Negro officials. During these years some members of the race were continually active in politics, although information concerning their activities is frequently fragmentary. In New York, as elsewhere, most Negroes were Republicans. But as the passing years continued to bring them scant rewards for their loyalty to the party of Lincoln and Emancipation, increasing numbers became Democrats. The experience gained during four decades of political participation, the beginning of a division of the Negro vote, and, most important, the rapid increase of the colored population caused by the migration from the South to Harlem during World War I, enabled Negroes to acquire the power to elect members of the race to office.

I

Between 1870 and World War I a variety of factors worked against the emergence of New York Negroes as a political force. Their numbers were small; until after 1910 they never constituted more than three percent of the population of the city. Moreover, the effect of their small numbers was heightened by their poverty; they had no money to contribute to the coffers of political parties. Discrimination also hindered Negro political participation. Race prejudice sometimes prevented them from participating in the activities of district clubs, which were the local party units. "Presidents of the different Republican organizations in New York City have not been overanxious for the attendance at their meetings of their colored brethren who have been members," lamented a group of Negroes in a letter to the *New York Times* in 1880, "or were

34

always sure to forget to place them on any of their committees and in case they did accidentally happen to get placed thereon, they were always found at the tail end."[1] As late as 1895 the New York newspapers carried a front-page story on the exclusion of a Negro from a district club despite the fact that Negroes numbered about one fifth of the voters of the district and usually furnished the margin by which the district went Republican.[2]

The political alignments of New York City and State prevented Negroes from getting much recognition. Most Negroes were Republicans, while most white New Yorkers were Democrats. Thus, Negro votes were not essential for the success of either party. Negroes were further limited because New York City political campaigns have usually been conducted around support or opposition to Tammany Hall rather than along strict party lines. City Republicans have not been strong enough to win elections by themselves. When anti-Tammany coalitions have been successful, they have included Democrats and independents as well as Republicans. Negroes along with other low-income segments of the community have generally supported regular party organizations because reformers did not seek to understand their special problems and needs. Therefore when anti-Tammany coalitions gained power, only those officeholders who were regular Republicans felt the need of rewarding Negro supporters. For example, when the Fusion mayor Seth Low was running for reelection in 1903 and Negro leaders asked him for more jobs, he replied that he had appointed a few messengers and these were enough.[3] Although state elections were conducted along party lines, the Republican Party of the state depended upon upstate areas rather than upon New York City for most of its votes, and most Negroes lived in New York City.

With political jobs and other forms of recognition scarce, feuding, jealousy, and competition frequently characterized the conduct of Negro leaders. A Negro minister might have been appointed a delegate-at-large to the Republican National Convention of 1884 if other Negroes had not opposed his selection.[4] T. Thomas Fortune, a New York newspaper editor, was one of the foremost Negro leaders in the nation during the 1880's and 1890's. Yet, in March 1899, Governor Theodore Roosevelt wrote that a meeting which Fortune had organized during the gubernatorial campaign the previous fall "was a complete breakdown, and I confess I went away saddened to think that the enmity to you among our fellow Republicans of color could be carried to such an extreme as to make them prefer to see the meeting an utter failure rather than to have you profit by it." Three days later, the governor again wrote to the editor, "Now, about the appointments...I have been able to see that a number of small appointments of colored men were made.... When we get to the large ones, my dear Fortune, the trouble lies in the rancorous factional feelings among the colored men themselves. For instance, when I suggested I wanted to put you up, I was met with a perfect chorus of opposition and so with every other colored man I deemed of prominence."[5]

Despite these handicaps Negro politicians wanted recognition, and white politicians wanted Negro votes. During political campaigns speakers of both races would address Negro audiences, describing the benefits which the Republican Party had conferred upon the race or forecasting the dire calamities which would result from a Democratic victory. At a typical gathering of this type at Cooper Union during the last week of the presidential campaign of 1876, 2,000 Negroes heard Henry Highland Garnett and John Mercer Langston, two Negroes who had formerly been abolitionists, speak on the subject "What a Solid South Means." During the presidential campaign of 1880 Garnett, Frederick Douglass, and Thurlow Weed of Albany, a leading white Republican, spoke at a similar meeting. In 1884 the Republicans carried New York State by slightly more than 1,000 votes. They naturally sought ways of increasing this lead in future elections. In 1888 a Negro newspaper reported eighteen colored clubs in various parts of the city supporting the Republican presidential candidate Benjamin Harrison. The next year marked the first time that a candidate for the State Legislature with a large Negro constituency advertised in a Negro newspaper.[6]

Political campaigning among Negroes was conducted on a segregated basis. White politicians would give money to Negroes who were expected to deliver the Negro vote. This practice frequently gave rise to disputes among Negro leaders and resentment among workers. "Here in New York where the white ward-heelers have controlled our votes ever since the [Civil] War, what have we to show for it?" wrote Thomas Fortune. "These white heelers have made millions of dollars and a widespread notoriety which we cannot call fame, but what have the colored voters gained?...Not one black man in New York State enjoys the respect or confidence of the

Republican politicians or can approach one of these sharpers on anything like equal footing." Ten years later, a Negro politician at the beginning of his career courted support from members of his race by complaining that the money was not being used wisely. "You can tell these Republican politicians who go to headquarters year after year and demand money to carry the colored vote," declared Charles W. Anderson in 1895, "that this money never reaches the colored voters, as a proof of which the Republican vote of this district has never varied for five or six years."[7]

Negroes would frequently demand jobs. After 1870 a few Negroes were always members of the Republican County Committee, the body which chose district leaders, and a Negro would sometimes represent the race as a delegate-at-large to the Republican State Convention. Periodically, Negroes would demand positions in city departments.[8] But they received little patronage from the city government as long as they were overwhelmingly Republican. In the 1880's Negro newspapers discussed the possibility of a member of the race running for the State Assembly. At least one New York City assemblyman appointed a Negro page, but the level of state jobs is better illustrated by the fact that in 1884 five men competed for the position of janitor of the State Senate.

Yet the passing years brought increasing Negro interest in politics. By the early 1900's many members of the race belonged to local Republican district clubs. In 1905, a year in which there was no Fusion movement, a Negro seconded the nomination of the Republican candidate for mayor at that party's city convention. The next year Negroes hoped to profit by the split among the white leadership of a district with a large number of Negro voters and nominate a black man for the Assembly. They formed an organization for this purpose, but it disintegrated when the black leaders disagreed among themselves. At the Republican National Convention of 1908 a Negro alternate-at-large represented New York for the first time. At least one New York Negro has attended every subsequent Republican national convention. In 1908 two Negroes were members of the Republican State Committee, fourteen were captains of election districts, and fifteen were members of county committees in various assembly districts.[9]

With the accession to the presidency of Theodore Roosevelt in 1901 Booker T. Washington became the patronage dispenser of Negro federal appointments. A New Yorker became one of his chief political lieutenants and the leading Negro political figure in the North. Charles William Anderson was born in Oxford, Ohio, April 28, 1866. While taking odd jobs to support a widowed mother, he attended the public schools of Oxford and Middletown, Ohio, the Spencerian Business College in Cleveland, and the Berlitz School of Languages in Worcester, Massachusetts. Then he came to New York and plunged into politics. In 1890 he was elected president of a citywide Negro young men's Republican club. The same year he received his first political job as a gauger in the Internal Revenue Service. Between 1893 and 1905, he served successively as private secretary to the State Treasurer, as chief clerk of the State Treasury, and as Supervisor of Accounts of the State Racing Commission. During the Republican presidential campaign of 1904, Anderson organized a group known as the Colored Republican Club which served as headquarters for the Negro Republicans of Manhattan for several years. The club owned its building. In his autobiography the poet James Weldon Johnson, who succeeded Anderson as president of the club, described the building as a three-story house in the heart of the then Negro neighborhood on West 53rd Street. A billiard and poolroom occupied the basement, while the main floor housed the assembly room, the second floor the lounge and card rooms, and the third floor the committee rooms. One night a week leading black entertainers performed for the membership, which came to include many of the business, professional, and social leaders of the Negro community.[10]

In 1904 Booker T. Washington wrote to Theodore Roosevelt suggesting Anderson as a delegate to the Republican National Convention. As early as 1901 the President had discussed with Washington the possibility of giving political appointments to Northern as well as Southern Negroes. The Tuskegee educator suggested Anderson as a possible recipient of such an appointment.

Ironically, Southern hostility enabled Roosevelt to give Anderson one of the most important Federal jobs held by a Negro up to this time. The President's selection of a Negro as Collector of the Port of Charleston irritated the Southern press, which dared him to make a similar appointment in the North. In March 1905, as one of the first acts of his second term as president, Roosevelt appointed Anderson as Collector of Customs of the 2nd District of New York, which included most of Manhattan and the Bronx.[11]

Anderson held the job for ten years. During the Panic of 1907 he was the only collector in the country to accept checks. Grateful businessmen wanted to give him a monetary reward. Since Anderson felt that he should not accept money, the merchants raised $5,000 which they donated to Tuskegee in his name.[12] Anderson was the only Negro Republican to be permitted to remain in office when Woodrow Wilson, a Democrat, won the presidency in 1912. During his term of office he collected over one billion dollars. When he left office, the New York *World* carried a complimentary editorial summarizing his work:

> Charles W. Anderson goes out of office today after holding for ten years this responsible post under the Treasury. Many millions of dollars have passed through his hands. His dealings have been practically all with white men of the keenest intellect and of substantial business standing. Capacity and courtesy have been the qualities marked in his conduct of an office maintained always in the highest efficiency. In Collector Anderson's time three complicated and important new revenues, the income tax, the corporation tax, and the war revenue tax have made this office the most difficult as it is the most important ever held by a colored man. He has stood the test.[13]

Anderson's interests went beyond the collection of revenue. Years later, acquaintances remembered his knowledge of English literature and of Irish history. He was a member of such diverse organizations as the Metropolitan Museum of Art, the Academy of Political Science, the New York Peace Society, the Japanese Franchise League, the National Geographic Society, and the Roosevelt Memorial Association. Mayors and governors frequently appointed him to hospitality and ceremonial committees such as those of the Hudson-Fulton and Catskill Aqueduct celebrations and committees to welcome various notables who visited the city.

Anderson's position as Collector of Internal Revenue gave him the power to dispose of a large number of jobs. He was responsible, directly and indirectly, for greatly increasing the number of Negro jobholders in government service. Professor Gilbert Osofsky, the historian of Harlem, wrote that Anderson found places for Negroes as mechanical draftsmen, state examiners of auto chauffeurs, deputy collectors and gaugers in the Internal Revenue Service, customhouse inspectors and clerks, messengers, immigration inspectors, attorneys to examine election frauds, referees in foreclosure suits, assistant superintendents in the Post Office, assistant district attorneys, deputy U.S. marshals, and stenographers. When a judge who was a former counsel for the Brewers Association came before the Bar Association as a candidate for a higher judgeship, Anderson presented the Bar Association with documentary evidence that he had refused to find bartenders guilty of violating the state civil rights act by refusing to serve Negroes. Anderson had access to politicians of both parties. In 1918, while an employee of the State Department of Agriculture under a Republican administration, he noticed trees being cut down and hauled to the city dump. He arranged with the Democratic city authorities to have five truckloads of cut trees carried to Harlem and deposited in front of his home on West 133rd Street. There they were distributed to people who needed stovewood. Anderson's correspondence with Booker T. Washington is preserved in the Washington Papers at the Library of Congress. His letters are filled with keen insights. A man who paid close attention to details, he could quote statistics on the exact number of registered voters in each Manhattan assembly district or list the positions held by Negroes in the Federal service and the salaries each job paid. Anderson was a careful reader of the society pages of daily newspapers. Years later, a Harlem resident remembered that Anderson had read that a wealthy contributor to the Republican Party, whom he knew by reputation but not personally, had become a grandfather. He sent him a congratulatory note. Although Anderson held an appointive job and possessed no power base among Negro voters, white politicians expected him to deliver the Negro vote. When Charles S. Whitman was running for District Attorney of New York County in 1909, he made an uncomplimentary remark about Negroes to a light-skinned Negro whom he thought to be white. The man to whom the remark was made reported it to Anderson, who confronted Whitman. Shocked, the candidate asked Anderson how he could remedy the situation. The Negro leader replied that Whitman should promise that if he were elected, he would appoint a black lawyer as one of his assistants. Whitman was elected, and the Negro lawyer got the job.[14]

II

Throughout this period the majority of Negroes remained Republican. But as the Republican Party increasingly subordinated the race question to other issues and failed to give Negroes the recognition which they felt they deserved, some members of the race urged political independence and a small but increasing minority took the then revolutionary step of becoming Democrats. From the time of the adoption of the Fifteenth Amendment in 1870, the Democrats made sporadic efforts to attract Negro votes. While the Tweed Ring had been aggressively proslavery before the Civil War, and Tweed had spoken of the political supremacy of the white race, Tammany wanted votes wherever it could get them. A Negro spoke at the Tammany Hall Fourth of July celebration in 1873. He charged the Republicans with neglecting their Negro supporters, and he praised John Kelly, Tweed's successor as Tammany leader, as an honest and efficient public servant. In 1880 a group of New York City Negroes announced that they would not vote for the Republican presidential nominee, James A. Garfield, because the Republican governor of the state had refused to pardon a Negro criminal. As part of a demand for patronage in the same year, a group of Negro Republicans asserted that Democrats sent Negroes from Albany with money "for the expressed purpose of demoralizing the colored vote, and one of the strongest arguments used by them and which is most likely to have an effect upon weak-kneed and wavering voters is that the Democratic Party is doing more for the colored man than the Republicans, and in support of these assertions they cite instances where the Democrats have actually placed colored men in positions for which many have sought at the hands of Republicans in vain." At least one Negro leader was criticized by other Negro Republicans for accepting an appointment as a deputy sheriff under a Democratic administration. The New York newspaper editor, T. Thomas Fortune, used the columns of his paper to plead for independent voting by members of his race. "The time has already come when necessity demands a division of the colored vote," he wrote in a typical editorial in 1884. "While we as a class confine ourselves to the narrow limits of either political party, we must expect to be ostracized. . . . I do not attempt to discourage Republicanism among us—but I cannot see why a man who is born black is of necessity a black Republican. No other race of men are so pronounced in their political preferences." When Grover Cleveland became the first Democratic president since the Civil War, in 1884, he appointed a New York Negro physician as ambassador to Haiti and gave another New York Negro a consular appointment. By the middle eighties black Democratic clubs had been formed in at least three assembly districts. During the 1891 gubernatorial campaign, leading Negro Democrats predicted that at least 1,000 members of the race would vote Democratic that year.[15]

One segment of the black population steadily supported Tammany Hall. The denizens of the underworld found favors from local politicians to be more profitable than political conformity or gratitude for the Emancipation Proclamation. For years the recognized Negro Tammany leader of the city was Henry H. (Hank) Anderson, the owner of several saloons and brothels in Greenwich Village. Anderson had begun his career as the body servant of "Boss" Tweed. Another early black Democrat was William Singleton, who arrived from Florida in the 1880's. Singleton became a friend of the steward of Tammany Hall, and in time he himself became steward. A Tammany district leader gave him financial assistance in opening a saloon and enabled him to remain open twenty-four hours a day without fear of police raids. In an election for District Attorney of New York County in 1886, a Negro Republican is quoted as saying, "My best friends come to me and say that they would like to vote the Republican ticket, but they have been offered four dollars for their vote, and that is too much of an inducement for them to withstand." The Negro went on to say that the owner of a colored saloon had been given $1,000 to divide among voters of his race.[16]

The founding of the United Colored Democracy in 1898 marked the beginning of the first permanent organization of Negro Democrats. The immediate cause of the new organization went back to 1896 when a New York Negro minister headed the colored section of the Republican Party. During the presidential campaign of that year party leaders promised that, if the ticket were successful, Northern as well as Southern Negroes would receive patronage. Although the Republicans won both the nation and the state, no jobs were forthcoming. The Democratic District Attorney of New York County died in 1897, and the Republican governor appointed a Republican as his successor. Negro leaders asked the new appointee to choose a black lawyer as one of his assistants. The District Attorney replied that he would make the appointment if the Republican County Chairman would give his consent. But when the County Chairman approved the appointment, the District Attorney changed his mind, giving as a reason that the time had not yet come when a Negro lawyer could get a conviction from a white jury in a criminal case. After this disappointment the Colored Republican County Committee, representing Negro voters in various assembly districts, passed a resolution declaring that Negroes would continue to support the Republican Party only if Dr. P. A. Johnson, a Negro physician who had been a lifelong Republican, received an appointment as Coroner. When informed of the resolution, Lemuel E. Quigg, the white county chairman, was reported to have said, "I know the Negroes better than they know themselves. You couldn't drive them out of the Republican Party with a sledgehammer." This cynicism naturally angered the Negro leaders, who disagreed among themselves on what course to follow in the 1897 municipal campaign. Three candidates were running for mayor that year.— Benjamin F. Tracey, a Republican lawyer, Robert Van Wyck, a Tammany judge, and Seth Low, President of Columbia University, the choice of the municipal reformers. At a stormy session the majority of the members of the Colored Republican County Committee voted to remain loyal to their party and support Tracey. James D. Carr, who the Negroes had hoped would receive the appointment as Assistant District Attorney, decided to cast his lot with Low. Two young Southerners who had recently come to the city, Andrew M. Robinson, a lawyer, and Eugene P. Roberts, a physician, resolved to organize Negro voters on behalf of Van Wyck. Since Roberts and Robinson knew that the Democratic label would not attract black voters, they called themselves Independents. After holding a meeting and passing a resolution on behalf of the Tammany candidates, Roberts, Robinson, and several of their friends obtained an interview with Richard Croker, leader of Tammany Hall. They informed him that they were dissatisfied with Republican treatment of Negro voters and prepared to organize support for the Tammany ticket. Croker replied that Tammany welcomed votes of any color and would gladly accept their support. But the Tammany leader was skeptical. He reminded them that Negro leaders had often promised votes, but few were forthcoming on Election Day. He sent them to the manager of the Van Wyck campaign, whose response was similar and who sent them to the leader of the district with the largest Negro population. The district leader said that he would gladly accept their support, since he was hoping to elect an assemblyman in a district which was normally Republican. He offered to furnish the Negroes with a clubhouse and to pay them for their services. Dr. Roberts replied that they were not primarily interested in money, but in jobs "just like white men, and not all cuspidor-cleaners." This request caused the leader to hesitate, but after getting the consent of Croker he accepted the Negro support on these terms.

Roberts and Robinson established campaign headquarters above a saloon, from where they dispensed free food and liquor. After fifty-five years Robinson remembered that on Election Day if a voter would show a Tammany worker that he had voted Democratic by displaying his unused Republican ballot, he would receive two or three dollars. After the election, Robinson was given a job as a diary clerk in the District Attorney's office, becoming the first Negro jobholder in that office who was not a menial. Roberts became a medical inspector in the Health Department. In 1917, Mayor John Purroy Mitchel appointed him as the first Negro member of the Board of Education of Greater New York (although three Negroes had served on the Brooklyn Board of Education when Brooklyn was an independent city).[17]

Although Van Wyck received only about 600 Negro votes, Croker decided to establish a permanent Negro auxiliary as well as a permanent Italian Tammany organization. Edward E. Lee, the Negro chosen as leader, was chief bellman at the Murray Hill and Plaza hotels. Although Lee remained illiterate throughout his life, he wielded influence in the Negro community by virtue of his ability to distribute what to Negroes were steady and well-paying jobs. Lee had undoubtedly met Croker at one of the conferences which Tammany leaders frequently held at the Murray Hill Hotel. Croker addressed the first meeting of the United Colored Democracy, as the new organization came to be known. "Follow Mr. Lee and you will make no mistake," the Tammany leader told the Negroes. "I have had occasion to come into contact with him frequently, and I have found him to be a straightforward man. I think he can be depended upon. We can treat the colored people in proportion to their work," he continued, "and give them patronage in accordance with their merit and representation, and that we will do for you. You understand organization as well as we do. If you don't, come to headquarters and we will be glad to give you all the information in our power...."[18]

Early Negro Democrats frequently faced the hostility of other

Negroes. They were regarded by many as traitors to the race. "The Negro who says that he can conscientiously support the Democratic Party in any state in this union must either be a fool or as ignorant of its history as a Choctaw Indian," wrote a black journalist in 1905. "The Negro Democrat is the political monstrosity of the present age. . . . The Democratic Party North and South is against the Negro, and every sane Negro should be against it."[19] During political campaigns Democratic speakers were sometimes stoned. Some Negroes were socially ostracized because of their party affiliation. At least one minister lost his pulpit because Negro Democrats held a meeting in his church. The Tammany appeal to Negroes was further weakened because a severe race riot occurred in 1900, two years after the founding of the United Colored Democracy. A Negro defense committee documented many instances of police brutality and even direct participation in the riot by members of the police force. A Tammany administration was in power in City Hall, and Tammany had close ties with the police. Negro demands of Democratic city officials for apologies and compensation were met with evasion. At least two New York newspapers went as far as to blame Tammany Hall for the riot.[20]

Yet the hostility of Negroes to Tammany diminished as with the passing years the United Colored Democracy filled a need in the Negro community. It gave the Negroes a place in the dominant political organization of the city which opened many jobs to them. "The Negro in New York has one vital need, steady decent work," wrote the social worker Mary White Ovington. "He dickers and plays with politics to get as much of this as he can." Tammany jobs ranged from Assistant Corporation Counsel and Assistant District Attorney to janitors and elevator operators in public buildings and streetsweepers. Moreover, Tammany leaders obtained jobs for their followers with private contractors doing business with the city. During the first year of the existence of the United Colored Democracy ten Negroes secured employment in the Dock Department, while forty members of the race found jobs as laborers and inspectors in the Streetcleaning Department. In 1900, during the Tammany administration of Mayor Van Wyck, the *Evening Post* reported that the builders of the subways were willing to give 500 construction jobs to Negroes. James D. Carr, a graduate of Rutgers and of the Columbia Law School, became the first member of his race to serve as an Assistant District Attorney of New York

County and as an Assistant Corporation Counsel. In 1911 Mary White Ovington found that the number of Negroes employed by the city almost equaled their percentage of the city's population.[21]

Lee organized branches of the United Colored Democracy in each assembly district with a sufficient number of Negro voters. The registered Negro Democrats of the district elected a leader, and the leaders of the districts formed the Executive Committee of the United Colored Democracy. The organization obtained funds from Tammany Hall and from assessments of members with city jobs. Although Lee may have maintained contacts with Negro Democrats of the underworld, his organization attracted members of unquestioned respectability and social standing. Besides Carr, at least two other lawyers were among the organization's earliest members—James L. Curtis, who was later appointed Minister to Liberia by President Woodrow Wilson, and J. Frank Wheaton, who had come to New York after serving a term in the Minnesota Legislature. Another early member who became a leader was Ralph Langston, son of the Negro abolitionist and congressman from Virginia, John Mercer Langston. In 1910 members of the United Colored Democracy's executive committee included a chiropodist, a salesman, a real estate operator, and a carpenter.

Lee remained leader of the United Colored Democracy until 1902 when he resigned, probably at the request of Charles F. Murphy, who had replaced Croker as leader of Tammany Hall in that year. Lee's successor, John J. Bell, a twenty-eight-year-old clerk in the Comptroller's office, lacked his predecessor's organizing ability and prestige. Bell resigned after serving as leader for a few months. The next leader was murdered by one of his lieutenants during a quarrel over the distribution of election funds. After more dissension Lee returned to power in 1907. He was appointed a deputy sheriff in 1910. After that year's election Charles W. Anderson admitted in a private letter that more Negroes had voted Democratic than ever before. Yet, Lee's opponents within the United Colored Democracy continued to be strong and vocal. The anti-Lee forces may have had the support of Tammany Leader Murphy because they were led by Robert N. Wood, who had been a boyhood friend of Murphy. In 1912 the Wood forces were able to replace Lee by their leader. When Wood died in 1915, the organization again split into two factions, one led by a court clerk named Thomas A. Church and the other headed by a lawyer, Ferdinand Q. Morton.

Murphy, who was friendly to Morton, decided in his favor under the pretext that an employee of the courts ought not to be a leader. As leader of the United Colored Democracy, as head of the Indictment Bureau of the New York County District Attorney's office, and as the first black member of the Municipal Civil Service Commission, and as a candidate for the first Negro district leadership in Harlem, Morton would remain one of the leading Negro Democrats of the city for a generation.[22]

III

Although by the second decade of the twentieth century Negroes had gained political experience both as Republicans and as Democrats, the migration from the South during World War I and their concentration in Harlem gave them the voting power necessary to elect a member of the race to office. Between 1910 and 1920, the percentage of Negroes in Manhattan increased from 2.6 to 4.8. Although 15 of the 31 Manhattan assembly districts were at least 2 percent Negro in 1910, the district with the largest concentration was only 18 percent black. By 1920 one district had become 50 percent black, while another was over one-third black.[23]

Until the settlement of Harlem, Negroes were scattered throughout the city because they frequently moved northward as the city expanded. With each move, some people stayed in the old neighborhood.

The earliest Negro settlement in New York was a row of clay houses on the fringe of what is now the Bowery. As the number of Negroes increased from eleven in 1626 to 3,000 by 1700, some moved from the original settlement to the site of the present-day Chatham Square. By 1850 the Negro population had expanded to 14,000, and they lived mainly on Carmine, Mercer, Lispinard, Broom, and Spring streets. Many Negroes were killed, injured, or impoverished as a result of the draft riots during the Civil War. Since the riots occurred in parts of Manhattan where Negroes were crowded together with poor white immigrants, many black people who had the money moved to the more roomy city of Brooklyn. Brooklyn remained the home of most upper-class Negroes for half a century. In the 1870's and 1880's Washington Square was the center of fashionable white society. Many colored servants lived near their employers, and a large Negro settlement sprang up in

Greenwich Village on Sullivan, Bleecker, Thompson, Carmine, Grove, and neighboring streets. As late as the 1930's Negroes who could not remember living anywhere else were found in this area. But most black people were forced to move again. The city was rapidly moving northward, and Washington Square gave way to upper Fifth Avenue as the chief abode of the wealthy.[24]

Between the sojourn in Greenwich Village and the settlement of Harlem, the center of Negro population shifted several times. For a short time in the 1880's large numbers lived in the upper twenties and the lower thirties west of Sixth Avenue. But they could not stay there very long because land was needed for the garment center and for other commercial activities. By 1900 two new Negro settlements had been established. Several of the big colored churches and most of the Negro entertainers and sporting figures of the era as well as thousands of other Negroes moved to 53rd Street west of Eighth Avenue. Others lived on 61st, 62nd, and 63rd streets between Broadway and the Hudson River. This second neighborhood was christened San Juan Hill because Negro troops had taken a prominent part in the capture of San Juan Hill during the Spanish-American War in 1898. But West 53rd Street and San Juan Hill proved unsatisfactory almost from the time of their settlement. The Negro areas were incredibly crowded, and rents were exorbitant. Sixty thousand black people lived in New York City in 1900, 5,000 of whom were jammed into one block on West 53rd Street. Other blocks on which Negroes lived were equally crowded. Thousands of people lived in dilapidated, ill-ventilated lodging houses or in cold-water flats, in which a washtub in the kitchen furnished the only bathing facilities. Two babies out of seven died before reaching their first birthday. "The area was a notorious red-light district," wrote James Weldon Johnson of West 53rd Street, "with bands of Negro and white whores roving the streets, like hungry wolf-packs. To make men follow them they would snatch their hats and run into dark hallways, where their victims were robbed by accomplices. Harlots in unbuttoned Mother Hubbards stood in front of churches on Sunday evenings and openly solicited men as they emerged." Moreover, the Negro districts were surrounded by thickly populated neighborhoods of whites who bitterly resented their presence. The worst race riot in the city's history up to this time took place in 1900, and many little riots occurred during the next few years. The growth of commercial establishments in the center of the city relentlessly encroached upon the residential areas of those without the financial means to move elsewhere. The Negroes would soon be forced to move again, but few at the time would have predicted that Harlem would be the place.[25]

Professor Gilbert Osofsky has written what will probably be the definitive work on the Negro move to Harlem. In 1900 the area had not lost its suburban atmosphere. Roi Ottley described it as "a cheerful neighborhood of broad drives, brownstones and large apartment houses, with the streets carefully laid out in the pattern of a gridiron."[26] For generations the area had been a playground for the wealthy. At the time of the American Revolution Alexander Hamilton and other social leaders had their country estates there. Seventy-five years later, the character of the area had not changed. It was so far from the city that only people with money ordinarily made the trip. Such men as Colonel Kip Rhinelander, Cornelius Vanderbilt, and Russell Sage drove thoroughbred horses on Lenox Avenue, and the Polo Grounds acquired its name because it was originally constructed as a place for playing polo. In the middle of the nineteenth century one Harlem resident created a public scandal by attempting to enroll the daughter of his black cook in a local school. During these years most travelers made the journey by stagecoach, with hostelries providing refreshments at convenient intervals along the route. The Third Avenue horse-drawn railroad began connecting Harlem with lower Manhattan in 1853. It used steam north of 42nd Street and horses south of it. The trip took an hour and twenty minutes, assuming that no horse balked or fell dead across the tracks. The Harlem Navigation Line covered the distance from 130th Street to Wall Street in an hour.[27]

The building of the Eighth Avenue elevated in the 1890's caused a rapid increase in population. Large numbers of Jewish immigrants settled in East Harlem along Madison and Park avenues. Within a few years this area was surpassed only by the Lower East Side in the number of Jews who lived there. A group of Irish immigrants lived at the northern end of Central Park. Their district became known as Goatville because some of them owned goats. The inhabitants of the area where Negroes were to move included second- and third-generation Germans, a few Jews, and people whose families had lived there for generations. The improvement of transportation caused Harlem to become the scene of a building boom. But the increase in population failed to keep pace with the construction of new houses and apartments. Under these conditions the Negroes gained their original foothold. A Negro real estate operator named Philip A. Payton has frequently been called "the father of Harlem." Payton came to New York from Westfield, Massachusetts, in 1900 at the age of twenty-six. He got the idea that if Negroes moved to Harlem, the downtown areas would not be so congested, while members of the race would live in modern buildings in a new and less crowded portion of the city. From the time of his arrival in New York until his death in 1917, the settlement of Harlem was the dominant passion of Payton's life. He began by opening an office in the neighborhood and by persuading the owners of two vacant apartments to make their property available to black tenants. Naturally, the apartments were quickly rented. Negroes soon bought or rented other houses and apartments on the same block and on adjoining blocks. The first apartments were on 134th Street near Fifth Avenue.[28] No one paid much attention to the Negroes until they moved west of Seventh Avenue. By 1905 enough of them were in the area to be noticeable. "An untoward circumstance has been injected into the private dwelling market in the vicinity of 133rd and 134th Streets," the New York *Herald* told its readers. "During the last three years the flats in 134th Street between Lenox and Seventh Avenues, that were occupied entirely by white folks, have been captured for occupancy by a Negro population, ... 133rd Street shows some signs of resistance to the blending of colors in the street, but between Lenox and Seventh Avenue it has practically succumbed to the stress of colored tenants." Half the block on 134th Street between Seventh and Eighth Avenues had already been occupied by Negroes, and the real estate brokers were predicting that the rest of the block would quickly follow. The writer concluded, "As the result of the extension of this African colony, dwellings in 133rd Street between Seventh and Eighth Avenues and in 132nd Street from Lenox to Eighth Avenue have depreciated from 15 to 20 percent in value, especially in the sides of those streets nearest 134th Street."[29]

The fear of declining property values caused white residents to organize in an effort to stop or at least to limit the Negro influx. Real estate dealers tried to buy leases on buildings in which Negroes lived. White Harlemites formed the Harlem Property-Owners Protective Association. This group circulated handbills showing that the presence of Negroes lowered property values. "The Negro invasion . . . must be vigilantly fought until it is permanently checked or the invaders will slowly but surely drive the whites out of Harlem," declared the president in a typical statement. "We now warn the owners of property on the outposts of the local commercial center that the invaders are clamoring for admission right at their doors and that they must wake up and get busy before it is too late to repel the black hordes that stand ready to destroy the homes and scatter the fortunes of the whites doing business in the very heart of Harlem." A writer in the *Indicator,* a real estate publication, proposed a solution. He felt that Negroes should not only be disfranchised, but also "segregated in some colony in the outskirts of the city, where their transportation and other problems will not inflict injustice and disgust on worthy citizens." Members of the Harlem Property-Owners Protective Association used their influence with downtown banks to prevent mortgage money from being given to extend the Negro settlement. The Association also encouraged the signing of restrictive covenants by which the residents of certain blocks agreed not to lease or sell their property to Negroes.[30]

But efforts to stop Negroes from spreading in Harlem were doomed to failure. Aside from moral reasons, many white property owners did not cooperate because they could make more money by letting Negroes occupy their buildings. As Negroes moved to Harlem in large numbers, they were frequently forced to pay higher rents than whites for the same living space, which made their presence financially profitable. Negroes began living in many buildings because of the now familiar pattern of panic moving. When one black family moved into a block or Negro tenants occupied a building, the other residents of the block would all move within months or even weeks. Landlords with vacant buildings were glad to find tenants of any color. Nonresident landlords were frequently more willing or even eager to lease or sell to Negroes than were landlords who lived in the area. Most important, the Negro move to Harlem could not be stopped because Negroes desperately needed housing. This need caused the expansion to be irresistible.

In the first decade of the twentieth century a group of black realtors and investors saw an opportunity to make money by helping members of the race. Such a group formed the Afro-American Realty Co. in 1904. James C. Thomas, a wealthy undertaker, was president, Payton was vice-president and general manager, and Wilfred T. Smith, a former attorney for Booker T. Washington, was general counsel. The company was capitalized at $500,000, $150,000 of which was subscribed immediately. All the subscribers were Negro. In managing the affairs of the Afro-American Realty Co. and in his other real estate ventures Payton used a racial appeal. The company's brochures had brown covers with the head of a Negro imprinted in the design. The original prospectus began with strikingly modern sentiments: "The idea that Negroes must be confined to certain localities can be done away with. The idea that it is not practical to put colored and white tenants in the same house can be done away with." Payton then appealed to racial solidarity. "The reason for the present condition of the colored tenancy in New York City today is because of the white owner and his white agent. When the owner becomes colored and his agent colored, then there is compelled to come an improvement in the condition. Race prejudice is a luxury, and like all other luxuries it can be made very expensive in New York City. With a cash capital of $500,000 the Afro-American Realty Co. can turn race prejudice into dollars and cents. The very prejudice which has heretofore worked against us can be turned and used to our profit." Although the company remained financially sound, the directors quarreled, and it disbanded within three years. Nevertheless, Payton and other Negro realists made small fortunes from the Harlem influx.

Negroes owned little real estate because they lacked the money to do much buying. They made their money by persuading the owners of property to rent their buildings to Negroes and employ them as the agents to collect rent. Occasionally, Negroes did have the money to buy apartment buildings. For seventy-five years St. Philip's Protestant Episcopal Church, one of the city's oldest and wealthiest Negro congregations, had owned land on West 33rd Street near Seventh Avenue. The church had purchased the land for $9,000. When the Board of Directors of the Pennsylvania Railroad decided to build Pennsylvania Station on its present site they wanted the land enough to pay $500,000. The agents of the church invested a large portion of the money in thirteen large apartment buildings on 135th Street near Lenox Avenue.[31]

Negroes moved to Harlem in ever-increasing numbers between 1905 and the end of World War I. By 1912 half the city's Negroes had moved uptown to an area which extended from 131st Street to 145th Street. During this year the Urban League conducted a survey of businesses and public institutions in the Negro area. Thirty-nine churches of eight denominations had already moved to Harlem. Negroes owned eight of the forty-four saloons in the district. The neighborhood also contained three public schools, ten groceries, ten restaurants, and one oyster house. Other businesses included one laundry, nine hairdressers, eleven barbershops, four undertakers, ten real estate offices, one bakery, nine employment agencies, one pharmacist, six ice, coal, and wood dealers, two confectioners, four expressmen, two whitewash and calciminers, one chiropodist, and six tailors.[32] Unlike merchants in Southern cities, New York merchants had never discriminated against Negro customers. As Negroes moved to Harlem, they found that they could make money regardless of the complexion of the neighborhood. Negro patronage apparently proved so profitable that in March 1913 the Harlem Board of Trade invited leading Negro realtors to a meeting to discuss community improvements. At the meeting, E. H. Koch, a leading 125th Street merchant, said that Negroes should live anywhere they can afford to pay the rent. The Property-Owners Protective Association was still trying to limit Negro residence in Harlem. When the president of this group tried to attend the Board of Trade meeting, Board members barred him, and he in turn accused the Board of using Negroes for political purposes.

By 1914, even the Harlem Property-Owners Protective Association recognized that Negroes were in Harlem to stay. While the Association tried to prevent further expansion of the Negro community, its leaders proposed cooperation with Negro leaders and offered to make financial contributions for the improvement of the Negro district. Members of the Association had several inconclusive meetings with Negro leaders. The meetings failed because the purpose of the Association was the limitation of the Negro community in Harlem, a purpose which no Negro leader could accept. But the meetings were important because they showed that even the Property-Owners Association was forced to acknowledge that blacks could not be driven away.

During the First World War thousands of Negroes left the farms and cotton fields of the South to enjoy the comparatively high wages and personal freedom of Northern cities. Although the Negro district in Harlem would have continued to grow if there had been no Negro migration, the arrival of thousands of Southern Negroes in New York gave the settlement of Harlem its final impetus. Negroes came North during these years for several reasons. A depression caused wages in some parts of the South to drop as low as $.75 a day. The depredations of the boll weevil further increased the difficulties of making a living. On the other hand high wages meant increasing opportunities in Northern cities. Agents traveled through the South recruiting migrants. "I witnessed the sending North from a Southern city in one day a crowd estimated at 2,500," wrote the poet James Weldon Johnson. "They were shipped on a train run in three sections, packed in day coaches with all their baggage and other impedimenta. The exodus was on," Johnson continued, "and migrants came North in thousands, tens of thousands, hundreds of thousands—from the docks of Norfolk, Savannah, Jacksonville, Tampa, Mobile, New Orleans, and Galveston; from the cotton mills of Mississippi and the coal mines and steel mills of Alabama and Tennessee; from the workshops and washtubs and brickyards and kitchens they came, until the number, by conservative estimate, went well over the million and a half mark. For the Negroes of the South this was the happy blending of desire with opportunity."[33] Those migrants who came to New York City naturally sought the area where space was most easily available. By 1917 70,000 Negroes lived in Harlem, and their zone of settlement had reached the Harlem River.

IV

The election of the first black officeholders resulted from a civic effort independent of the regular party organizations. A group of middle-class Negroes were among the earliest residents of Harlem. Moreover, the settlement of Harlem by Negroes enabled a number of black businessmen to make money as owners and managers of property and as investors. Several of these men assumed the leadership of organizations designed to bring about neighborhood improvements as well as general racial goals. The Equity Congress was an organization of this type, founded in 1911 by James C. Thomas, an undertaker, Burt Williams, an entertainer, and J. Frank Wheaton, a lawyer. Its members, leading figures of the Harlem community, met each Sunday afternoon at Thomas's mortuary to study community issues. The organization conducted a long and ultimately successful campaign to obtain a black national guard regiment in New York State. The Equity Congress also financed suits against white property owners who adhered to restrictive covenants, led an attack on the spread of vice in Harlem, and encouraged members of the race to patronize black businessmen.

Leaders of the Equity Congress also formed the United Civic League for the purpose of conducting a "civic, industrial, political, and educational campaign among members of the race" in 1913. The League, which raised money by regular monthly and annual dues, came to include some of the wealthiest members of the Harlem community. Of its hundred members in 1918, three were said to be worth $30,000 each, five $100,000 each, and twenty-five between $5,000 and $10,000. The League bought a $30,000 brown-stone building for its headquarters and completed payment for the building in six years. The organization brought about the establishment of a milk station at 135th Street and Fifth Avenue, campaigned for more playgrounds and for black attendants at playgrounds, for free movies and band concerts, and for better housing. John M. Royall, a Virginia-born Harlem real estate operator, was the moving spirit behind the formation of the United Civic League. The election of black officeholders was one of Royall's objectives from the beginning. He had been active in Theodore Roosevelt's effort to win the presidency on the Progressive Party ticket in 1912. Because of Roosevelt's popularity among members of the race, he received about 73 percent of the vote in black areas, far outdistancing the regular Republican candidate, William Howard Taft. Royall tried unsuccessfully to persuade the Progressive county chairman to nominate a black candidate for the State Assembly in 1912 and one for the Board of Aldermen in 1913. Royall also blamed the prejudice of the State Superintendent of Banking for refusing to allow him to charter a bank.

Spending a large amount of his own money, Royall ran as an independent candidate for the Board of Aldermen in 1913. Leaders of the United Civic League employed several strategies to arouse the race-consciousness of black Harlemites. The League held mass rallies at the Palace Casino, a large auditorium in Harlem, on Sunday afternoons. Race-consciousness was probably highest on Sundays, since many Negroes would have been to a church in the morning and would be returning there for an evening service. Although every Negro was encouraged to attend the League rallies, Royall made a special effort to stimulate attendance by representatives of clubs, churches, and fraternal organizations. In a typical speech he said that if he were a politician, which he was not, he would be controlled by the principle of "a black man first, a black man last, and a black man all the time." He went on to say that a black man who did not stand up for his race was either a fool or a traitor. Finally, he declared that as long as it was time for the Negroes to pay taxes and to help support the government, it was time for them to be given representation in the administration of government. At the close of one Sunday rally it was announced that another mass meeting would be held in two months, and meanwhile the audience was admonished "to carry on an active campaign to bring about the realization of the hopes of the race." Although Anderson and Wood, the black Republican and Democratic leaders, failed to support Royall, and Anderson actively opposed him, he did obtain the support of Fred R. Moore, editor of the New York *Age,* and of other leaders of the black community. He received about half the registered race vote in a district which was about 10 percent black.[34]

After the first campaign the United Civic League continued to enter candidates in Republican primaries, usually a candidate for assembly in one district and one for alderman in the adjoining district. Assembly and aldermanic districts were reapportioned in 1917. The Republican organization intended to have a black man elected as alderman. In this way the race would be given elective representation on the lowest level, since membership on the Board of Aldermen was regarded as a less important job than membership in the State Assembly. Although the Republican clubs of both districts nominated white candidates to run against those of the United Civic League in the primary, the Negroes won both races. Edward A. Johnson, a lawyer who had come to New York after serving as dean of the law school of Shaw University in Raleigh, N. C., received the nomination for assembly. The aldermanic nomination was won by James C. Thomas, Jr., also a lawyer, who had been a track star at Cornell. Thomas's father was an undertaker, investor in Harlem real estate, and leader in both the Equity Congress and the United Civic League.

Reaction to the black candidates varied. In the district in which Johnson, the former law school dean, was the candidate, a rumor was spread that a Negro janitor had been nominated. The campaign literature of the white Democratic aldermanic candidate opposed to

Thomas included the following statement: "Do you want your alderman to be a Negro? James C. Thomas, Jr. is a colored man. Vote for Frank Mullen, who has been your alderman for four years." On the other hand the Harlem *Home News*, a neighborhood weekly, reported, "At a meeting held last Saturday evening in the Manhattan Republican Club, 139th Street and Seventh Avenue, the members all pledged themselves to work just as hard and put as much vigor into their efforts to elect James C. Thomas their colored candidate for alderman as they would for their white candidates."

In Johnson's district, the 19th, which was approximately 30 percent black, the Republican vote in 1917 dropped 4.6 percent below 1916; in 1918 it dropped 4 percent more, while in 1919, when both candidates were again white, it rose to its 1916 level. In Thomas's district, the 21st, which was about 45 percent black, the Republican vote dropped 10.4 percent in 1917, but rose to its 1916 level in 1919, when both candidates were black.

In the general election Johnson defeated his Democratic opponent by about 300 votes out of 7,300 cast. He could not have won if he had not received some white votes. Thomas took an early lead, but when the returns from six missing election districts were discovered, his opponent proved victorious.[35]

Elected officials symbolized group progress for Negroes as for European immigrants. By electing officeholders who are like themselves racially or ethnically, members of a group gain added dignity and self-respect. Moreover, they come to feel that they possess a stake in the democratic process which exists and operates for them as well as for others. At least one Negro has always held office since 1917. The election of Edward A. Johnson gave black New Yorkers tangible proof of the promise of equality and first-class citizenship.

CHAPTER 4

The Recognition of Harlem

When Edward A. Johnson became the first elected Negro official in New York in 1918, the fact was barely mentioned by the papers which deigned to notice it at all. In the fall of 1967 the *New York Times Magazine* devoted an entire article to "A Political Tour of Harlem."[1] The half-century that intervened calibrates the slow but sure increasing role that Negroes have played in the political life of the city. For blacks, as for other ethnic groups, recognition has meant an increase in the number of elected and appointed positions and an increased voice in the councils of party organizations. Today, Negro state legislators and district leaders represent every borough except Staten Island. Members of the race are regularly elected to the City Council from Manhattan and Brooklyn. Every court except the Court of Appeals has at least one black judge. Since 1953 a Negro has been president of the borough of Manhattan, while others are regularly appointed to city and state boards and commissions. Most significant for Negroes as for other groups, the attention given to grievances by government is directly proportional to political power.

Population statistics tell some of the story of this increase in black political power. According to the census of 1920, the Negro population of New York City was 152,467—2.7 percent of the whole. Negroes were less than 5 percent of the population of Manhattan. Today there are approximately 2,000,000 Negroes in New York City—25 percent of the whole. Today, several assembly districts are over 90 percent black.[2]

Added to the increased size and concentration of Negro neighborhoods and the increase of black skills and wealth, the style of politics in New York City has aided Negroes in gaining political power. James Q. Wilson, a student of Negro political activity in Chicago, has compared Chicago and New York and concluded

58

that the New York Negroes have garnered more high-level jobs than in Chicago because of frequent factional disputes within the Democratic Party.[3] They have been able to bargain for recognition with the opposing factions.

I

In 1917 members of the New York State Assembly were elected annually. When Johnson ran for reelection in 1918, he was defeated by his white Democratic opponent, Martin J. Healy. During the campaign, Johnson favored prohibition, while Healy not only opposed it but made campaign appearances in Negro saloons. The same year another Negro Republican lawyer, John C. Hawkins, was elected to the Assembly from the 21st A.D., the area north of 135th Street. Hawkins was reelected in 1919 and in 1920, while in the preceding year two Negroes were elected to the Board of Aldermen. They were Charles H. Roberts, a dentist, and a newspaper editor, George W. Harris. As the result of a change in district boundaries in 1921, Roberts was defeated. By this time Tammany had begun running Negro candidates, and John W. Smith, a black lawyer, was declared the victor over Harris after an election dispute which occupied most of the aldermanic term between 1921 and 1923.[4]

The decision by Tammany to run Negro candidates and the success of local Democratic candidates in Harlem came about because Negroes, while continuing to give large majorities to Republican presidential candidates, were voting Democratic in local elections in increasing numbers. In 1917 John F. Hylan, the successful Democratic candidate for mayor, received about 27 percent of the Negro vote. When he ran for reelection four years later, he garnered a majority of black votes, perhaps as much as 70 percent. The staunchly Republican New York *Age* admitted that the defeat of Roberts, the Negro Republican alderman, "is attributed mainly to the defection of the vote in the colored section of the district.... He was given the united party support in the white sections...." In 1922 Alfred E. Smith, the Democratic gubernatorial candidate, received between 60 percent and 70 percent of the black vote in New York City. The *Age* reluctantly conceded that "in New York City the majority of the race vote went to the Democrats."[5]

There are several reasons for the Democratic success among

Negroes. While the majority of Negroes continued to vote Republican in other parts of the country during the first half of the 1920's, the number of black Democrats was increasing. For decades Negro leaders had complained of neglect by Republicans. The *Age* attributed the New York Democratic success of 1922 to the failure of President Harding to give patronage to blacks. In 1922 Delaware blacks gave a majority to the Democratic senatorial candidate because his Republican opponent refused to support an anti-lynching bill. The next year the Negroes of Baltimore gave majorities to the Democratic candidates for mayor and governor, while two Negro Republican members of the City Council were defeated.[6]

However, the local situation was more important than lack of national patronage in causing New York Negroes to vote Democratic. Through Tammany influence, blacks obtained jobs in city departments and with contractors doing business with the city. Moreover, Mayor Hylan campaigned as the poor man's friend and made the five-cent subway fare his chief campaign issue. During his campaign for reelection he spoke to Negro meetings in Harlem. "This city administration has steadfastly insisted that the Negroes have a square deal and the protection to which they are entitled," he told one gathering. He went on to claim credit for the admission of the first Negro interns to city hospitals and for an increase in the number of Negro policemen. At this time Marcus Garvey, the leader of the Back to Africa movement, was at the height of his power. Garvey, who maintained his headquarters in Harlem, openly allied himself with Tammany Hall. He probably took this action because the Democrats were in power in the city and because Garvey, being a West Indian, had no traditional attachment to the Republicans. He did, however, support Harding and Coolidge in 1920 and 1924. Garvey's followers filled at least one Democratic meeting during the campaign of 1922. In the same year William H. Ferris, a Yale graduate who edited Garvey's newspaper, the *Negro World,* ran as an independent candidate for Congress and siphoned off votes from the Republicans. Two years later, Garvey supported a white Democrat who was opposed by a Negro Republican.[7]

The most important reason for the success of the Democratic Party among Negro voters was undoubtedly the attitude of Tammany Leader Charles F. Murphy and his relationship to Ferdinand Q. Morton, leader of the United Colored Democracy. Murphy, who led Tammany Hall from 1902 until his death in 1924, enjoyed the respect of Negroes regardless of party. In an editorial printed at the time of his death the New York *Age*, ever a bulwark of Republicanism, assessed Murphy's contribution: "It may have been his humble beginnings that endowed the leader of Tammany Hall with the human touch in politics. At all events it was clearly manifested that he was free from any bias of race or color prejudice in his dealing with his fellow-citizens." Murphy "increased the places opened to the race in the city service, and it was with his approval that they grew of greater importance.... The moral effect of this attiutde on the part of the head of a great political organization governing the greatest city in the world cannot be overestimated. It imbued all of his followers with the same humanizing spirit of broadness and liberality." The *Age* admitted that "the motive which underlay this policy may have been political, but the effect was not only to make votes, but to make good will. Even those members of the race who never voted the Democratic ticket could not refrain from feeling respect for the head of Tammany Hall."[8]

Murphy was attracted to the Negro lawyer Ferdinand Q. Morton because Morton was the first college-trained Negro the Tammany leader had known. A native of Mississippi, Morton had spent his boyhood in Washington where his father was a government employee. After graduating from Phillips Exeter Academy and attending Harvard, he came to New York to practice law. Morton prepared for admission to the bar in the office of another Negro lawyer who happened to be a Democrat. In this way he became involved in Democratic politics, and he became acquainted with Charles F. Murphy. As a young lawyer Morton felt that his talents were going to waste. He almost decided to move to Brazil where he believed the opportunities for a black lawyer to be greater than in the United States. But by his ability he rose to leadership in the United Colored Democracy. At the time of a factional dispute within the organization in 1915, Murphy decided that Morton should be leader. At the same time Murphy secured an appointment for him as Assistant District Attorney. Within five years Morton had become head of the Indictment Bureau. In the fall of 1921 a committee of Negroes met with Murphy and asked for the appointment of a Negro as a magistrate. After the spectacular Democratic success of that year Murphy offered the appointment to Morton, but the Negro leader felt that he would be more useful politically if he were not a judge. Almost fifteen years were to elapse before a Negro would be appointed as a magistrate, but Morton did become a member of the Municipal Civil Service Commission, a job which he held for a quarter of a century. Negroes have been represented on the Commission ever since. In the District Attorney's office and as a member of the Civil Service Commission Morton's competence is universally acknowledged. But his personality made him a controversial figure in the Negro community. George Furniss, a student of black political assimilation, describes him as "aggressive, egotistic, intellectual, and dedicated; stubborn and outspoken, yet an organization man." As Civil Service Commissioner he went to great lengths to avoid a possible accusation of being biased in favor of Negroes. At times he would deliberately ask another commissioner to make a decision in a case where a member of the race was involved. With this attitude his presence on the Commission did not open many jobs to blacks. Moreover, even Morton's personal friends admit that he was not popular with rank-and-file party workers. One who knew him well described him as speaking Harvard English everywhere, even in political clubhouses. Ironically, Morton was accused both of snobbishness and of having close friends with shady reputations. He may have been unable to relax with his equals.[9]

While Murphy was Tammany leader, all black patronage was channeled through Morton and the United Colored Democracy. In the early twenties Morton's power was at its height. He constantly emphasized the number, quality, and financial rewards of the jobs given to Negroes by Tammany.[10] Although Morton remained as Civil Service Commissioner until 1947 and later ran for a district leadership post, his power declined after the death of Murphy. The Negro Democratic vote also declined, although the Republican majorities were smaller than they had been before 1920. A conflict arose between Morton and the white leaders of the Harlem districts. When the Negro vote was small and scattered, the United Colored Democracy had served as a rallying point for Negro Democrats. But when Negroes constituted a substantial portion of the voters of several assembly districts, the existence of a separate organization cutting across district lines undercut the power and influence of the district leaders. George W. Olvany, Murphy's successor as leader of Tammany, distributed patronage through the regular district clubs. Although the next Tammany

leader, John F. Curry, tried to restore the power of the United
Colored Democracy in 1930, the Negroes had become the majority
in two assembly districts, and a separate Negro organization had
lost its reason for being.[11]

During the 1920's the number of black officeholders fluctuated
very little. Throughout the period any of four positions, two assembly and two aldermanic, might be occupied by a Negro. Although
both parties sometimes chose Negro and sometimes white candidates
for these positions, the number of Negroes in elective office never
rose above two between the 1921 reapportionment and 1929. The
Republicans nominated more Negro candidates than the Democrats because Negro districts usually gave the Republicans a majority and because, being out of power both in the city and state, they
had little to lose by nominating black candidates. In 1929 four of
the seventy members of the Board of Aldermen were Republican,
two of the four being black. In 1918 a Negro minister ran as an
independent candidate for Congress, and in 1922 a follower of
Marcus Garvey did likewise. From 1920 to 1922 Martin C. Ansorge,
a Republican, represented the congressional district which included
Harlem and Washington Heights. Defeated by his Democratic
opponent in 1922, he preferred a federal judgeship to renomination
in 1924. In that year the Republicans nominated Dr. Charles H.
Roberts, the Negro dentist who had previously been a member of
the Board of Aldermen. Although Roberts carried black districts,
his white Democratic opponent was elected. The *Age* charged white
Republican district captains with working for Roberts' defeat. The
Republicans also nominated Negro congressional candidates in 1928
and 1929. Both of them were defeated.[12]

Blacks also received some recognition in the form of appointive
jobs. In 1921 James C. Thomas, a young lawyer who had almost
been elected to the Board of Aldermen in 1917, became the first
member of his race to be appointed an Assistant United States
District Attorney. In the same year John C. Hawkins, a black Republican lawyer, who was a member of the State Assembly, did not
run for reelection and received an appointment as Associate Counsel
of the United States Shipping Board. One or two Negro lawyers
continually served as assistant district attorneys of New York City,
assistant corporation counsels, and assistant attorneys general of
New York State. The highest appointments of Negroes who were
not lawyers were probably in the Post Office and in the Internal

Revenue Service, the latter under the influence of Charles W. Anderson. Anderson himself was appointed as Collector of Internal Revenue in 1923. He held the post until 1935. In 1924 the New York *Age* credited the Republican leader of one Harlem district with obtaining 400 jobs for Negroes.[13] The next noticeable sign of increased black voting strength and recognition came with their election as district leaders—the key policy-making positions of the county organizations of both political parties.

II

In the years when Negroes were a significant minority of the voters in the Harlem districts, white district leaders treated them with varying degrees of recognition and integration. In each district a black subleader was either appointed by the white leader or chosen by the black county committeemen. The power of the Negro leader depended upon the structure of the district and the personality of the white leader. Henri W. Shields, a Negro lawyer who was a member both of the Board of Aldermen and the State Assembly and who acted as the lieutenant of Edmund P. Holahan, Democratic leader of the 21st A.D. in Upper Harlem, wrote of the latter job, "I did most of Mr. Holahan's work. If a constituent would get in trouble, Mr. Holahan would send me to see the Police Commissioner, the Commissioner of Docks, judges, etc., to plead for leniency. He sent me to court to fight hundreds of rent cases, for which I was never paid a cent, and I was even sent to Syracuse to represent Mr. Holahan at a Democratic State Committee meeting." In the other largely black district, the 19th, led by Martin J. Healy, the Negro leader was William "Kid" Banks, a man with underworld connections. Banks maintained a separate club. Darwin W. Telesford, now a judge, then a young immigrant from the West Indies, remembers going to Healy's club and being told that he was in the wrong place. By persisting in his desire for membership in the white club, he was eventually accepted. Negroes who were allowed in Healy's club were segregated. When J. Raymond Jones became New York County Democratic leader in 1964, he told a *New York Times* reporter that his initiation into politics was going to Healy's club and finding that Negroes were not allowed. In 1924 the New York *Age* complained that in this club Negroes were instructed about the primaries but not permitted to remain for the dinner which followed.[14]

The Republican leaders of the 19th and 21st districts permitted blacks to participate in all club activities, but pursued contrasting policies in other ways. Robert S. Conklin, leader of the 21st, had to contend with a demand for Negro leadership as early as 1923, when a group of blacks formed a club which opposed the regular club of the district. At this time the voters of the district elected county committeemen, and the county committeemen chose the leader. Since twenty-eight county committeemen out of approximately 200 were black in 1923, the Negroes could do little more than raise the issue. Conklin countered by attempting to organize a party among the Negroes of the district who would be loyal to him. In 1925 he deposed one black associate leader and named another. Many Negroes resented this action because the black associate leader had previously been chosen by Negro county committeemen or by black and white leaders in conference. The next year Conklin's Negro opponents nominated a separate slate of delegates to the state convention. The leader responded by removing fourteen district captains and at the same time appointing a black woman as his co-leader. The struggle continued until 1929, when the Republicans divided the district, which was then about 70 percent black. Conklin retained the predominantly white districts, while a Negro was made leader in the black areas.[15]

David B. Costuma, Republican leader of the 19th, possessed the best reputation among Negroes of any white Harlem political leader of the period. The officers as well as the membership of his club were interracial. Fred R. Moore, the publisher of the New York *Age*, was a member of his club. Costuma was given credit for securing many jobs held by blacks. A white assemblyman who was president of his club repeatedly introduced legislation desired by the black community. No demand for black leadership arose while Costuma remained as leader. In 1926 he engaged in a dispute with Republican County Chairman Samuel S. Koenig. Whether as an aftermath of the disagreement or for personal reasons, Costuma resigned as leader in February 1927.[16] He was replaced by Abraham Grenthal, the president of Costuma's club, who had represented the district in the Assembly since 1925. As an assemblyman Grenthal had introduced bills relieving tenants from making payments to landlords who had not made repairs and reapportioning the municipal court districts so that two black justices would be elected. When Costuma resigned, Grenthal was unanimously elected leader. The following November he was reelected to the Assembly despite the fact that his opponent was a Negro. Yet in February 1928 the *Age* began a campaign for Negro leadership of the district. Week after week the paper told its readers that the district was 70 percent Negro and that most lucrative patronage jobs were held by whites who had formerly lived in the district and who had moved away. Its editor, Fred R. Moore, who had been the unsuccessful candidate for alderman in 1927, accused Grenthal of instructing his white district captains to promise Republican votes for the white Democrat in exchange for Democratic votes when he had run for reelection to the Assembly. In 1954 Costuma told the writer that irregularities had been discovered in the club treasury after Grenthal had become leader. In 1928 the anti-Grenthal forces nominated a candidate to run against him in the Republican primary, but Grenthal won reelection. The next year the Grenthal opponents nominated candidates for the Assembly, for the Board of Aldermen, and for district leader. In 1928 Negroes throughout the country had been stirred by the election of Oscar DePriest of Chicago as the first black man to sit in the House of Representatives since 1901. During the 1929 campaign to unseat Grenthal, DePriest came to New York and addressed a rally at the Abyssinian Baptist Church: "None can lead you but one who has been Jim Crowed," DePriest told his audience. "Never ask any fellow to give you what belongs to you. Take it. You can only get leadership by electing a man who will fight your battle. It is said the present leader intends to spend a lot of money for the coming election. Take his money and defeat him. Whoever heard of politicians giving up anything? White men select Negroes whom they can control." Costuma and other white residents and jobholders of the district supported the black slate. It was victorious. Francis E. Rivers, a young Negro lawyer, defeated Grenthal for reelection to the Assembly. Fred R. Moore was elected to a second term on the Board of Aldermen, defeating the editor of a rival paper who was supported by Grenthal. The first Negro to head a full assembly district was Charles W. Filmore. Filmore, a native of Ohio, was a veteran of both the Spanish-American War and of World War I. He was well known in the black community because he was a lieutenant-colonel of the National Guard. Filmore had won in the September primary; in the general election in November four Negroes were elected to office for the first time, two to the State Assembly and two to the Board of Aldermen.[17]

The Negroes gained two more elective positions in 1930. Beginning five years earlier, assemblymen from Harlem districts had introduced bills reorganizing the municipal court districts to enable the Harlem area to choose two new judges. In some years the bills were defeated in the legislature, while in other years they were vetoed by Democratic governors who feared the election of Republican judges. But in 1930 a compromise was made by which districts were carved out for four new judges, two in Harlem and two downtown. The Harlem judgeships were expected to go to black Republicans, while the downtown jobs were slated for Democrats. Governor Franklin D. Roosevelt signed the bill in 1930. Each party nominated two Negro judicial candidates. Francis E. Rivers, the Republican assemblyman who had introduced the bill, received a judicial nomination, along with John C. Hawkins, the former assemblyman who at this time was a member of the Board of Aldermen. The Democrats chose Charles E. Toney, Ferdinand Q. Morton's law partner, and James S. Watson, an immigrant from Jamaica who had become Assistant Corporation Counsel. In 1929 the four elected black officeholders had been Republicans; in 1930 two Democrats were elected to the Assembly, and the two Democratic judges were elected. The change was probably caused by the coming of the Depression and by the fact that the Democrats who were in power in the city and state controlled the dispensing of relief. In 1932 Harlem Negroes gave Franklin Roosevelt 48 percent of their votes, while the figure skyrocketed to 79 percent by 1936. The only Negro Republican to be elected to office in Harlem from 1929 to the present was Conrad A. Johnson, a lawyer who was elected to the Board of Aldermen in the LaGuardia victory of 1933. LaGuardia himself ran strongly in black neighborhoods in his 1937 and 1941 campaigns for reelection.[18]

The success of black Republicans in gaining district leaderships in 1929 and the Democratic victories in 1930 encouraged Negro Democrats to seek district leaderships. Clubs formed for this purpose opposed the white leadership in both the 19th and 21st districts in 1931. But both clubs were led by relative amateurs, and they were badly defeated. By 1933 a club known as the Beavers had been organized for the purpose of bringing black leadership to the 21st. The club was headed by Henri W. Shields, a former member of the State Assembly and the Board of Aldermen. Although the club did not have much money, the members were dedicated to the principle of black leadership. In 1933 Herbert L. Bruce attended his first meeting of the Beavers. Bruce, an immigrant from Barbados, had held odd jobs, eventually becoming a redcap at Pennsylvania Station. He and another redcap pooled their money and opened a cabaret, the Monterey. Mrs. Shields came to the Monterey seeking ads for the Beavers' journal. She succeeded not only in getting an ad but in persuading the proprietor to attend a meeting. At one of Bruce's first meetings the members discussed the problem of where to find enough money to pay next month's rent. Impressed by the Beaver dedication, Bruce agreed to guarantee the rent. He subsequently joined the club and took on the job of finance chairman.

Shields became the district leadership candidate in 1933. His campaign literature stressed the fact that while two thirds of the voters were black, they received only about 10 percent of the salaries of the district's patronage. When the votes were counted Shields had carried sixteen election districts and his opponent eighteen. Shields believed that his opponents had won by the use of repeaters and by spreading a rumor that people on relief would lose their food tickets if they voted for him. In 1934, for a reason which remains obscure, the Beavers expelled Shields, and he returned to the regular Democratic district club. Bruce now controlled the Beavers.

Another club was formed in the district in 1934. The leadership and membership of the new club, the Ramapo, were interracial. William A. Dodge, the Manhattan district attorney, provided the impetus for the formation of the Ramapo, but he never ran for office in the district. The Ramapo was probably formed to extend the influence of the powerful West Side district leader James J. Hines. In the Ramapo's first campaign William T. Andrews, a black lawyer who was its candidate for assembly, defeated his opponent in the primary and went on to win in the general election. Dodge sponsored a white man named McIntosh to oppose the Beavers and the regular club of the district, the Chicopee, in the 1935 district leadership contest. Two weeks before the voters were to go to the polls to choose county committeemen, McIntosh was so badly injured in an automobile accident that he could not continue in the race. Andrews took his place as the candidate for district leader. The Ramapo suffered another severe setback when they were ruled off the ballot in thirty election districts because their petitions were found to be defective. In the election of county committee-men the Chicopee elected the most, the Beavers were second, and the Ramapo third. Between the selection of county committee-men and the meeting at which a leader was chosen, the Ramapo decided to unite with the Beavers. The two clubs merged. Bruce became the candidate for district leader, while Andrews ran for the Assembly. The meeting of county committeemen to choose a district leader began an hour and a half late. Three Tammany officials and thirty policemen kept order. The election resulted in Bruce receiving 252 votes and his white opponent garnering 212. Herbert L. Bruce became the first black man to be a member of the executive committee of Tammany Hall. Negro newspapers drew lessons from Bruce's election. The *Age* told its readers, "The success of the Democratic voters in this fight should serve as an object lesson for all Harlem on the value of unity and working together for a common cause. A little more united action will mean that many problems which have vexed the Negroes in New York for so long will vanish, and that a new day will dawn for them on the political horizon." The *Amsterdam News* believed that Bruce's election marked "a seven-league stride in the progress of Harlem voters toward political emancipation. It signalized also the smashing of one of the barriers which has prevented whites and blacks in the district from co-operating as citizens for the mutual good of the community."[19]

The leadership contest in the 19th was complicated by factional disputes within the Democratic Party. For several years the Demo-cratic organization of Manhattan had been feuding intermittently with the national and state organizations. In 1934 Democratic National Chairman James A. Farley and Governor Herbert Lehman had helped to replace John F. Curry by James J. Dooling as leader of Tammany Hall. At the beginning of 1935 Governor Lehman submitted a plan for the apportionment of state legislative dis-tricts which Tammany leaders felt would reduce their power. News-papers predicted that the vote on the bill might be so close that the two Negro assemblymen, James E. Stephens and William T. Andrews, might hold the balance of power.

In 1935, 300,000 Harlemites lived in the area bounded by 110th and 155th streets, Amsterdam Avenue, and the Harlem River. If the population of the rest of Manhattan had been equally dense, the entire population of the United States could have been squeezed on Manhattan Island. Despite the fact that the unemployment rate in Harlem was about twice that of the rest of the city Negroes were almost completely excluded from skilled trades and white collar jobs. Many of the stores in Harlem refused to employ blacks. On the other hand, overcrowding caused rents to be higher than in other parts of the city. When a boy was arrested for stealing a penknife at Woolworth's on 125th Street, a riot broke out during the same week that the Legislature was considering reapportionment. One hundred people were injured, an equal number arrested, and millions of dollars of property was destroyed.

Stephens and Andrews issued a statement opposing the reapportionment plan because under it Harlem would lose an assemblyman and fail to gain a state senator. "I'm here by the suffrage of Negroes," Stephens declared in a speech on the Assembly floor, "and I'm serving notice on Speaker Steingut to tell the Governor that he has two Negroes here who can block Democratic measures yet to come. We are holding our seats by the votes of Negroes and we intend to fight for them." The reapportionment plan was defeated by ten votes, but this was one of the first instances when the press and party leaders feared that black voters might hold the balance of power.[20] The reapportionment plan caused a permanent break between the Tammany leadership and the supporters of Farley and Lehmann.

Martin J. Healy, who had been leader of the 19th A.D. since the early 1920's, was a supporter of James J. Hines, and the latter was allied with Farley and Lehmann. Moreover, because of his long tenure he was entrenched in his district. On the other hand he was injured by charges of corruption, charges which were later proved and for which he went to jail. In the district leadership contest of 1935 the Tammany leadership supported Harry C. Perry against Healy. Until 1931 Perry had been leader of the 2nd A.D., that section of the Lower East Side which included the "Little Italy" Mulberry Street settlement. When threatened with a primary fight led by Albert Marinelli and his ally, the Mafia chieftain Charles "Lucky" Luciano, Perry had resigned. He now attempted to regain his position as a district leader, this time in Harlem. Perry was related by marriage to the Sullivan family, which had been politically active in lower Manhattan since the turn of the century. He was the brother-in-law of Congressman Christopher D. Sullivan, who would become leader of Tammany

Hall in 1937. The third candidate was Ferdinand Q. Morton. Negro newspapers frequently mentioned other possible Negro candidates, but Morton was the only one who put up a slate of county committeemen to be chosen by the voters. In the primary Healy elected most committeemen, Perry was second, and Morton was a very poor third. Between the primary which chose county committeemen and the meeting to elect a leader, Healy and Perry decided to join forces and divide the district. During the meeting their decision was revealed. Their supporters left the meeting, and Morton was declared leader by default.

But Morton found that he could not retain the leadership if he were to remain as Civil Service Commissioner. Consequently, another meeting proved necessary. An Oklahoma-born black real estate broker, Fred Dickens, whose family was to play a role in Harlem politics for a quarter of a century, tried to enter the contest as heir to Morton. But Dickens was declared ineligible because he had not participated in the primary to choose county committeemen. At a second meeting held in February 1936, the only eligible candidates were Healy and Perry. Perry won the leadership, retaining it for four years. In 1937, as many as six candidates, five of them black, opposed him at the same time. The next year Perry supported a black member of his club, Daniel L. Burrows, in a successful bid for the Assembly. By 1939 the demand for black leadership and opposition to Perry was so great that he resigned the leadership in favor of Burrows. The western half of the 17th A.D. in Southern Harlem also obtained black leadership in the early forties, again following a factional dispute among the white leadership of the district.

George Furniss concludes that several conditions seem to have been necessary for blacks to become district leaders, both Republican and Democratic, in Manhattan. Black district leaders were chosen when members of the race constituted two thirds to three fourths of the voters of the districts. Negroes became district leaders in each party when the other party was in power in the city. Successful bids by blacks for leadership were supported by experienced politicians of both races as well as by members of the Negro middle class. Finally, the selections of both Filmore the first Republican and Bruce the first Democrat followed intense campaigns fostering race-consciousness.

Since 1929 the Republican County Committee has included black members, as has the executive committee of Tammany Hall since 1935. Whatever the changing power relationships within the political organizations were, Negroes have not relinquished district leaderships once obtained.[21]

III

In demanding members of the race as district leaders, Negroes had frequently complained of lack of patronage. They had contended that former residents of the districts who had moved away received most of the lucrative jobs. Yet when Negroes became district leaders, the number of jobs available to them did not immediately increase. Most blacks voted Democratic, and Tammany was out of power in the city until 1945. Moreover, Democratic leaders frequently feuded with each other. While intraparty disputes worked to the advantage of Negroes at other times, this was not the case in the late 1930's and the early 1940's. Herbert Bruce frequently opposed the leadership of Tammany Hall, a group consisting of William Solomon, Edward Loughlan, Clarence Neal, Burt Stand, and their sometimes ally Congressman Vito Marcantonio. The disagreement was one of personalities as much as of issues. The Neal-Stand-Loughlan group was accused of cooperating with members of the underworld and with leaders such as Marcantonio and the young Adam Clayton Powell, who were frequently supporters of left-wing causes. Bruce wanted to maintain an image of incorruptibility at all costs. In any case these disagreements limited the number of jobs Negroes could get from the Democratic organization until that organization regained power and black leaders arose who worked more in harmony with the Democratic leadership.[22]

Although appointments emanating from political organizations were relatively rare in the late thirties and early forties, the first appointed black judges took their seats on the bench during these years. They were Republicans appointed by Mayor LaGuardia and Governor Dewey. In September 1936 the Mayor chose Myles A. Paige as a magistrate. Thirty-seven years old at the time of his selection, Paige, who was a native of Montgomery, Alabama, had graduated from Howard University and the Columbia University Law School. In 1928 when Negroes were demanding a member of the race as Republican district leader, Paige had been the assembly candidate against Abraham Grenthal, the white incumbent.

Grenthal had won, but the next year Paige had received an appointment in the State Attorney General's office. He had the added advantage of being a Catholic so that his appointment could serve a religious as well as a racial purpose. During the swearing-in ceremony, the Mayor said that he had decided to name a black magistrate the previous year. "You just have to make good because the attention of the city will be focused on you," LaGuardia told the new judge. "You will probably have a very difficult time, but you have the balance and control to do the job. If you make good the credit is all yours and if you don't the fault is mine for appointing you." Paige responded that he knew he would have a heavier burden than if he were white, but he felt that he could do the job as well as any other magistrate. In 1940 he became the first Negro to be appointed to the Court of Special Sessions. His predecessor in this job had come from Brooklyn, and he moved from Harlem to Brooklyn to accept the appointment.

In 1939 Mayor LaGuardia appointed another black judge, this time a woman to the Court of Domestic Relations. She was Jane Bolin, a thirty-two year old native of Poughkeepsie who had graduated from Wellesley and the Yale Law School. She became the first black woman to be a member of the Association of the Bar of the City of New York. In 1941 the Mayor appointed Hubert T. Delany to the Court of Domestic Relations. Delany was a native of North Carolina, where his father was a Methodist bishop. The younger Delany had been married to the daughter of Booker T. Washington's secretary. Before his appointment to the bench, he had served in the New York County district attorney's office and as Tax Commissioner in the LaGuardia administration.

The black judicial appointment which attracted most attention was the selection by Governor Dewey in September 1943 of Francis E. Rivers as a city court judge. The *New York Times* gave this selection front-page coverage as well as an editorial entitled "An Excellent Appointment" in which the new judge was complimented for his competence. Rivers, son of a minister and a native of Washington, had earned a Phi Beta Kappa at Yale. He had graduated from the Columbia Law School and had served as an officer in France during World War I. As a member of the New York State Assembly, he had introduced a bill which made possible the election of the first two black judges in 1930. Serving as one of Thomas E. Dewey's assistants in the New York County district attorney's office, he had been the first Negro to be a full assistant district attorney, and one of the first two to apply for membership in the American Bar Association. His brother, a dentist, had been a Republican district leader in Harlem from 1933 to 1939, and Rivers himself had headed the Negro division of the Republican National Committee during the 1940 presidential campaign. He received an interim appointment which made it necessary for him to run for a full ten-year term in November 1943. He ran with the support of the American Labor Party as well as of the Republicans. The Democrats nominated a white man to oppose him. Nevertheless, Rivers won, with the American Labor Party providing the margin of victory. Rivers became the first black candidate in New York to win in a predominantly white constituency.[23]

Other candidates who ran for offices not previously held by Negroes lost. The American Labor Party ran black candidates for a variety of offices. In 1938 a Negro Republican was nominated for Congress, and in 1942, Ludlow Werner, though supported both by the Republicans and the American Labor Party, lost his race for the State Senate to the son of the former white district leader Harry C. Perry.[24]

About 1940 the two leaders who were to gain national reputations and to symbolize Harlem politics for a generation came into at least local prominence. The careers of Adam Clayton Powell and J. Raymond Jones require more detailed analysis than this chapter can give, but no general account of the period can ignore them. Powell ran for his first political office, that of city councilman, at the age of thirty-three in 1941. First as assistant to his father as minister of Harlem's largest church, then as minister himself, Powell earned his reputation by ten years of social work in Harlem during the height of the Depression. His most widely known achievement was as co-chairman of a committee which secured jobs for Negroes with public utilities and stores doing business in Harlem. The state constitutional convention of 1937 created a city council to replace the Board of Aldermen. Members of the council were elected by a system of weighted voting known as proportional representation. Although other black candidates both from Manhattan and from Brooklyn ran for the council in 1937 and 1941, Powell with the support of liberal and left-wing groups was the first member of the race to receive the 75,000 votes necessary for election. He served one two-year term in the City Council, keeping himself before the black public by attacking discrimination on a wide variety of fronts while maintaining his ties with labor and left-wing supporters. Gambling on the hope that the first Negro would be sent to Congress in 1944, he declined to run for reelection to the City Council in 1943. The state legislature did reapportion congressional districts in 1944, and Powell won the congressional nominations of the Republican, Democratic, and American Labor Parties as well as the general election.[25]

Jones, a native of the Virgin Islands, first came to Harlem in the 1920's. He mastered the technical aspects of party machinery in the predominantly white 22nd A.D. which included upper Harlem and Washington Heights. His career was characterized by an almost uncanny ability to choose the winning side in political controversies. In 1939 he ran against Harry C. Perry for the district leadership of the 19th A.D. Largely becaues of the Jones campaign, Perry was forced to resign in favor of Daniel Burrows, a Negro. In 1943 Congressman Michael Kennedy, leader of Tammany Hall, was opposed by a group of district leaders headed by Edward Loughlan, Burt Stand, and Clarence Neal. In that year Jones, supported by the Neal-Stand group, ran against Herbert Bruce for the leadership of the 21st. Although Bruce retained the leadership of the district, Loughlan replaced Kennedy as leader of Tammany Hall in January 1944. In that year assembly districts as well as congressional districts were reapportioned. The number of assembly districts was reduced from twenty-three to sixteen, and Jones was given leadership of half of the new 13th. In the 1944 congressional contest Jones and the Tammany leadership supported Powell, while Bruce opposed him. After reapportionment, Bruce's district became known as the 12th. It was the most populous district in New York County. In the 1945 leadership contest Jones and the Tammany leadership supported Bruce's opponents. Three opponents, two black and one white, successfully contested his leadership in various parts of the district. After his defeat the district was divided among them.[26]

In 1945 William O'Dwyer was elected mayor of New York to succeed Fiorello LaGuardia. Jones was one of his campaign managers. After O'Dwyer's election the Harlemite was one of a group of district leaders who supported the Mayor in a successful bid to unseat Tammany leader Loughlan and replace him by Frank Sampson, a leader who owed his position to O'Dwyer. In return for his support, Jones secured an appointment in 1946 for Vernon Riddick, president of Jones's Carver Democratic Club. In the same year Harold Stevens, another black lawyer who was a member of Jones's club, was nominated for the Assembly from the 13th A.D. Between 1946 and 1950 four of the sixteen Manhattan assemblymen were black, while Negroes made up about 15 percent of the borough's population. In 1947 Mayor O'Dwyer appointed Jones Deputy Housing Commissioner with the understanding that he would be the Mayor's liaison with Harlem.[27]

One Harlem officeholder proved a striking exception to the continuous Democratic majorities piled up in black neighborhoods. Proportional representation permitted two avowed Communists to be elected to the New York City Council. They were Peter Kaccione from Brooklyn and Benjamin J. Davis, Jr., from Harlem. Davis, born in Dawson, Georgia, in 1903, was the son of the publisher of a Negro newspaper who became a member of the Republican National Committee. After graduation from high school young Davis enrolled at Morehouse College, where he was one of the leaders of a student strike in his freshman year. After one year at Morehouse, he transferred to Amherst. There his violin playing brought him the position of concertmaster of the Amherst–Mt. Holyoke symphony and his football prowess brought him recognition as all-Eastern tackle in 1923. After graduation from Amherst and from Harvard Law School Davis became the second black man to be admitted to the Georgia bar since Reconstruction. He hung out a shingle in Atlanta, but few Georgians wanted a Negro lawyer. One of his first cases was the defense of Angelo Herndon, a black Communist. Herndon had led an interracial group of protesters who demanded that the Atlanta Community Chest give larger relief payments. Although Herndon and his followers won more money, he was indicted for inciting to insurrection, an offense under a statute of Reconstruction days which was punishable by the death penalty. Davis began by challenging the absence of Negroes on the jury. In 1949, when Davis along with other Communist leaders were on trial for violation of the Smith Act, he told the court that the Herndon case was the turning point of his life. "The Judge referred to me and my client as niggers and darkies, and threatened many times to jail me along with my client. I was treated in such a way that I could see before me the treatment of the whole Negro people in the South. The fact that

I had been luckier than most people in education and income did not shield me from what all Negroes suffer. So I felt that if there was anything I could do to fight against this and identify myself fully with my own people and strike a blow at the lynch system, I was determined to do it. In defending Herndon I had to familiarize myself with many of the Communist books and they made sense to me." Angelo Herndon was eventually freed by the United States Supreme Court. In 1933 Benjamin Davis joined the Communist Party, and two years later he moved to New York. He quickly advanced in party councils. By 1943 he had become editor and publisher of the *Daily Worker* as well as party chairman both in Harlem and Manhattan. When Adam Clayton Powell, hoping for a congressional nomination the following year, announced that he would not seek reelection to the City Council, Davis declared his candidacy.[28]

He won a seat on the New York City Council because he obtained the support of non-Communist Negro and labor groups as well as of the Communist Party. In 1943 the United States and Russia were allies in the fight against Germany. The conviction of Communist Party leaders, the expulsion of the Communists from the CIO, and McCarthyism were of a future era. Davis received wide support from non-Communist Negroes because he constantly identified Negro aspirations with the goals of Communism. In his own emotions the two were indistinguishable. He would frequently tell audiences, "I am a Negro. I am a Communist. I am an American. I am proud of all three." His position as a Communist gave him an identity which most black people living in a white society lacked and still lack. Ironically, the Communists of the 1930's and 1940's were almost the only group on the American scene who advocated complete racial equality and who tried to practice what they preached.

While the vast majority of black people were too steeped in the American tradition to accept Communism, they could not feel much hostility toward a group which made the redress of their grievances a major aspect of its program. Negroes who disagreed with Davis politically or who were indifferent to his political views could identify with him as a person because he had achieved status and position in a predominantly white organization and because he used his position as a sounding board for black aspirations. When he announced his candidacy for the City Council, the New York *Age* listed his Communist Party activities in the same sentence that it told its readers of his membership in the exclusive black college fraternity Alpha Phi Alpha and in the Negro Elks. The president of the Philadelphia chapter of the NAACP termed his election "a wonderful achievement." The *Amsterdam News* described his victory as "in many respects the most outstanding feature of the recent councilmanic contest.... The most important of all points to make about the election of Mr. Davis is that he is thoroughly qualified for his membership in the council. A close student of social problems, courageous, honest, and highly dedicated ... [he] should be a real asset to the entire citizenry of New York as a member of its legislative body." Roy Wilkins, at this time Assistant National Secretary of the NAACP, thought that New York was "fortunate to have him in the city Council.... It is to be doubted if there is a single council member of any higher caliber."[29]

As a member of the City Council, Davis introduced resolutions and demanded investigations on such subjects as segregation in the Stuyvesant Town housing development which was being built by the Metropolitan Life Insurance Company with city funds, alleged police brutality, inadequate fire protection in Harlem, the color bar in major league baseball, and the celebration of Negro History Week. Moreover, he acquired a reputation for availability to his constituents and a willingness to listen to their problems. When he ran for reelection in 1945 all the Harlem Democratic leaders and the leadership of Tammany Hall favored his endorsement by Tammany. That organization did endorse him. Only last-minute pressure from mayoralty candidate William O'Dwyer caused the endorsement to be rescinded. The New York *Age* suggested that the Republicans nominate him. Adam Clayton Powell, elected to Congress the previous year, served as co-chairman of his campaign, while J. Raymond Jones appeared at a Harlem ball in his honor. From the world of entertainment his endorsers included Lena Horne, Jose Ferrer, Olin Downes, Leonard Bernstein, Hilda Simms, and Langston Hughes. He won reelection with the second highest total of any candidate.[30]

Proportional representation was abolished in 1947, and the system of electing councilmen was changed to single-member constituencies. Davis's district ran from 97th Street to 160th Street on the West Side. About 40 percent of the population was black. In 1949 Davis, along with other Communist Party leaders, was tried for conspiracy to advocate the overthrow of the United States Government. The City Council changed its meeting time to late afternoon so that he could attend its sessions after court. Yet Davis's days as a city councilman were numbered. The Republicans, Democrats, and Liberals (the latter having split from the American Labor Party in 1946) united upon the candidacy of Earl Brown to oppose him. Brown, a native of Virginia, son of a minister, and graduate of Harvard, was a journalist. After serving a stint on the *Amsterdam News* he had become a reporter for *Life* magazine. Many people who lived outside the district and some who lived outside the city made financial contributions to his campaign. On the other hand the *New York Times* reported that some of the Harlem Democratic district leaders were not doing all they could for Brown. The leaders of the Communist Party were convicted on October 14. The party redoubled its efforts to reelect Davis. The only party member holding political office in the United States and a symbol of the party's concern for racial equality, his return to office now became a symbol of the repudiation of the verdict in the Smith Act trial. On November 3 he was released from jail on $20,000 bail. His homecoming to Harlem caused a riot which resulted in the arrest of six people. On Election Day Brown won by a 3–1 majority getting 63,000 votes to Davis's 21,000. Yet Davis received a majority in the 11th A.D., which included central Harlem and which was over 90 percent black.

At the time of his conviction an effort was made to expel Davis from the City Council. It could not be done by unanimous consent since American Labor Party Councilman Eugene Connally objected. On November 28, a month before his term expired, he was expelled by a 15–0 vote with two councilmen abstaining. Davis's expulsion was the first in the eleven-year history of the Council.

Davis served three years and four months in the Federal penitentiary at Terre Haute, Indiana, and two months in a jail in Pittsburgh on a contempt charge stemming from his appearance as a witness in the trial of a secondary party leader. While in Terre Haute, he was the plaintiff in a suit to desegregate the federal prisons. After his release, he became New York state secretary and in 1959 national secretary of the Communist Party. He died of cancer in 1964.[31]

Up to this time Manhattan was the only area in New York with a large enough black voting population to elect office holders. Beginning in the late 1940's and early 1950's enough Negroes had crossed the river into Brooklyn and made the move to the Bronx to give the blacks sufficient muscle to exact increased political recognition and to elect local officials and officeholders in those boroughs. In some ways the pattern of gaining political recognition paralleled that of Manhattan, while in others it reflected the unique political situation in each borough.

CHAPTER 5

To the Present

I

The first elected Negro officeholder from Brooklyn took his seat in the New York State Assembly in 1948. His election resulted from an increase in the borough's black population from 68,921 or 2.7 percent of the total in 1930 to 210,570 or 7.6 percent of the total in 1950, and from their concentration in the area known as Bedford-Stuyvesant. Yet the black community of Brooklyn is as old as that of Manhattan. Francisco the Negro was one of the original patentees of the town of Bushwick, while Swaen Janse, known as Van Luane, who had migrated from Sierra Leone in 1657, gained clear title to 500 acres of land in the present-day Bay Ridge section. Seventeenth-century newspapers describe Brooklyn Negroes as holding a wide variety of jobs. In 1698 the population of Brooklyn was 2,013, of whom 296 were black. Brooklyn remained 10 percent black a century later. A Negro church held services as early as 1818, and in 1831 a group of Kings County Negroes held a meeting to protest against colonization. Until the 1820's black children attended integrated public schools. Then a separate school was established, supported by a combination of public and private funds. As a result of the draft riots during the Civil War, many middle- and upper-class Negroes moved to Brooklyn. Some, such as the newspaper editor T. Thomas Fortune, worked in Manhattan but lived and participated in the social and civic activities of the Brooklyn Negro community. "In the 1890's," wrote Ralph Foster Weld, "there were families sufficiently well-to-do to afford to buy large houses and to furnish them lavishly. They could drive in expensive carriages, employ servants and go abroad on annual trips."[1] Most Brooklyn Negroes lived on or near Fleet Street and Fort Greene Park. From 1881 until Brooklyn merged into Greater New York in 1898, three successive Negroes served on the city's Board of

81

Education, under both Republican and Democratic city administrations. Probably in an effort to win black votes from their traditional Republican allegiance, a Democratic mayor of Brooklyn, who held office from 1889 to 1891, appointed two black men to the city's Department of Public Works. The first Negro became a Brooklyn patrolman in 1891, while a member of the race did not secure a similar position in Manhattan until 1911.[2]

Despite these beginnings the black community of Brooklyn remained smaller, less developed, and more scattered than that of Manhattan. As Harlem developed, middle- and upper-class Negroes, or those with such aspirations who came to the city, settled in Manhattan while others who had lived in Brooklyn moved back across the river where the center of racial activity was concentrating. In 1918 the Brooklyn *Eagle* reported that approximately 50,000 Negroes lived in the borough and that they worshipped in eleven churches. The paper went on to enumerate eight areas in which members of the race lived in substantial numbers. They resided in parts of the present-day sections of downtown Brooklyn, Bedford-Stuyvesant, East New York, and Flatbush. The next year the same paper reported, "President Isaac Ellman of the Brownsville Landlords Protective Association met a delegation of four Negroes from the American African Protective Association to consider the proposition of replacing ousted tenants in Brownsville with Negroes from the Harlem district of Manhattan. Mr. Ellman stated that he was much impressed with the businesslike methods of the delegation who said that they had sufficient money backing to purchase 100 of the largest double-deck apartment houses in the community and were ready to offer $2,000 more than the price so far asked." Subsequent issues of the *Eagle* do not indicate whether Negroes eventually purchased the buildings. In any case, the Brownsville–East New York section eventually became the largest concentration of Negroes in Brooklyn next to Bedford-Stuyvesant.[3]

The section of central Brooklyn known as Bedford-Stuyvesant was first settled in the seventeenth century. In 1668 Thomas Lambert was granted a license "to establish an inn for men and beasts" in the little hamlet of Bedford to sell beer, wine, and other liquors. At the same time Dutch farmers began buying land in the vicinity of Bedford and the adjoining hamlet of Stuyvesant-Heights. One of the oldest public schools in the borough was built on the site of the present-day corner of Fulton Street and Bedford Avenue in

1663. The area remained largely agricultural until the late nineteenth century. At this time row after row of three-story houses were built and sold to upper-middle-class families, largely English, German, Irish, and Italian. In 1954 an old Bedford-Stuyvesant resident reminisced, "I remember these houses fifty years ago when the owners had their own carriage houses, and the butlers wouldn't let you in the front door unless you put your card in a silver plate."[4]

As in Harlem, the area was overbuilt. The cost of operating the big homes skyrocketed after World War I. During the Depression many of the older people moved to smaller quarters. "Although real estate has been affected throughout the entire city," reported the Brooklyn *Eagle* in 1930, "it has been doubly affected in the great central area of Brooklyn, largely through lack of new modern improvements for the past many years . . . and also because of depreciation and obsolescence which have continued for many years. . . ."[5] As the overbuilding of Harlem had offered Negroes an opportunity to escape from crowded conditions downtown, overbuilding in Bedford-Stuyvesant offered them an opportunity to escape from overcrowded Harlem. Moreover, the Independent subway connected central Harlem with Fulton Street, the main business street of the district, while the Seventh Avenue connected Harlem with Eastern Parkway, the southern boundary of the district. The other boundaries of Bedford-Stuyvesant were, roughly, Flushing Avenue on the north, Broadway on the east, and Vanderbilt Avenue on the west. Black Harlem became as overcrowded as it did partially because the area was surrounded by the Harlem, Hudson, and East rivers, and by Morningside Park. Thus, expansion proved difficult. No such natural boundaries hampered the growth of the black community of Brooklyn. Negroes moved not only to Bedford-Stuyvesant, but spilled over into the surrounding neighborhoods of Crown Heights, Bushwick, Brownsville, and East New York. The black population of Bedford-Stuyvesant increased fivefold, from 30,000 in 1930 to 155,000 in 1955. This area became the first black neighborhood in Brooklyn to demand and ultimately receive political representation.

In the early years of the twentieth century most Negroes in Brooklyn, as elsewhere, voted Republican. As late as 1931 the only Republican assemblyman elected from the borough represented the district with the largest concentration of blacks. For almost a half century George E. Wibecan was undoubtedly the leading black political leader in Kings County. Wibecan's failure to win more than local recognition was probably due to the weakness of the Brooklyn Republican organization and to the small number of black votes in Brooklyn during most of the years of his leadership. He worked in the Brooklyn Post Office for forty-six years, retiring in 1933 as supervisor of the inquiry department. Yet his organizing ability, his militancy, and his knowledge of German at a time when Germans were a political factor not only in Brooklyn but throughout the city won him respect and influence both within and outside the black community. In 1912 he organized a boroughwide Negro Republican organization with 200 members. He attended every Republican state convention and several national conventions between 1910 and 1940. When he retired from the Post Office, he was appointed as a confidential inspector by a Democratic borough president. He seconded Thomas E. Dewey's gubernatorial nomination in 1938 and was appointed vice chairman of the Kings County Republican Committee in 1946, but died before the appointment could be announced.[6]

Although Negro newspapers occasionally reported the existence of black Democrats in Brooklyn before the 1930's, their effectiveness really began with the founding of the United Action Democratic Association headed by Bertram L. Baker in 1931. Baker's organization was a predominantly black political club in the district with the largest number and percentage of Negroes. Although Baker never attained the political power enjoyed by J. Raymond Jones, his rise to political leadership in Brooklyn resembles that of Jones in Manhattan in several important respects. Baker was a native of the West Indies and Jones of the Virgin Islands. Both arrived in the country without money or political connections. Both obtained political preferment by working their way up through the ranks of regular party organizations. Finally, both arrived upon the political scene at a time when the black population of their districts was beginning to increase and thus a need for black political leadership was arising. They saw the need and carved out careers for themselves by satisfying it.

Bertram L. Baker was born on the island of Nevis in 1896, the son of a minister. His mother died when he was two, and he was brought to Brooklyn to be raised by a grandmother. While working as an elevator operator and as a messenger, young Baker took correspondence courses in bookkeeping and accounting and became head of the accounting department of a chandelier-making firm. He was also a tennis player, and served as executive secretary of a national organization of Negro tennis players before the sport was integrated. Baker became an American citizen in 1924, and entered politics the next year. In 1932, six Negroes in Baker's district served on the Kings County Democratic Committee, the body which chooses district leaders. Largely owing to the influence of Baker's organization, the number had increased to thirty-two by 1934 and thirty-nine by 1936. In the latter year Baker was instrumental in the defeat of an incumbent district leader. In 1939 Baker became a Deputy Collector of Internal Revenue. Five years later, he obtained a job as a confidential inspector in the borough president's office. He ran unsuccessfully for the City Council in 1941 and 1945. The Republicans and the American Labor Party nominated black candidates for the Assembly in 1944 and 1946. The ALP withdrew its candidate in 1946 and supported the Republican. The white Democrat won by 77 votes. In 1948 the incumbent withdrew in favor of Baker. With both candidates being black, the district produced its normal Democratic majority, and Baker triumphed by a 2–1 margin. In January 1949 the first black legislator in New York City or State outside Harlem took his seat in Albany.

By 1950 Baker's club had attained a membership of 1,600. The next year Clarence Wilson, a Brooklyn Negro lawyer, was appointed a magistrate. Two years later, he was promoted to the Domestic Relations Court.

In 1953 the Democratic Party nominated Benjamin Schorr, a white man, as the candidate for Municipal Court Judge. Municipal court judges, who were elected, handled landlord-tenant cases and suits below $3,000. Louis Flagg, a Negro lawyer, challenged Schorr in the primary and received wide support from the black community. Baker went along with the party organization and supported Schorr. Nevertheless Flagg won by a narrow margin.

In the same year as Flagg's election the veteran white district leader of Baker's district died. The next year districts were reapportioned, and Baker was given the leadership of the old 17th A.D., which was renamed the 6th. The new district, which was shaped like a horseshoe, was gerrymandered in such a way that several years were to elapse before a Negro would lead another district in Brooklyn, and then only after another challenge to the party organization.[7]

II

Between 1950 and 1953 Negroes were elected to the Court of General Sessions, the New York State Senate, the State Assembly from the Bronx, and the borough presidency of Manhattan for the first time. All these jobs except that of Bronx assemblyman came as the result of factional fights within the Democratic Party.

In 1949 Tammany district leaders agreed that an Italian should be nominated as a surrogate, but they disagreed as to which Italian. Frank Sampson, the then Tammany leader, supported Impelleteri, while a group of leaders headed by Carmine DiSapio supported Valenti. J. Raymond Jones agreed to support Valenti if DiSapio would support a Negro for the next vacancy in the Court of General Sessions. The vacancy occurred in 1950, and Harold Stevens, a member of Jones's Carver Democratic Club and assemblyman from the 13th A.D., received the nomination. Stevens has since been elevated first to the Supreme Court, then to the Appellate Division. Since Stevens is both a Catholic and a Negro, he helps to give the judiciary both racial and religious balance.[8]

The state senatorial district with the largest black population was that of Jacob Panken. It included the 7th A.D. on the Upper West Side, which was approximately 15 percent black and Puerto Rican, the 13th, which was half Negro, and the 11th, which was over 90 percent Negro. Robert Blaikie, leader of the 7th, was fighting the Tammany leadership. In 1952 he supported Julius Archibald, a Negro who was a lawyer and teacher, in opposition to Panken. Joseph Pinkney, district leader and assemblyman from the 11th, supported Archibald, while J. Raymond Jones, leader of the black half of the 13th, did not come out strongly for Panken. Archibald won both in the primary and in the general election, thus becoming the first race member to sit in the upper house of the New York State Legislature.[9]

The election of the first black officeholder from the Bronx reflected the political situation in the borough, and the method by which he was chosen differed markedly from the way in which the first elected members of the race were selected in Manhattan and Brooklyn. In the former two boroughs Negroes had had to defeat an entrenched organization in the primary or at least bring it to its knees in a general election to gain elective office. On the other hand the Bronx political machine of Edward J. Flynn recognized the changing population trends and granted Negroes and Puerto Ricans at least token representation without a struggle.

Between 1940 and 1957 the Negro population of the Bronx increased by 315 percent. The majority settled in an area of the South Bronx which included the Morrisania section and parts of Hunt's Point and Crotona Park. This district, whose main thoroughfares were Prospect Avenue and Boston Road, was on a direct IRT subway route from central Harlem. Moreover, the district had had a radical tradition. In the late 1940's its assemblyman, Leo Isaacson, had been the only member of the American Labor Party elected to the State Assembly from the Bronx. As early as 1944 a Negro had run as an independent candidate for assembly. He received about 1,000 votes. By the early 1950's, the 6th, the assembly district with the largest number of blacks in the borough, was one of the most heavily Democratic districts in the city. The Republicans appointed a black woman as co-leader in 1951. In 1953 the Bronx democratic organization recognized the increasing black and Puerto Rican vote by designating Negro and Spanish candidates for the State Assembly in adjoining districts. The first elected black assemblyman was Walter Gladwin, while the first Puerto Rican was Torres. Gladwin, a native of British Guiana, was a lawyer who had previously served as deputy collector of internal revenue and had held jobs in the offices of the Bronx District Attorney and of the Corporation Counsel. At the time of Gladwin's selection his district was approximately 45 percent black, 15 percent Puerto Rican, and 40 percent Jewish.[10]

The most important political gain made by Negroes during these years was the election of a member of the race as borough president of Manhattan. The borough presidency provided the logical next step on the ladder of political recognition because it was halfway between a local and a citywide job. Except for the four years between 1917 and 1921, a borough presidency of Manhattan had been continuously held by a Jew between 1909 and 1949. By the latter year Jews were being nominated for city-wide and state-wide offices, and the borough presidency no longer served as a token of group recognition. The city charter divides New York into five boroughs: Manhattan, Brooklyn, Bronx, Queens, and Richmond. Each borough is headed by a borough president who supervises the repair of streets and sewers, helps plan construction projects, and presides over ground-breaking ceremonies within the borough.

The most important responsibility of the borough president is as a member of the Board of Estimate which draws up the city budget and, together with the City Council, constitutes the legislative arm of the city government. The nomination of a black man as borough president in 1953 came as a direct response to pressure from members of the race. As early as 1947, Lloyd Dickens, a Harlem real estate broker who was then a candidate for district leader, suggested that Negroes might be numerous enough in a few years to elect a borough president. In 1949 the American Labor Party had nominated a black man, Ewart Guinier, as borough president of Manhattan, and he had received about 16 percent of the vote. The same party had nominated a Negro as borough president of Queens in 1951.

A citizens group known as the Harlem Affairs Committee was formed in 1953. Led by ex-Assemblyman Robert W. Justice, its object was either to get a major party to nominate a candidate for borough president or to run one independently either in the primary or in the general election. A newspaperman named Carl Lawrence who was active in the Harlem Affairs Committee suggested to the Harlem Republican leader Harold C. Burton that the Republicans nominate Elmer A. Carter. After graduation from Harvard, Carter, a Democrat, had served as an official of the National Urban League. He had accepted an appointment from the Republican Governor Thomas E. Dewey as a member of the State Commission Against Discrimination. In 1950 he had run as the Republican candidate for Congress against Adam Clayton Powell. Hoping to attract Democratic voters in Harlem, the Republicans nominated him for borough president in July 1953. A split within Democratic ranks again aided the Negroes. Vincent R. Impelleteri served as mayor from 1950 to 1953. When he ran for reelection Tammany Leader Carmine DiSapio did not support him, but chose the then borough president of Manhattan, Robert F. Wagner. Twelve of the thirty-five Tammany leaders supported Impelleteri; the others supported Wagner. Among the Impelleteri adherents were Joseph Pinkney, leader of the 11th, and Herbert L. Bruce, who in 1951 had regained leadership of the 12th. Immediately following the designation of Carter, the Impelleteri forces chose Chauncey Hooper, a black lawyer who at this time was Deputy Comptroller and who was a lieutenant-colonel in the National Guard. During the last two weeks in July and the first

two weeks in August newspapers speculated on whether the
DiSapio-Wagner forces would also choose a black man. Their first
choice was a white assemblyman, but after the Liberal Party chose
Rev. James H. Robinson, Negro pastor of the Church of the Master, the DiSapio group withdrew their candidate and substituted
Hulan Jack, assemblyman and district leader from the 14th A.D.
in East Harlem. In this way the election of a Negro as borough
president of Manhattan was assured. Wagner and Jack both won
in the primary and in the general election. Jack became the first
black borough president of Manhattan. The job has been held by
a black man ever since.[11]

In February 1954, the *Daily Mirror* reported that every daily
paper outside the Iron Curtain had printed Jack's biography. The
Voice of America beamed his story to the world. His election to the
borough presidency was treated as the culmination of a Horatio
Alger saga. Born in British Guiana in 1906 and raised at St. Lucia
in the Windward Islands, he was the son of an Anglican minister
who taught in a Catholic school and who later became bishop of
the African Orthodox Church in Barbados. One of five children,
young Hulan helped to support his family as a "printer's devil" on
a weekly paper in St. Lucia, doing some printing but mostly
cleaning up the place. Coming to New York at the age of sixteen,
he found a job at $18 a week as janitor of the Peerless Paper Box
Co. He eventually became vice-president of the company. In his
spare time he took business courses at night at New York University. In 1930 he joined the racket-ridden Owasco Democratic
Club in East Harlem, whose leader, Alderman William Solomon,
was later sent to jail for bribery. In Jack's early years black people
were confined to the club's basement. The district became more
and more black and Spanish, and in 1937 a Cuban Fusionist, Oscar
Garcia-Rivera, supported by the Republicans, defeated the Tammany assemblyman. Running as the Democratic candidate, Jack
defeated Rivera in 1940, and remained in the Assembly for thirteen years, becoming the ranking Democratic member of the Committee on the affairs of New York City. Although he introduced a
number of bills against racial discrimination, he became primarily
known as a loyal party organization man. When Mayor Impelleteri
tried to oust Tammany Leader Carmine DiSapio and Jack supported the Tammany leader, he was reported as giving as his reason,
"I am in the organization now. Why should I fight to get in?"

As borough president, critics accused him of lacking a strong will and imagination, while Negroes accused him of being subservient to the white Tammany leadership. In 1959, when the New York *Post* disagreed with Jack on other matters, it told its readers that "he had made his way among politicians by hard application to the tasks at hand, amiability, and obedience to party rule.... On the political stump the normally mild Mr. Jack turns into a thundering proclaimer of party loyalties. He denounces non-Democrats with splendid fervor." The writer went on to credit Jack with being "a man of easy temper and more than perfunctory friendliness, who seems to enjoy pleasing the party and people."[12]

Jack's image in Harlem reached its low point because of his role in the political campaign of 1958. In 1956 many Negroes were dissatisfied with the civil rights plank of the Democratic platform. On October 11, Adam Clayton Powell announced that he would support President Eisenhower for reelection, and two weeks later he announced his support for Jacob Javits against Mayor Wagner for the United States Senate. After the election there were rumors that Powell as well as several Southern congressmen who had supported Eisenhower would be deprived of their committee seniority. This did not happen. But in 1958 Tammany Leader DiSapio decided to punish Powell by not supporting him for reelection. Whether from conviction or from what they felt to be political necessity, all the Harlem leaders but one went along. Because of his position in the city administration, Hulan Jack became the spokesman for the anti-Powell forces in Harlem. City Councilman Earl Brown somewhat reluctantly accepted the task of trying to defeat Powell in the Democratic primary. J. Raymond Jones, who had resigned his district leadership in 1954 and since then had been politically inactive, emerged as Powell's campaign manager. The Liberal Party supported Brown, while the Republicans, despite the opposition of Republican County Chairman Thomas Curran, supported Powell.[13]

The attempt to purge Powell proved a boomerang. It enabled him to charge the Tammany leadership with trying to dominate the politics of Harlem. This charge struck a responsive chord with black people, who hold smouldering resentment against white businessmen, landlords, and policemen who work in the black community and take money from it but live elsewhere. Powell dubbed DiSapio a "plantation boss" and raised a storm of controversy when he warned DiSapio and Jack not to come north of 110th Street. Jack was booed at a rally in front of the Hotel Theresa. On Election Day Powell won with a 3–1 majority.

The 1958 campaign marked the beginning of the end of Carmine DiSapio's power in the city. His insistence upon Frank Hogan as the nominee for the United States Senate and the subsequent defeat of Hogan and of Governor Harriman for reelection gave rise to an opposition group, the Reform Democrats, led by Eleanor Roosevelt, Herbert Lehman, and Thomas K. Finletter. The dominant black group led by Powell and Jones since Powell's 1958 victory remained aloof from the controversy. They continued to oppose DiSapio, and in the 1959 district leadership contests Powell, Jones, and one of their supporters defeated incumbents backed by DiSapio. On the other hand the issues raised by the Reform Democrats did not raise a sympathetic response among Negroes. Mrs. Roosevelt, Lehmann, Finletter and their colleagues charged DiSapio with bossism and appealed for more democracy in the selection of candidates and party officials. Although Negroes had responded to charges of bossism against DiSapio when the charges were put in racial terms, the abstract questions of political democracy and of honest and efficient government were issues to which they could not easily relate. The Reform Democrats aimed their appeal at middle-class voters, but the percentage of middle-class Negro voters is small. To most black people, politics means the politics of recognition as it did to the Irish, Italians, Jews, and other ethnic groups before they moved into the middle class in large numbers. Under this philosophy the purpose of politics is to get jobs which result from group power and which in turn increase group power. Moreover, the political power structure serves people in practical ways such as getting favors from government agencies, helping those in trouble with the law, aiding tenants who have problems with their landlords, or helping people to get on relief. In a typical speech illustrating this point of view, made in January 1960, J. Raymond Jones told the Riverside Democrats, a leading Manhattan reform club, that black people wanted patronage and recognition and that they would be glad to work with the reformers when they could agree upon a common objective.

Because black people could identify neither with DiSapio nor with his opponents, Powell and Jones tried to form what they hoped would be a third force, calling themselves the Harlem leadership team. During the district leadership contests of 1959, when Powell and Jones were successfully attempting to win leadership posts, the New York Times reported that Harlem leaders were distributing more patronage and performing more services for their constituents than usual. When DiSapio sought reelection as New York County leader in 1959, he was successful, but Powell and other Harlem leaders refrained from voting. The formation of the Harlem leadership team by Powell and Jones did not lead to a permanent alliance. During the next open factional confrontation within the Democratic Party, that of the mayoralty campaign of 1961, Powell and Jones were on opposite sides, and Jack no longer possessed power.[14]

After the abortive attempt to purge Powell, Jack tried to rebuild his image and mend his political fences in Harlem. He hired a black public relations adviser. Becoming interested in Harlem housing conditions, he made publicized visits of inspection. In the spring of 1960 he broke with DiSapio and joined with Powell and Jones. But it was a seemingly small indiscretion rather than a political setback which for a time at least, halted the career of Hulan Jack.

While investigating housing conditions, a reporter for the New York Post discovered that Sidney Unger, a long-time personal friend of Jack and a real estate operator with a slum clearance project up for approval by the Board of Estimate, had paid $5,500 for the redecoration of the borough president's apartment on West 110th Street. The discovery was made because Unger and the contractor who did the job disagreed about the price, and the contractor was disgruntled because Unger had withheld what the contractor felt to be some of his money. Jack was accused of violating several sections of the city charter. When the matter was made public in December 1959 Powell and other black leaders rallied to the borough president's defense. Aside from their personal feelings about Jack, Negro leaders defended the borough president both because of what he symbolized and because of their fears. Jack occupied the highest political office held by a black man at this time. Accusations against him seemed vaguely like an attack on racial progress. Moreover, Negroes feared that if Jack were removed, a white man might get his job.

The case went to a grand jury. At first, Jack maintained that his wife had paid for the renovation from household money, and only later did he admit that Unger had paid. Although Board of Estimate records showed that Jack had voted against Unger three times, he was indicted for conspiracy to obstruct justice and for three violations of the city charter.[15]

The governor has power to remove a borough president. In January 1960, when Jack was indicted, he suspended himself from office. The next month, a justice of the state supreme court, the court of original jurisdiction despite its name, dismissed the indictment on the ground that the charges of conspiracy and of violation of the city charter were improperly joined. The district attorney appealed, and the joint indictment was sustained both by the Appellate Division and by the Court of Appeals. The first Jack trial lasted a month in June and July 1960. After deliberating for twelve and a half hours, the jury reported that it could not agree whether the borough president was guilty beyond a reasonable doubt. During the trial the *Post* printed a feature on Jack entitled "Man in the Spotlight." "There is a quality about the composed bearing and the unforced sweetness of nature that invests with pathos the figure of Manhattan Borough President Hulan Edwin Jack these days. . . . Small and, at fifty-two, running to paunch, he is one of those well-tailored quietly dressed men who always looks as if they automatically repel lint and dust without the aid of accessories." The district attorney was given a second chance to try Jack. The second trial occurred in the last week of November and the first week of December 1960. After deliberating for four hours and thirty-five minutes, the jury convicted him of three of the four counts with which he had been charged. He was given a suspended sentence of a year in jail. The Appellate Division and the Court of Appeals later sustained the conviction. At the time of his conviction he told reporters that he would not leave politics. He remained as Tammany leader of the 14th A.D., and in 1967 he was reelected to the State Assembly.[16]

Since Jack's conviction automatically made him ineligible to serve as borough president, speculation naturally arose as to his successor. The new borough president would be chosen by the Manhattan members of the City Council, with the Mayor voting in case of a tie. Jack's successor would need to be acceptable to the Mayor, DiSapio, the Reform Democrats, and the Harlem leaders. The *New York Times* editorially opposed the establishment of a tradition that the borough presidency should be reserved for a black man. In 1957 the Republicans had nominated a white man to oppose Jack. Although newspapers mentioned several white candidates, none were seriously considered. Until he accepted an appointment by the Kennedy Administration, the most prominently mentioned Negro was Dr. Robert C. Weaver. Then Councilman Earl Brown became the leading candidate. He might have gotten the position if the Corporation Counsel had not ruled that the members of the City Council could not choose one of their number. On February 1, 1962, the choice fell upon Judge Edward Dudley. Dudley is the nephew of Edward A. Johnson, the first Negro elected to the State Legislature. After graduation from college in North Carolina and from St. John's Law School, he joined the legal staff of the NAACP in 1945. He held this job for ten years, with an interruption to serve as Minister to Liberia. In this latter capacity he administered the first Point Four program to an African nation. In 1955 Mayor Wagner decided not to reappoint Justice Hubert Delaney to the Domestic Relations Court, reputedly because the Mayor felt that some of Delaney's positions and organizational affiliations were too far to the left. Since Delaney was chairman of the NAACP Board of Directors, the Mayor replaced him by Dudley, a member of the NAACP legal staff. Dudley was a justice of the Domestic Relations Court at the time he was chosen borough president.[17]

The 1961 mayoralty campaign found the Democratic Party divided. In a bid for a third term the Mayor allied himself with the Reform Democrats, while the five county leaders supported State Comptroller Arthur Levitt. Powell supported Levitt, while Jones became the only district leader not a Reform Democrat to declare for Wagner and one of the chief strategists of the Mayor's successful campaign. Both the Mayor and DiSapio nominated black men for the borough presidency of Manhattan. The Mayor supported Dudley for reelection, while DiSapio supported the veteran Harlem district leader Lloyd Dickens. In Harlem the Mayor won by a 2–1 majority in the primary and a 3–1 majority in the general election.[18]

Carmine DiSapio's defeat for the district leadership in 1961 made him ineligible to continue as county leader. In the maneuvering to succeed him Jones obtained the support of the Harlem district leaders and of those leaders who were not reform Democrats. The Reform Democrats opposed him because he was not one of them, while Negroes interpreted their opposition as racially motivated. Edward Costikyan became County Leader, while Jones was appointed as the Mayor's liaison with the five county leaders.[19] In 1962 Dudley was nominated for Attorney General. Other states also nominated Negroes for statewide office. Otis Smith had been elected State Treasurer of Michigan in 1960. In 1962 the voters of Massachusetts chose Edward Brooke, who was later to become United States Senator, as Attorney General, and a black man was chosen State Treasurer of Connecticut. But in New York Governor Rockefeller, Lieutenant-Governor Wilson, and Attorney General Lefkowitz all won reelection, and Dudley did not run ahead of his ticket. No black man was nominated for statewide office in 1966. In 1970 the Democrats nominated State Senator Basil Patterson for Lieutenant-Governor, but the Republicans were victorious.[20]

The number of Negroes representing Harlem districts in the State Legislature declined from four to two. In 1950, when Harold Stevens became the first race member to be nominated to the Court of General Sessions, his place in the legislature was taken by a white man. When Hulan Jack became borough president, he was replaced by Kenneth Phipps, a black member of his club. In 1958 Phipps received a judicial appointment, and his seat in the Assembly was taken by José Ramos Lopez, a Puerto Rican. Although some Negroes wanted to replace Ramos Lopez by a black man in 1960, and for some time Jack gave them his support, they were unsuccessful, and Ramos Lopez was renominated and reelected.

Earl Brown remained on the City Council until September 1961, when he accepted an appointment as a member of the Housing and Redevelopment Board. He was succeeded by Herbert Evans, a lawyer. In 1963 Brown became deputy borough president, and Evans took Brown's job on the Housing and Redevelopment Board. J. Raymond Jones was elected to the City Council in 1963, and held the job until 1969.

During the Wagner Administration the first two black men became heads of city departments. In 1954 Arthur C. Ford, a civil engineer who had worked in the borough president's office for many years, became Commissioner of Water Supply, Gas, and Electricity. Later, when this department became a board, Ford was chosen its chairman. In 1959 James R. Dumpson, a social worker who had been a deputy commissioner in the Department of Welfare, became Welfare Commissioner. Since the time of Ferdinand Q. Morton, a

Negro has been one of the three members of the Municipal Civil Service Commission, and since the time of Mayor Impelleteri one has served as a deputy police commissioner. In 1961 the *Amsterdam News* printed a list of the leading black appointive city officials. They included a member of the Parole Board, secretary to the Board of Estimate, and deputy commissioners of the departments of Police, Hospitals, and Corrections, the last of these having two.[21]

J. Raymond Jones ran both for City Councilman and for district leader in 1963. Powell and several other Harlem district leaders opposed him. The political disputes between Powell and Jones were sharpened by disagreements over business matters, and they entered into a bitter public controversy. Warren Moscow, a political reporter for the *New York Times*, maintains that Powell and Jones disagreed in public, but privately remained partners, so that one could always win regardless of the result. In any case, 1963 was Jones's year. He defeated opponents both for the district leadership and for the City Council and emerged as one of the most powerful Democrats in the state.[22]

In 1964, Constance Baker Motley launched her meteoric political career, and Harlem leaders successfully maneuvered to obtain the nomination and election of two state supreme court justices at the same time. Julius Archibald, the first black man to sit in the New York State Senate, had served a two-year term and had been defeated in a 1954 primary contest by James L. Watson, the son of one of the first two elected black judges. After ten years in the State Senate, Watson was appointed to the Civil Court and subsequently to the United States Customs Court. Three aspirants sought Watson's Senate position. On the face of the vote the successful candidate was Noel Ellison, president of the Riverside Democrats, a leading reform club, and the operator of several dry-cleaning establishments. After Ellison's nomination, the fact that he had several policy convictions was made public. Nevertheless, the Riverside Democrats determined to keep him as the candidate. Harlem leaders and New York County Leader Edward Costikyan opposed him. Discovering irregularities in the choice of county committeemen by the Riverside Democrats, the Tammany leadership began a lawsuit to disqualify him. The lawsuit, combined with pressure from Mayor Wagner, finally forced him to withdraw. Mrs. Motley was then chosen as the candidate. She had obtained national recognition by her work

with the NAACP Legal Defense Fund, but she had had no previous
political experience.[23]

She is only the most prominent of many NAACP lawyers and
other officials who combine civil rights activities with politics. In
1966 black state senators from Manhattan and the Bronx had both
been elected to office while serving as presidents of NAACP chapters, and a state senator from Brooklyn had been a leading NAACP
lawyer of the borough. The participation of many Negroes in
NAACP activities and later in politics was not surprising. Until
very recently civil rights was one of comparatively few ways for
black lawyers both to make money and to obtain recognition. In
New York, as elsewhere, the Negro community has had few businesses which could offer lucrative retainers to black lawyers. Most
white law firms have traditionally been closed to blacks. Because of
these barriers, civil rights has become a major path for talented and
ambitious black lawyers to distinguish themselves while, at the
same time, identifying with racial aspirations. Moreover, the white
power structure has turned to civil rights leaders more often than
to political leaders as being representative of Negro opinion. During
a riot in Harlem in 1943 Mayor LaGuardia toured the city not
with a politician, but with Walter White, who was then National
Executive Secretary of the NAACP. During the 1964 disturbances
in Harlem and Brooklyn, Mayor Wagner conferred with a group
of Negro leaders headed by Dr. Martin Luther King, who had
flown to New York from Atlanta for the purpose. Finally, civil
rights leaders are frequently rewarded because of an ambivalence
toward them by white society. White people feel that Negroes
should fight for their rights, while at the same time hoping that
recognition might take the edge off their militancy.

Three state supreme court judges for the district which includes
Manhattan and the Bronx were chosen in 1964. By skillfully assuming the balance of power in a factional dispute, Harlem leaders
obtained two of the three nominations. Mayor Wagner and the
Liberal Party supported Borough President Edward Dudley and
Gustav Rosenberg, president of the State Board of Higher Education. Bronx leader Charles Buckley, who was antagonistic to the
Mayor and the Liberal Party, supported a member of his own organization. The Harlemites led by Adam Clayton Powell joined with
the supporters of Dudley and at the same time made an agreement
with Buckley that they would support the Bronx choice if the

Bronx delegates would support Civil Court Judge Darwin Telesford. Telesford and the Bronx judge were nominated. Although the Liberal Party did not support Telesford in the general election and some Manhattan Democrats were lukewarm in their support, he and Dudley both won judgeships.[24]

Edward I. Costikyan resigned as New York County Democratic leader in 1964. Relations between regulars and reformers had improved while he had been leader. At the time of Costikyan's resignation the reformers controlled six and five sixths votes of the sixteen on the Democratic County Executive Committee. Jones was the personal choice of the Mayor to succeed Costikyan. On December 3 he was chosen county leader. The Harlemite had become so powerful that the only reference to his race in the press was the mention that he was the first black county leader in the state and perhaps the only one in the nation.[25]

One of the new county leader's first problems was the choosing of a borough president to succeed Edward R. Dudley. Earl Brown, who at this time was serving as deputy county leader, was acceptable to the Mayor and to most of the Harlem leaders, but not to Jones. A smouldering enmity between the two men was fanned into flame when Brown supported Jones's appointment for City Council in 1963. To block the selection of Brown, Jones gave his support to Constance Baker Motley. Despite the opposition of most of the Harlem leaders who felt that she lacked experience, Jones pushed Mrs. Motley's election through the ·Manhattan delegation to the City Council.[26]

His knack of selecting winning candidates in elections seemed to desert Jones once he became county leader. In 1965 the Democratic Party in New York City was divided between regulars and reformers, with only the vote-getting ability of Mayor Wagner to hold it together. The Mayor's announcement in June 1965 that he would not run for reelection resulted in a scramble for the nomination. Jones and the Mayor supported City Council President Paul Screvane, while City Comptroller Abraham Beame won the nomination. The Republicans nominated their popular congressman from the "silk stocking" district, John V. Lindsay, and the Liberal Party, who usually support Democratic candidates, gave Lindsay their endorsement. Many blacks had become dissatisfied with Mayor Wagner between 1961 and 1965. They criticized his general indecisiveness, his failure to appoint more race members to high-level city jobs, the behavior of the police during civil rights demonstrations, his failure to advocate a complaint review board composed of civilians to process grievances of citizens against the police, and his conduct during the disturbances in Harlem and Bedford-Stuyvesant during the summer of 1964. During the campaign Lindsay frequently visited black neighborhoods, sometimes speaking and often merely walking through the streets and shaking hands. He promised more jobs and came out in favor of an independent civilian complaint review board. On the night before election he answered questions on a black radio station. On election day Lindsay garnered about one third of the votes of Negroes, almost doubling the vote of Lefkowitz in 1961.[27]

The new mayor's most conspicuous Negro appointment was that of Robert Lowery as Fire Commissioner. Lowery, a Democrat and friend of J. Raymond Jones, was a career fireman. He had served as president of the Vulcans, the society of black firemen, and vice-president of the Federation of Negro Civil Service Organizations. The other widely publicized appointment of a Negro by Lindsay was that of William Booth, president of the NAACP State Conference of Branches, as chairman of the City Commission on Human Rights. In the conduct of his office Booth gave eloquent articulation to black grievances, but members of other minority groups frequently complained that the Commission was neglecting them. In February 1969 the Mayor appointed Booth a criminal court judge, and he was replaced by Simeon Golar, a Negro lawyer who had run as the Liberal Party candidate for Attorney General in 1966. Golar was subsequently appointed chairman of the New York City Housing Authority and replaced as chairman of the City Commission on Human Rights by Eleanor Holmes Norton, another Negro lawyer.

The Lindsay victory weakened Jones's position; the surrogate contest of 1966 made his retirement inevitable. Although the choice of surrogate is important to politicians because surrogates probate wills and thus control millions of dollars of patronage every year, their selection usually attracts little public attention. In 1966 both Jones and Republican County Chairman Vincent Albano supported Supreme Court Justice Arthur Klein, while Senator Robert Kennedy, reform Democrats, and the Liberal Party supported another State Supreme Court Justice, Samuel Silverman. In the course of the campaign the candidates were all but forgotten, while Jones and

Kennedy became the principal protagonists. Most Negro leaders supported Klein, and some tried to raise a race issue, by claiming that Jones faced opposition because he was black. The Silverman campaign was headed by Steven Smith, a Kennedy brother-in-law, and it included veterans of the campaigns of both the Senator and the late president. Silverman won by a 3–2 majority. Jones's continuation as county chairman for ten months after the Silverman victory bears witness to his strength as a leader. He resigned in March 1967, admitting that his inability to work with Senator Kennedy was the reason for his resignation.[28] Coincidentally, early 1967 witnessed the loss of power by both leading Harlem politicians. Within a month Adam Clayton Powell was denied his seat in Congress and J. Raymond Jones resigned as New York County leader.

Powell's difficulties stemmed from the combined effect of his own activities with the state of American public opinion on civil rights. In 1960 the Harlem congressman was tried for income tax evasion, but acquitted when the jury failed to agree. Two years later, he shocked large segments of the public by traveling to Europe at government expense accompanied by two female members of his staff. The legal maneuvers which followed the much-publicized libel suit by Mrs. Esther James forced him to continually absent himself from his district. In the fall of 1966 an examination of the payroll of the House Education and Labor Committee of which Powell was chairman revealed that Powell's wife was receiving a $20,000 annual salary although she lived in Puerto Rico and the law required that those on the payrolls of congressmen must work either in Washington or in the congressman's home district. In December 1966 a subcommittee of the House Administration Committee investigated the use of House Education and Labor Committee funds. The committee criticized Powell for payroll padding, for misuse of committee credit cards, for the submission of fraudulently signed vouchers, and for generally loose spending. Yet Powell might not have been disciplined and certainly would not have been expelled from Congress if the temper of the American public had not worked against him. By late 1966 the civil rights movement of the early 1960's and the interracial thrust for integration and equality had been all but spent. In the summers of 1964, 1965, and 1966 riots had broken out in the ghettos of many American cities. Many white Americans, liberals as well as conservatives on the race issue, reacted to the hostility and violence borne of black frustration with their own hostility and fear. Powell had achieved a position as a racial folk hero by his articulation of Negro defiance of white America. Beginning in the spring of 1963 when he had appeared on a Harlem platform with Malcolm X, he had frequently made speeches which many white Americans interpreted as being sympathetic to black separatism and "black power," the latter term in its context of hostility and defiance of integration. Powell's conduct and the temper of the times caused congressmen's mail to reflect increasing dislike of Powell and demands that his power be curbed. The first action came in September 1966 when members of his House Education and Labor Committee revolted against his leadership. By a vote of 27–1 the committee deprived him of most of his power as chairman. When the 90th Congress convened in February 1967, the House rejected a compromise supported by the Democratic leadership which would have allowed him to take his seat until a committee of investigation decided what action should be taken. Instead, the House adopted a resolution supported by the Republican leadership which declared his seat vacant while the committee was investigating. In the same month the committee recommended that Powell be seated, but that he be censured for gross misconduct, that he be stripped of his seniority, and that he pay $40,000 as a punishment. The House voted to disregard the recommendations of the committee and to oust Powell. Although the Harlem congressman was reelected in a special election to fill his unexpired term, he did not attempt to take his seat. In the fall of 1968 he won his usual overwhelming victory. When the 91st Congress convened in January 1969, he was permitted to take his seat, but without seniority. During 1969 and 1970 he seldom appeared in Harlem, and his influence in Congress and in the civil rights struggle was minimal. By the spring of 1970 opposition to his reelection had arisen within the Harlem community. In the primary in September of that year he was defeated by a Harlem state assemblyman, Charles Rangell. In this way the career of Adam Clayton Powell came to an end.[29]

In 1966 Constance Baker Motley became a federal judge. She was succeeded as borough president of Manhattan by Percy Sutton, the fourth member of his race to hold this office and the third in three years. With the decline in power of Powell and Jones, Sutton became the most powerful Harlem political leader. His power is based as much on the force of his personality as upon the office which he holds. Percy Sutton was born and raised on a farm in Texas. Although born into slavery, his father eventually became the principal of a San Antonio high school. Percy was the youngest son and one of fifteen children. During World War II he was the first Negro to enter Air Force intelligence. As a pilot, he rose to the rank of captain and won combat stars in the Italian and Mediterranean theaters. In 1944 he was arrested for sitting at a table with a white colonel, and seventeen years later he was again arrested, this time in Mississippi as a Freedom Rider. Sutton studied law. His clients ranged from Malcolm X to civil rights demonstrators. In 1961 and 1962 he served as president of the Harlem branch of the NAACP. Sutton founded the first reform Democratic club in Harlem. After several unsuccessful attempts he defeated the long-time assemblyman Lloyd Dickens in 1964, despite the fact that Dickens was also a district leader. As a freshman legislator in 1965, Assemblyman Sutton co-sponsored a resolution for the creation of a committee to investigate the liberalization of the state's divorce law. He served on the committee and introduced bills to liberalize both the state's divorce and abortion laws. In August 1966 the *World-Journal-Tribune* referred to him as "the most articulate defender of minority rights in the Assembly" and "Perhaps the most listened-to lawmaker in this house." In March 1966 the *Times* described an incident: "Assemblyman Percy Sutton, normally a poised, controlled speaker no matter how emotional the issue, became so incensed that his voice almost broke as he replied to an argument against school bussing by a Nassau Republican. 'It seems to me,' Mr. Sutton said, glaring at Assemblyman John E. Kingston, 'as though someone is saying that in chipping away at segregation and discrimination, we are intruding on the rights of others.' A hush fell over the chattering assembly as the Harlem Democrat spoke. 'All we are asking,' Mr. Sutton went on, his angry eyes still on Mr. Kingston's face, 'is that you give another man what you enjoy daily. You behave as though you were giving him something special and he should be grateful to you.' His voice thickened with emotion in his final sentence: 'We wouldn't come asking for anything if we had what you had.'" Although Sutton had been elected to the legislature with the support of reform Democrats, he united with other Harlem leaders in support of Arthur Klein and J. Raymond Jones in the surrogate primary of 1966. Sutton's articulateness and his acceptability to various groups both in the Harlem community and in the Democratic Party brought about his selection as borough president despite the fact that he had less than two years of experience in elective office.[30]

III

The increase in the black population and in the black percentages of the population of Brooklyn, Bronx, and Queens brought about increased political recognition in the late 1950's and in the 1960's.

The black district in the south Bronx has continued to be one of the most heavily Democratic in the city, and its leadership has remained loyal to the regular party organization headed after the death of Edward J. Flynn by Congressman Charles Buckley and his successors. Walter Gladwin, chosen to be the first black elected official from the Bronx in 1953, remained in the State Assembly for four years, when he was appointed a City Magistrate. His successor, Ivan Warner, one of Bronx Leader Buckley's chief lieutenants, has been the most important Bronx Negro political leader to date. Warner was born in New York City in 1920, the son of West Indian immigrants. His father was a shipping clerk in a candy factory. A drop-out from Haaren High School, he worked as a shoeshine boy and pushed a handcart in the garment district until deciding to complete his education at the age of twenty-six. By this time he had moved to the Bronx and had become interested in politics. He earned money to complete high school and to attend college and law school by working as a typist and as an aide to Bronx Congressman Isidore Dowlinger. Warner was admitted to the bar in 1955, and within two years he was a member of the State Assembly. Elected to the State Senate in 1960, he became the first Bronx Negro to be a district leader in 1963, the same year he was elected vice-president of the Bronx County Democratic Committe. The next year he was elected president. In the State Senate Warner became chairman of the Education Committee and of the Joint Legislative Committee on Housing and Urban Development. During the intraparty struggle over the Democratic leadership of the legislature in 1965, Warner was Buckley's candidate for the Senate leadership, although he stood little chance of winning.

In the 1965 election for Bronx borough president Warner was nominated on the ticket headed by Abraham Beame, while Commissioner of Relocation Herman Badillo ran on the mayoralty ticket of Paul Screvane. Badillo won by about 200 votes. His nomination was the most important given to a Puerto Rican up to that time. In 1965 the State Legislature was reapportioned, and a special election was held, in keeping with the Supreme Court's "one man one vote" decision. Therefore Warner had to relinquish his seat in the State Senate to run for borough president. However, he regained his Senate seat in 1966. Two years later, Warner obtained the Democratic designation for a state supreme court judgeship. Despite an unfavorable recommendation by a committee of the Association of the Bar of the City of New York, the voters of Manhattan and the Bronx put him on the bench. Members of his club replaced him in the State Senate and as district leader. These jobs, along with one seat in the State Assembly, were held by the black Bronx-elected and party officials in 1971.

In recent years Negroes have been moving to an area in the north Bronx extending roughly from Dunhill Road and from 233rd Street and from White Plains Road to the New England Throughway. According to a resident who is familiar with the pattern of settlement, this neighborhood is about 10 percent black. To date, the area has no black elected officials or district leaders, although Andrew C. Parks did run unsuccessfully for councilman-at-large in 1969.[31]

In Queens Negroes have largely settled in two areas which do not adjoin each other, South Jamaica-St. Albans and Corona-East Elmhurst. About 200,000 blacks live in the former area, in which an assemblyman and the Republican and Democratic leaders of a portion of a district are black. In the 1930's Hugo Heydorn, a black realtor, challenged restrictive covenants in the courts and succeeded in integrating the Addisleigh Park area of St. Albans. This neighborhood became the home of some of the city's wealthiest blacks. The extension of the Independent subway from Kew Gardens to Jamaica in 1937 was a spur to Negro migration to the borough. The South Jamaica district of Queens, like the Bedford-Stuyvesant section of Brooklyn and the black neighborhood in the South Bronx, is on a direct subway route from central Harlem. The building of the Triboro Bridge, which connected 125th Street with Queens, brought blacks into Corona and East Elmhurst, while jobs in aircraft plants on Long Island during World War II proved to be an additional reason for Negroes to move to the borough.

In 1933 Negro newspapers reported black participation in a

Republican district leadership fight as well as the existence of a Negro Democratic club. A former district attorney was among the members of the Democratic club. In 1935 J. Foster Phillips, a native of the West Indies who was a funeral director, became the first member of his race to be a member of the Democratic County Committee. Twenty-three years later, he became the first Negro district leader. As early as 1952 a Negro ran as an independent candidate for the Assembly from a South Jamaica district. In 1957 the Republicans designated a black woman as a candidate for the City Council in opposition to a popular liberal Democratic incumbent. The Democrat won easily. Queens districts were reapportioned in 1958, and Phillips was named as leader of part of a district. The Democrats nominated a black assembly candidate, but he was defeated. In 1964 Kenneth Brown, a Negro lawyer, defeated both a white Democratic opponent in a primary and the Republican incumbent to become the first member of the race elected from the borough.

The leading black Democrat in Queens in recent years has undoubtedly been Guy Brewer. Brewer, a native of Atlanta and a graduate of Morehouse College, began his political career in the 1930's as an aide to Herbert L. Bruce in his efforts to bring black Democratic district leaders to Harlem. Later, Brewer and Bruce quarreled, and in the 1940's Brewer served for a time as a Harlem district leader. He then moved to Queens and continued his interest in politics. In 1958, when J. Foster Phillips became the first black district leader, Mrs. Brewer became his female co-leader. In 1967, when Phillips died, Brewer became district leader, and the next year, when Assemblyman Brown received a judicial nomination, Brewer took his place in the Assembly.[32]

The most significant gains in black political representation occurred in Brooklyn. Bertram L. Baker remained the only black district leader and assemblyman in the borough until 1962. He and a Republican assemblyman from Auburn, George Metcalf, introduced and gave their names to bills making housing discrimination illegal. In 1957 J. Daniel Diggs, president of Baker's political club, became the first Negro from the borough to be nominated and elected to the City Council.

By 1960 the assembly district adjoining Baker's was over half black. In June of that year a predominantly black but interracial group formed the Unity Democratic Club to bring black leadership and legislative representation to the district. The club was led by Thomas R. Jones, a lawyer with a radical image and record who had been active in the American Labor Party in the 1940's and was that party's candidate for the State Supreme Court in 1946. In the mayoralty campaign of 1961 the Unity Democrats allied themselves with the reform Democrats and supported Mayor Wagner for reelection. The next year Jones ran both for assemblyman and district leader against Samuel Berman, the white incumbent of both positions. Wesley Holder, a Negro who was not affiliated with the Unity Democratic Club, announced that he would oppose the white incumbent for the State Senate. Then Berman withdrew from the Assembly race in Holder's favor. Jones won both the district leadership and the Assembly nomination. The strength of the demand for racial representation is shown by the fact that Jones was the only leadership candidate allied with the reform Democrats to win in Brooklyn that year.

Jones's victory was quickly followed by other gains. The first Brooklyn Negro was nominated and elected to the State Supreme Court in 1963, and the next year the first member of the race was elected to the State Senate. The legislative reapportionment of 1965 brought about a black district leader and assemblyman from a district adjoining Bedford-Stuyvesant in East New York.[33]

But by far the most significant political gain for Brooklyn Negroes in the 1960's was the election of the first black candidate to Congress from Bedford-Stuyvesant in 1968. For nineteen years the congressional district in Brooklyn with the largest black constituency was that of Edna Kelly. Mrs. Kelly's congressional record displeased liberal whites as well as blacks. She was almost defeated in a 1966 primary. In the summer of 1967 she walked into a police command post during disturbances in Bedford-Stuyvesant and disagreed with orders that policemen should only shoot in self-defense. "I give you permission to shoot to kill," she is quoted as having said, although she later denied it. At another time she said, "There has to be a willingness on the part of lower economic groups to help themselves. All ethnic groups have done so. We have to give them a helping hand, but they have to help themselves to a large degree."[34]

Early in 1968 the State Legislature under a federal court order to correct population inequities in some congressional districts redrew lines. A new district emerged which included a large part of Bedford-Stuyvesant along with portions of Crown Heights,

Bushwick, and Williamsburg. The new district was about 80 percent Democratic and 70 percent black. It contained 10,000 more registered women than men. While Congresswoman Kelly conducted an unsuccessful primary campaign to unseat Congressman Emanuel Cellar in an adjoining district, three Negroes vied for the Democratic nomination in the new district. Assemblywoman Shirley Chisholm proved victorious. In the general election she faced James Farmer, former National Director of CORE. Farmer gained Republican and Liberal Party support. Farmer had not only to buck the normal Democratic majority and the predominance of women, but he had never lived in the district. Chisholm won by a two and a half to one majority.

Shirley Chisholm was born in Brooklyn in 1925. Her father was an unskilled laborer and her mother worked as a domestic. Both her parents were natives of Barbados, and she spent her childhood years from three to eleven on that island. After graduation from Brooklyn College and Columbia, she taught at and directed a day-care center.

After serving one term in the State Assembly and as a district leader, Thomas R. Jones accepted a judgeship. Shirley Chisholm ran successfully for his assembly seat in 1964. She was reelected in 1965 and 1966 with larger majorities than the candidates at the top of the ticket. Her name was attached to the first bill enabling domestic workers to obtain unemployment insurance, and she was instrumental in the passage of the SEEK program, a higher education plan which enables worthy disadvantaged students who make low aptitude scores to enter universities and receive intensive remedial aid. Albert Blumenthal, who served as deputy minority leader during these years, described her to a *New York Times* reporter as "a very tough lady, likeable, but a loner. Unlike other women in the legislature, she was never afraid to jump into a debate. She knew what she wanted to say and she said it well. She wasn't quick to make up her mind, but when she did, you couldn't blast her out of it." Her husband, who is one of her chief advisers, is a former private investigator and now a senior investigator for the New York City Department of Social Service. After her election to Congress, she replaced Edna Kelly as the woman member of the Democratic National Committee from New York State. As the first black woman elected to Congress and because of her own articulateness, she has been in constant demand as a speaker and she has furnished good copy for publications as diverse as political reporters, European journalists, the black press, women's pages, the college press, and Washington's regular Capitol Hill corps.[35]

In 1969 Mario Procaccino and John Marchi, two avowed conservatives, won the Democratic and Republican mayoralty primaries. Shirley Chisholm was the first black political leader and one of the first Democrats to announce her support for John Lindsay in his bid for reelection on a third-party ticket. Most Negro leaders and liberal white Democrats followed her example.

Two events of political importance to the black community of New York occurred in 1970. An era was ended when Adam Clayton Powell was defeated by Assemblyman Charles Rangell in the Harlem congressional primary, and State Senator Basil Patterson became the Democratic Party nominee for lieutenant-governor.

CHAPTER 6

Adam Clayton Powell

Undoubtedly most people who are unfamiliar with the New York political and racial scene will equate politics in Harlem and perhaps all Negro politics in America with the name of one man. A recent biographer described Adam Clayton Powell as one of the most controversial figures of the century.[1] Loved and hated, identified with and vilified, social worker, minister, radical, race leader, powerful congressional committee chairman, and *bon vivant*, he was a public figure for a quarter of a century. Yet his place in history will stem neither from his antics nor his accomplishments, but from the feelings of black people about him.

External̇ly, the career of Adam Clayton Powell has almost nothing in common with the life of the average Negro. His skin was so light that he could, and for a time did, pass for white. He never knew material poverty, and he enjoyed educational opportunities which, until the past few years, were open only to a handful of members of the race. Yet despite these differences Powell not only said and did things which black people would like to say and do, he shared their aspirations, their limitations, and their feelings of inferiority. Many reasons have been given for his biennial reelection to Congress regardless of what he said or did, whether he campaigned, or what others said about him. Although various factors contributed to Powell's continuation for a century as a black leader, the underlying reason was that Negroes saw him as an image of themselves. Despite his light skin, his power in Congress, and his trips to Europe, Powell could not break the ghetto walls which formed his personality.

Adam Clayton Powell inherited ability, strength, egotism, and craftiness from his father. Born in Virginia in 1865, the elder Powell worked as a coal miner and lost money as a gambler before getting religion. The father attended Yale and occupied pulpits in Philadelphia and New Haven before becoming pastor of Harlem's

Abyssinian Baptist Church, one of the city's oldest Negro congregations, in 1908. "He was three men in one," a deacon reminisced to a writer for *Esquire*, "a great leader, a great preacher, and a great financier." When Powell became minister, the church was located on 40th Street between Seventh and Eighth avenues, and it was $150,000 in debt. By 1911 he had decided that the church should move to the up-and-coming neighborhood of Harlem. Some of the elders opposed the move, and it was delayed for a decade. The church bought property in 1920, and the next year the minister threatened to resign unless the move was made. The church did move the following year, and a mortgage of a third of a million dollars was paid off in four years.

The legacy which the father bequeathed his son had many facets. "Father was against dancing, motion pictures, and card playing," the congressman later recalled. "He used to preach a lot against whiskey." One weekend when young Powell was home from college he did not have a dress shirt for a formal dance. "I started rummaging around in his chest of drawers for a shirt—and turned up three or four empty gin bottles. I was shocked, and immediately confronted the old man. The father took the discovery with great equanimity. "You've heard me preach against whiskey," he told his son, "but I've never said a word against gin." The son was soon to learn the same dexterity when met with an embarrassing question. Hickey and Edwin in their biography of the son describe the father's autobiography as "compounded of reminiscence, exhortation, and an extended catalogue of tributes to himself. The old pastor had carefully clipped all newspaper reports of his lectures and sermons, all editorials lauding him for public service, the complete texts of testimonials tendered him in his honor. These he scrupulously included . . . in page after page of verbatim transcription. But it was precisely this prideful thrust that made him so tireless a worker for Negro betterment." He remained as pastor until 1937 and died in 1953.[2]

Adam, Jr., was born in 1908, the year the family moved to New York. His maternal grandfather was white, and he was of mixed French, German, and Choctaw Indian ancestry. The Powells lived in a neighborhood where juvenile white and black gangs sometimes fought. Powell remembered being beaten up by a white gang and a short time later being asked what he was by members of a Negro gang. When he replied that he was mixed, the Negroes thought that he had said that he was a "Mick," so they beat him up, too. In his book *Marching Blacks* he claimed that his earliest awareness of racial differences occurred when as a child he stood on a chair and traced with his fingers the letter "P" branded on his slave grandfather's back. Powell attended PS5 and Townsend-Harris High School, where he graduated at the age of sixteen. Starting at City College, he flunked out in his freshman year and transferred to Colgate. At Colgate he first thought that he wanted to be a doctor, but then changed to a theology course. At the beginning of his career at Colgate he tried to pass as white, rooming with white students and pledging a white fraternity. This attempt ended when his father came to Colgate to preach a sermon. Powell's childhood coincided with the heyday of Marcus Garvey, leader of the Back-to-Africa movement. Garvey made a deep impression on both Powells, father and son. The latter described him as "one of the greatest mass leaders of all time." The future congressman was most impressed by Garvey's oratorical ability and by his sense of pride in being black.[3]

After graduation from Colgate and a world tour, Powell took up his duties as assistant pastor of the Abyssinian Baptist Church in 1930. He began his career during the height of the Depression. New York had no Department of Public Welfare. The young minister was put in charge of the social and educational program of the church. A soup kitchen in the church basement fed as many as 1,000 people some weeks. Powell also distributed shoes, and found work for men three days a week. When running for re-election in 1921, Mayor Hylan had claimed credit for the acceptance of the first black doctors at Harlem Hospital. But in 1931 Harlem Hospital was known as the "butcher shop." Its mortality was the highest in the city. The dismissal of five black doctors triggered a protest by Negroes. Powell assumed the leadership, organized meetings, picket lines, and delegations to medical and city officials. The protest culminated with a march of 6,000 people to City Hall. Powell acted as their spokesman, demanding an interracial staff. The demands were granted.[4]

In 1933 Powell married Isabel Washington, former Cotton Club chorus girl, actress, and divorcee with a young son. Although some members of the church were hesitant about their pastor marrying a woman with this background, his father performed the ceremony, and Mrs. Powell became deeply involved in church work.

"The Harlem in which he moved was a mean and deflated community," wrote Hickey and Edwin. "In the middle 1930's Harlem newspaper readers were fed a diet of five major ingredients: the Scottsboro boys, Ethiopia, Father Divine, Joe Lewis, and mayhem." Harlem rents were 25 percent higher than anywhere else in the city. On February 15, 1936, Powell began writing a column for the *Amsterdam News* called "The Soapbox." "What Harlem needs is a year-round air-conditioned soapbox," he proclaimed in his first column. "It is my intention to try to supply this need. I hearby set up my soapbox in this corner." Assuming a leftist posture, he discussed everything which might interest Negroes, ranging from the invasion of Ethiopia to the Negro church to Joe Lewis. "Powell's column was a goad to the Harlem conscience," wrote a biographer. "He instructed his readers dutifully, like a New England schoolmaster, in spite of his youth and inexperience. His precocity was apparent in every column: the well-developed historical sense, the cosmic concerns that extended far beyond the bounds of parochial Harlem politics, the recurring light touch, and easy communicativeness." The most consistent theme was that Negroes should unite with other workers and go left. He recommended books for Harlemites to read, and condemned middle-class Negroes who copied middle-class white aspirations.[5]

On Lincoln's birthday, 1938, Powell and a group of Harlemites announced the formation of the Greater New York Co-Ordinating Committee for Employment. The other co-chairman was a Presbyterian minister. The Co-Ordinating Committee formed picket lines, with picketers chanting, "Don't buy where you can't work." As the result of the committee's efforts, Consolidated Edison, the New York Telephone Campany, and bread and milk companies agreed to hire more Harlem residents. By picketing the World's Fair, members of the committee forced the hiring of a substantial number of Negroes in jobs other than menial. The organization of a bus boycott and the threat to march on the New York Omnibus Company's downtown offices resulted in the hiring of black drivers and mechanics for the first time. The committee's greatest victory came when it made an agreement with the Uptown Chamber of Commerce guaranteeing one third of all jobs in Harlem stores to blacks. Powell gained added publicity by refusing to serve on a committee to celebrate President Roosevelt's birthday because of discrimination against crippled black children at Warm Springs. The

Co-Ordinating Committee's employment victories insured the fame
which Powell's church work and newspaper column had begun.[6]
   The membership of the Abyssinian Baptist Church and of the
Co-Ordinating Committee gave Powell a base from which to try
for public office. As part of a new constitution drafted in 1937,
the City Council had replaced the Board of Aldermen. Members
of the new body were elected by a system of weighted voting known
as proportional representation. Although two Negroes had continuously represented Harlem districts on the Board of Aldermen since
1929, none were elected to the City Council in 1937 or 1939. In
1941 Powell announced his candidacy. His slogan was "One people!
One fight! One victory!" The candidate described his campaign
organization as being composed of "about the finest bunch of honest
thieves and corrupt Christians in captivity." He tried to convince
the three major parties, the Republicans, Democrats, and American
Labor Party, that they should withdraw their own black candidates
and solidify the race vote behind him. But Powell did not confine
his appeal to blacks. Although he never became a member of the
Communist Party, he had been co-operating with the Communists
since the party had tried to organize a united front around the
Scottsboro case in the middle thirties. His support, most but not
all left-wing, came from the CIO Trade Union Council, the League
of Women Voters, the Trade Union Committee to Elect Labor's
Candidates, the United City Party, and the Transport Workers
Union. Repeatedly he emphasized the point that a Harlem representative in the City Council would be to everyone's advantage.
He told street-corner audiences and civic groups, "I am not seeking
a political job. I am fighting for the chance to give my people the
best representation in the affairs of their city, to help make Harlem
the No. 1 community of New York." "It was his baptism as a
campaigner and a moment of discovery for both himself and the
Harlem voters," wrote Hickey and Edwin. "The latter were struck
by his energy, his apparent sophistication, and his determination
to beard the white man in his own arena—in this case the City
Council chamber." The Powell organization distributed 200,000
sample ballots. On Election Day Powell came in third among six
successful Manhattan candidates. Although some intellectuals assumed a "wait and see" attitude, Harlem was generally jubilant.
The *Amsterdam News* editorialized, "With an earnest, kindly word
of caution, we congratulate New York's first colored councilman . . .

as he begins his first two-year term in office. It is a grand opportunity for service to his people, city, and country that confronts him. He has the ability, courage, and popular support to render that service.... How effective his tenure in office will be depends entirely on how effectively in and out of the council chamber he uses these natural advantages."[7]

"He commenced agitation immediately on a broad front, demanding resolutions condemning alleged discrimination in a dozen areas," wrote a recent biographer. A month after Powell's election, the Japanese attack on Pearl Harbor brought the United States into World War II. Powell attacked the Federal Government for its internment of Japanese Americans. The new councilman declaimed against the treatment of Negroes in the armed forces and in war production. When the city of New York agreed to turn over the campus of Hunter College as a training center for WAVES and SPARS—outfits which refused to accept Negro women—Powell introduced a resolution condemning the pact, which was passed. He demanded the impeachment of Mayor LaGuardia for approving the construction of the lily-white Stuyvesant Town housing development, announced that not a single Negro was among the 2,232 faculty members at New York's city-supported colleges (a fact which was later proven untrue) and managed to have the presidents of the colleges questioned by the council. He also introduced a resolution to have newspapers forbidden from identifying the race of criminals. "The energy of Powell's denunciations left an impression of high activity and accomplishment on his Harlem constituents," wrote Hickey and Edwin. "The Harlem press, however, frequently accused him of failing to follow up on his attacks, of losing interest in a cause once the speeches had been made and the news coverage exhausted. He was not, in fact, well liked by many of his fellow councilmen, but the reasons were less racial than parliamentary. He was voluble from the outset, instead of maintaining the customary freshman's reticence."[8]

On February 14, 1942, Powell and Charles Buchanan, the owner of the Savoy Ballroom in Harlem, began publication of the *People's Voice*. The weekly, smaller than tabloid size, was more radical than Harlem's two older weeklies, the New York *Age* and the *Amsterdam News*. Eventually, the *People's Voice* would become a regular follower of the Communist party line. Powell severed his connection with it in 1947, and it ceased publication in 1948. In the early days

Marshall Field may have subsidized it, because it was printed on the same presses as *P.M.*, the liberal weekly of which the department store heir was a major supporter.[9]

In June 1943, eighteen months after Powell's election to the City Council, he announced that he would not seek reelection and that he would be a candidate for the new congressional district which the State Legislature seemed likely to create in 1944. His gamble proved justified. The 22nd congressional district was created (changed to the 16th in 1952 and the 18th in 1962), containing about 300,000 people, 90 percent of whom were black. Some Harlemites made efforts to persuade A. Philip Randolph, president of the Brotherhood of Sleeping-Car Porters and leader of the March on Washington, or Channing Tobias, nationally known Negro YMCA worker, to run against Powell. In 1944 the Democratic Party in the city had been out of office and disunited for eleven years. Herbert L. Bruce, who in 1935 had become the first black district leader, supported Randolph and remained cool to Powell even after he became the party candidate. Thus Powell was forced to rely largely on his own resources. The self-reliance which characterized Powell's first congressional campaign led to the comparative independence of party control which marked his later career.

Randolph and Tobias declined to enter the political arena. Powell ran in the Republican, Democratic, and American Labor Party primaries. His opponent was Sarah Pelham Speaks, a Republican lawyer, who was the daughter of a Washington Negro newspaper publisher and wife of a physician. The Powell platform included the ending of segregation in the armed forces, a permanent FEPC, a Federal law prohibiting discrimination in interstate travel, and an end to the poll tax and the white primary. Powell was unclear about his conception of his role as a black congressman. In one speech he declared, "I will never be a machine man. I will represent the Negro people first. I will represent after that all the other American people." A few days later, he modified this point of view: "I promise to represent this district first—not only the Negroes, but each and every citizen of this area, irrespective of race, creed, or political affiliation." His supporters included Tammany, the American Labor Party, a large group of Negro entertainers, the CIO Political Action Committee, the Transport Workers Union, and the Communist Party. The *Amsterdam News* supported Mrs. Speaks. Powell swept all three primaries and went on to become the first black congressman from New York and, to date, the only one from Harlem. The *Herald-Tribune* noted that Powell had "traveled to national political reputation through fourteen years of unreserved defiance of what he sees as 'undemocratic practices.'

"His crusade has been accompanied by incessant pulpit-pounding and much fist-shaking at his pet peeves which include 'prejudiced merchants,' 'weak-minded public officials,' 'poll tax lynchocrats,' and 'blood-sucking imperialists.' He has made use of opportunities to lead a picket line, promote a mass meeting, and to dispatch a wire of protest either to Congress or to the President. He has given articulation in a belligerent tone to the wants and grievances of a large following, with whom he has achieved popularity, while incurring the distrust of some of the more conservative Negro leaders.

"These leaders have said he is 'a bit too radical,' that he shows no regard for the counsel of other Negro leaders, and that many of the economic gains which he says he has won for Harlem were either highly exaggerated or resulted in large measure from the work of other Negroes. . . ."[10]

While he was a candidate for Congress, Isabel Powell sued her husband for divorce. She had opposed his entrance into politics, although she later described him as a model husband. He married the pianist Hazel Scott in 1945.

The year after his election to Congress, Powell wrote a book entitled *Marching Blacks*. Hickey and Edwin describe it as "a shrill polemic cum autobiography which sketched in the American Negro's history and attempted by the energy of its exhortation to get America's black men on their feet and marching up Freedom Road." With a neo-Marxist tone, it tied the Negro destiny to that of the working class. Roy Wilkins disliked the flamboyant oratorical style and the personal egotism of Powell's book, yet he wrote: "It is not to be denied that he [Powell] played a leading role in mobilizing inarticulate sections of the Harlem population during the dark and seemingly pathless days of the great depression. He taught them how to ask and work for what they needed, and what, it may be added, was due them. Now patiently, now in frenzied, near demagogic speeches, he taught them and he led them. If he asked them in return to send him to the City Council and then to Congress they still, in all honesty, have the best of the deal. The new power he has taught them to use is cheap at the price."[11]

During his first term in Congress Powell introduced measures supporting a permanent FEPC, abolishing segregation on the railroads, and giving Virgin Islanders the right to vote. He bombarded the heads of the military services with the demand that black nurses be accepted, and he demanded that black journalists be allowed to sit in the congressional press gallery. Congressman Dawson of Illinois, the only other black man in Congress at this time, had accepted exclusion from facilities, but Powell directed members of his staff to use the steam room and the barber shop and to go to the cafeteria and eat whether they were hungry or not. Bilbo and Rankin, the conservative segregationist Senator and Congressman from Mississippi, symbolized what he was fighting against. "American fighting men are coming back from the foxholes of the earth to meet American Fascists emerging from rat-holes," he wrote. "Bilbo and Rankin are two political degenerates and rat-hole Americans." He attacked Jim Crow in the District of Columbia. In his first session he proposed a four-point program including equal and unsegregated schools, desegregated federal buildings, a civil rights bill for the District of Columbia, and enfranchisement of Washington residents. He tried to secure a commission for Joe Lewis.

Detractors criticized him for not showing tangible results in the form of legislation. He responded, "The way of the legislator is hard, and especially if he is black. If he happens to be a Negro, he must virtually build a way out of no way. For one thing however there must never be an excuse—and that is silence. In these days of challenge silence is no longer golden." In 1946 Earl Brown, a black journalist, wrote that Powell "is one of the few politicians extant who is not wanted by any party but is sought by practically all of them." He called the congressman "the champ soapbox demagogue. He can even make a preacher part with a dollar bill."

When Powell ran for reelection in 1946, his opponent was Grant Reynolds, at that time State Corrections Commissioner. Julius J. Adams, a black newspaperman who later became a member of the Republican State Committee, wrote that Reynolds was "logical, studious, and gives close attention to form and strategy, while Powell is rash, blustering, strong-willed, and is constantly off on a tangent and half-cocked. Reynolds works methodically for permanent and lasting gains; Powell is more opportunistic and will capitalize on a situation for temporary advantage." Powell categorized the campaign as one between an Uncle Tom and the "New Negro." He won a 4–1 victory, and he continued to defeat his opponents biennially, never receiving less than 70 percent of the vote.[12] In 1948 Powell said of his opponent, the veteran Harlem Republican leader Harold Burton, "Harold knows he has no chance of beating me and he's only in it for the money. He remembers that Dewey gave the last guy who ran against me a big campaign kitty and a liquor store license, and Harold hopes to do as well."[13]

In the early and middle 1940's Powell had cooperated closely with the Communists. In 1944 he had shared top billing at a rally with Earl Browder and William Z. Foster. Yet he had never been a party member. He was to insist that in any Red association he was never duped, and to add, "We used the Communists more than they used us." As anti-Communist sentiment increased, the Harlem congressman gradually broke his left-wing ties. In 1946 he severed his connection with the *People's Voice,* the Harlem weekly he had helped to found four years earlier, declaring that it had become Communist-dominated. Although he voted against the Marshall Plan, he did not support the Presidential bid of Henry Wallace in 1948 or the mayoralty campaign of Vito Marcantonio the following year. When Paul Robeson in 1949 announced that Negroes would not fight against Russia, Powell publicly declared that Robeson was not speaking for all blacks. In his contest for the City Council and in his first three campaigns for Congress, Powell ran with the support of the American Labor Party, and he frequently worked closely with its leader, the congressman in the adjacent district, Vito Marcantonio. In 1950 Carmine DiSapio, who had become Tammany leader the previous year, announced that no candidate accepting ALP nomination could get the Tammany designation as well. Faced with this choice, Powell remained a Democrat.[14]

In 1952 Powell became Vice-Chairman of the preconvention effort of Averell Harriman to receive the Presidential nomination. In that year he became the first Negro to be chosen a delegate-at-large to a Democratic national convention. Many black people were dissatisfied with the civil rights plank of the Democratic platform and with the nomination of Senator John Sparkman of Alabama as the candidate for Vice-President. Powell sent Sparkman a telegram, asking for his views on changes in the Senate rules to prevent filibusters and on FEPC. Sparkman's answer was evasive. Powell threatened to bolt the ticket, but he did not carry out the threat in 1952.

Herbert L. Bruce had opposed Powell as far back as Powell's first campaign for Congress in 1944. Bruce, who had been elected as the first black Tammany district leader in 1935, had continued in this position for ten years. In 1945 the district had been divided, but Bruce regained leadership of the entire district in 1949. During the 1953 mayoralty contest between Wagner and Impelleteri, Bruce had supported the latter. His final mistake was running against Powell for Congress in 1954. The Tammany leadership supported Powell, who won by a 2–1 majority. Bruce resigned his district leadership in the spring of 1955.

Powell's role at the Bandung Conference brought him international as well as increased national recognition. In 1955 nonaligned nations of Asia and Africa held a conference at Bandung in Indonesia. The United States took no official part in the conference. When Powell applied to the State Department to attend as an observer, he was told that the United States had not been invited to the conference and that because he was a congressman his presence might be misunderstood. Powell replied that he would make clear that he was neither an official representative nor an official observer. The State Department granted him a passport, and he went to the conference as the correspondent for the black weekly newspaper the New York *Age*. On the first day of the proceedings Powell called a news conference which was attended by 100 reporters from all parts of the world. The Harlem congressman began by assuring the correspondents that the American government was not hostile to the conference. He then launched into a discussion of American race relations. "Racism in the United States is on the way out," he told the assembled correspondents. "Second-class citizenship is on the way out. A peaceful revolution has occurred over night. . . . A few years ago Washington was an open cesspool of United States democracy. . . . Today it is a place of complete equality. Every hotel, restaurant, amusement place, school and golf course is completely integrated." He continued, "It is a mark of distinction in the United States to be a Negro. To be a Negro is no longer a stigma." After pointing to black city officials in Atlanta, Richmond, and Norfolk, he said that if one judges the United States by the nine or ten backward states of the South, one is making a very unwise judgment. The Powell press conference naturally elicited praise in the American press, while Communist Chinese papers accused him of trying to sabotage the conference.[15]

Beginning in the late forties Powell had been introducing riders to appropriation bills which became popularly known as Powell amendments. These amendments made the legislation inoperative unless administered on a nonsegregated basis. Powell attached his riders to government-subsidized programs such as education, health insurance, and the maintenance of the military reserve. The non-segregation amendments severely embarrassed and sometimes divided liberal advocates of social welfare legislation. Sometimes opponents of such legislation would vote for the Powell amendments knowing that Southerners would vote against the legislation if the Powell amendments were included. The first bill with a Powell amendment was passed in 1960.

In 1956, when a Powell amendment was instrumental in defeating a federal aid to education bill supported by the Eisenhower Administration, the *New York Times* made Powell the subject of its daily feature entitled "Man in the News." Readers were told of Powell's dedication to the cause of civil rights, of his ownership of three homes, and of his statement that his annual income was $115,000. He was described as casual, friendly, and a good conversationalist, as the owner of an Italian racing car and a Jaguar, and as a devotee of the theater and of classical music. The article also noted that the Internal Revenue Service was investigating Powell's income tax payments, and that one of his aides had been convicted of tax evasion.[16]

Powell did not attend the Democratic convention in 1956. Instead, he spent the summer in Europe. Upon his return to nearby coastal waters on October 2 he conducted a ship-to-shore telephone interview with the press, in which he said that he would come down the gangplank at New York with an open mind on whether or not he would support the Democratic nominees. As a condition of his support, he wanted a commitment from the nominees against continued use of Federal funds in states that defy Federal law. "And," he added, "I don't want that pledge confined to education." He demanded nothing less than an endorsement of the Powell amendment by the Democratic Party. On October 12 Powell had a thirty-minute conference with President Eisenhower. He emerged from the conference with the announcement that he would support the Republicans. Powell said that Stevenson had snubbed him by refusing to see him and by not inviting him to a rally in Harlem. According to the Harlem congressman, three main points had helped him to make his decision: (1) the President had agreed not to oppose a school aid bill which Powell would introduce in the next session of Congress; (2) Eisenhower had promised to give priority to a bill protecting voting rights in federal elections; and (3) a procedure would be devised for enforcing court integration orders with Federal marshalls and for arrest and trials of persons in contempt of court decisions. In his announcement Powell added that he would speak for the Republican ticket, but would remain a Democrat.

The Harlem congressman's announcement shocked and angered other Democrats. Eleanor Roosevelt accused him of making a deal. A group of Harlem Democrats issued a statement blaming his defection on pressure from the White House, since his former secretary, Hattie Freeman Dodson, had been convicted of income tax evasion, and Acy Lennon, another member of his staff, was on trial for the same offense. The charge that Powell had agreed to support the Republicans in exchange for legal concessions was repeated in a syndicated article by Drew Pearson and Jack Anderson and in an article in the *National Review* in 1957 (Lennon was later convicted; the evidence at his trial included his declaring as dependents two nonexistent sons). On October 25 Powell announced his support of the then State Attorney General Jacob Javits who was the Republican candidate for the United States Senate against Mayor Robert Wagner.

A Harris poll and a survey made by the New York *Post* found that gratitude for the New Deal outweighed the importance of Powell's switch in the minds of Harlemites. "They done more for me than anybody," a workman told the *Post* reporter Irwin Ross. "They gave me work when I didn't have it, they gave me food when I was hungry." "A plumpish housewife in an incredibly dingy kitchen, graced with a massive spanking new refrigerator" told the reporter that she was for Stevenson because the Democrats favored poor people and "There ain't no sense changing." She doubted if Powell's switch would have much effect. "First he's a Democrat, then he's a Republican. . . . Reminiscent gratitude to the New Deal was a glowing and substantial thing," concluded Ross, "undiminished by controversies over civil rights—a typical attitude in the slum areas of Harlem." In 1956 the Democrats carried the big city black areas, but by reduced majorities. Their loss in New York was about average. Whatever Powell's influence or lack of influence on others, his own popularity remained undiminished. He received 77.8 percent of the vote.[17]

Several Southern congressmen also defected to the Republicans in 1956. Rumors circulated that Powell and the Southern congressmen would be deprived of their seniority. This did not happen. The Baptist Ministers Alliance, Roy Wilkins, and other black leaders rallied to Powell's defense. The *Amsterdam News* editorialized about the reasons for Powell's retention of his seniority: "There's no doubt that the Democrats planned to chastise Mr. Powell and there's no doubt in our minds that they planned to do it simply because he was a Negro. . . . A few years ago the Negro in this country would have sat idly by like a toad-frog on a mushroom while the Democrats pulled off this dirty trick. But those days are gone forever. Instead of sitting by and letting the Democrats get away with it, Negroes rallied around Congressman Powell as if he were their long lost brother. Thousands of Negroes who had never agreed with Mr. Powell rallied to his defense. They did it not because they had suddenly fallen in love with Mr. Powell but because Mr. Powell is a Negro whom white people were trying to 'put in his place.' "[18]

In the mayoralty contest of 1957 the Harlem congressman remained neutral. The next year Tammany Leader Carmine DiSapio decided to purge him. Six district leaders, one of whom was white, voted for the purge, while Lloyd Dickens, a Negro, voted against it and William Fitzryan, who is white, abstained. Powell announced that he would run independently. Hickey and Edwin describe the campaign which followed as "a political campaign which is a classic study in minority politics. . . . The classic character of the 1958 purge attempt grew partly out of its nature as a confrontation between an entrenched leader of a minority group—which had not yet been assimilated—and a political organization whose power derived from the assimilation of minorities; partly out of the revelation that Negroes bitterly resented any attempt by the white power block to force a leadership upon them."[19]

The line-up for and against Adam Clayton Powell during the 1958 campaign divided more clearly along racial lines than any other issue in recent years. White liberals were almost all against him, while virtually every major Negro was for him. Jackie Robinson called the Powell campaign a chance for black America to show its unity. Joe Louis became a Powell partisan with the pronouncement, "I like a man who is a fighter." J. Raymond Jones came out of political retirement to manage Powell's campaign, which also resulted in the renewal of his own career.[20] Throughout the Harlem congressman's years in public life a part of his genius had been his ability to make himself the symbol of black protest. The day after the leaders of his district voted not to support him, he was indicted for income tax evasion. At his arraignment two hundred of his followers appeared, lifted him on their shoulders, and gave him $275 as a start toward the expenses of his election campaign. He pleaded not guilty and was released without bail in his own custody. "I am purged because obviously I am a Negro and a Negro should stay on the plantation," he told reporters in the courthouse pressroom. Asked about the fact that party leaders in Harlem had voted to drop him because he was not a Democrat, he called DiSapio a "Mississippi boss" and added, "The Negroes left Mississippi to get away from the white bosses, but they found them here in Harlem."[21] Because of his position in the city administration, Hulan Jack became the spokesman for the anti-Powell forces. On one occasion Powell characterized the borough president as "the house Negro who curried favor with the plantation overlords at the expense of his fellow Negroes." Jack was booed at a public meeting in front of the Hotel Theresa. Powell calmed the crowd, but later he said of Jack, "Send that Uncle Tom back downtown," and warned DiSapio and Jack not to come north of 110th Street. Since the rally was officially sponsored by the NAACP, that organization protested Powell's statement, but it received so many letters from Powell supporters that it had to issue a statement asserting that its protest had been misconstrued.[22]

Despite the opposition of Republican County Chairman Thomas Curran, the Harlem Republicans voted unanimously to support Powell. The Democrats had difficulty in finding a Negro with stature in the community who would be willing to oppose him. Thurgood Marshall, Rev. James H. Robinson, and Hulan Jack were offered the nomination but declined. Finally, City Councilman Earl Brown reluctantly agreed to make the race. In a discussion with white Tammany leaders before accepting the nomination, Brown said that Harlem leaders really favored Powell but that their judgment had been warped by DiSapio. Disliking Hulan Jack,

Brown finally agreed to oppose Powell only if Tammany paid all the bills and if Jack stayed out of the campaign.[23]

Throughout the contest Powell emphasized the idea that the real struggle was between black Harlem and white downtown, between an outspoken advocate of black rights and the Southern Democrats eager to purge him. Powell inaugurated training courses to instruct volunteers in door-to-door electioneering, and he sent out mailings advising Harlemites to scrutinize nominating petitions carefully before signing—and, coincidentally, to sign only those bearing Powell's name. The rules for preparing nominating petitions are rather technical. Since Acy Lennon, the member of Powell's staff who knew about such matters, sat out the campaign in jail for income tax evasion, J. Raymond Jones played a crucial role.[24]

Powell's church was his chief source of manpower and woman-power. Three days after his ouster, the *New York Times* reported that he had talked to 800 people in the church basement and that he had planned to hold political training courses in the church for three nights. For a century and a half the black church has been a center for a wide variety of activities. James Q. Wilson analyzes why a church can easily serve as the nucleus for a political campaign: "A church can be an ideal source of...strength. It directly recruits and organizes the masses, it can be financially independent, it has a variety of channels throughout the community, and it has the luster of an indisputably good institution." Moreover, church members are normally organized into committees. Powell's church included about 10 percent of the registered voters in his congressional district. According to Wilson 4,000 people heard his Sunday sermons, while 1,000 came to the church or community house every day of the week. "The mingling of political, religious, and civic roles is seen in the organization of his headquarters. The secretary of the church's board of trustees acts as financial secretary of Powell's political club; his congressional administrative assistant charged with handling local political affairs has an office adjacent to that of the church's full-time social worker, and the two share the task of dealing with voters-parishioners." In addition to providing volunteers, the church raised $30,000 for Powell's 1958 campaign.[25]

Powell referred to his opponent as "Lookdown" Brown, a reference to Brown's habit of looking down when he spoke, which Powell interpreted as a distant ivory-tower attitude toward Harlem and its problems. When questioned about his absentee record, which was one of the worst of any congressman in the House, Powell replied, "In the first place I carry too much of a load as compared with most of my other colleagues, because in addition to serving the 400,000 people of my district I frankly have to serve about eight million Negroes who are behind the color curtain in the South. I have more requests, more correspondence from Negro people outside my district than those within. It keeps me overly busy; therefore, it has been my rule since I went to Congress not to answer quorum calls unless I happen to be in the area of the Congress." The insensitive white press called Powell "demagogic," "racist," "rabble-rousing," and "irresponsible." Powell read such attacks to Harlemites from a sound truck. Hickey and Edwin described a rally at the Hotel Theresa on August 9: "For thirty minutes Powell held them rapt. It was a strange and highly charged scene. Powell was to the crowd not only the principal actor in a passion play—which few of the whites present could have been expected to understand—but also their confessor, their high priest, and their lover. His words, gestures, intonations, and appearance were almost calculatedly sensual. At one instant he roared his plaint so that it rumbled across the black faces; at the next he was silent; unbreathing, and tentative until the next rush of passion. . . . He worked over them with the attention and fastidiousness of an amorist. When the end came, they were ready for it, having been prepared skillfully. There was a pause, and then suddenly, 'I appeal to your manhood! Harlem is on the march.' They met like willing brides. A great swell of shouting and applause, mounting to a tumult, broke from them. Powell waved and smiled, then quickly departed from the microphones, leaving the crowd relaxed and satisfied in the afterglow of his presence." The next day, Powell told a church rally: "On Tuesday we'll march to the polls; not as Uncle Toms, but free men and women under God."

Brown lacked Powell's dynamism and charisma. He felt most comfortable addressing small groups and concentrating on Powell's record. By Election Day all predictions favored Powell. On Primary Day, August 12, the polls opened at three P.M. At Powell's church headquarters campaign workers stood by, awaiting commands to defend the polls in Harlem. Powell charged that Tammany planned to send in hoodlums from other districts to subvert the balloting. He ordered poll-watchers to inspect the fingers of Tammany men to prevent any invalidation of the paper ballots by the use of sharp rings. Like a field general he had organized his workers into numbered squads. When trouble was reported at a polling place, he ordered out Squad 2 or Squad 3 to deal with the matter. Actually, the balloting was orderly and the turn-out quite light. Powell carried every election district except a few white ones. He won by a 3–1 majority. The victorious candidate thanked his supporters and declared that his election meant a rejection of bossism by the black community. DiSapio announced that he would support Powell in the general election. Then the congressman took a vacation in the West Indies.

In the general election Powell supported Governor Harriman's bid for a second term. However, the disputes in Harlem and some of Powell's charges proved an embarrassment to the governor. During the campaign Powell alleged that the Republicans had offered him a $50,000 cash bribe for his support. At another time he charged the Republican gubernatorial candidate Nelson Rockefeller with not being a life member of the NAACP because such a membership was not tax deductible. Rockefeller not only replied that he was a life member, but pointed to his family's long tradition of contribution to causes working for racial equality.[26]

The district leadership contests of 1959 demonstrated Powell's control of Harlem. He proved victorious in four of the five contests which involved his prestige. He, J. Raymond Jones, and a supporter, Mark Southall, overturned incumbent leaders, while Lloyd Dickens, the only Harlem leader who had backed Powell in 1958, won reelection. Only Hulan Jack survived the Powell landslide.[27]

In the spring of 1960 Powell was tried for income tax evasion. His trial in a crowded courtroom lasted for seven weeks. Malcolm X was among the spectators. The congressman and his attorney, the noted criminal lawyer Edward Bennett Williams, produced figures to show that, instead of evading taxes, Powell had overpaid. During his cross-examination he was asked if he had listed as a deduction $1,000 for his son's tuition at Riverdale School. "Everybody knows that Adam Clayton Powell is for federal aid to education," the congressman answered. The court broke up, from the judge on down. As usual, the defendant was able to evoke in black people a feeling that his prosecution possessed racial overtones. A reporter heard such comments in the courtroom as: "This trial has made Adam a martyr." "No matter what they do, he's a bigger man." "Adam says what he thinks. That's why they're out for him." "Nobody can hate Adam. They might not like him, but they can't hate him." "No, they hate him. They can't control him. They're out to get him."

The Powell jury was out for twenty-six hours. After taking twenty ballots, it reported itself unable to agree, the vote being 10–2 for acquittal. A Powell aide said that the trial had cost the congressman $70,000. Although Hazel Scott divorced him seven months later and he married his Puerto Rican secretary in 1961, she refused to testify against him during the trial. Eventually, the charges were dropped. Powell had Edward Bennet Williams made Man of the Year in Harlem. Williams was presented with a large gold trophy at a meeting on the steps of the Hotel Theresa. In introducing the lawyer, Powell said, "Ladies and gentlemen, I give you a man who is greater than Abraham Lincoln. Abraham Lincoln freed the slaves, but Edward Bennett Williams freed Adam Clayton Powell." [28]

In the maneuvering which preceded the 1960 Democratic national convention most Negroes distrusted John F. Kennedy. The senator from Massachusetts had voted to send a civil rights bill back to the Judiciary Committee in 1957. Moreover, as part of his effort to obtain the nomination, he had a breakfast meeting with the segregationist governor and state chairman of Alabama. In addition, Powell pointed to Kennedy's uncertain record during the McCarthy era. The Harlem congressman announced himself in favor of Senator Stuart Symington of Missouri, although he made clear that he would support the nominee of the party. During the campaign he worked hard for the Kennedy-Johnson ticket.

In January 1960 Representative Graham Barden of North Carolina, chairman of the House Education and Labor Committee, announced that he would not run for reelection. As the second-ranking Democrat on the committee, Powell was in line for the chairmanship. The *New York Times* editorialized about the irony in the fact that Southerners who had always profited by and defended the seniority system now found that the system had given the chairmanship of one of the most important committees to Powell. Southerners were not the only ones who opposed Powell's getting the chairmanship. George Meany, president of the A.F.L.-C.I.O., felt that he would be self-serving and unreliable. But the system worked impartially, and Powell became chairman of the House Education and Labor Committee in January 1961. The same month the church gave Powell a testimonial dinner. Secretary of Labor Arthur Goldberg and Secretary of Health, Education, and Welfare Abraham Ribicoff were among the speakers. A telegram from President Kennedy was read. In his speech Ribicoff said that the President had asked him "to make sure I extend his personal best wishes to Adam and all his friends." Coming at a time when the President did not want to be associated with the New York Democratic Party because the party was so badly split, the presence of two Cabinet members at the Powell testimonial shows that the President regarded Powell as a major power in Washington.[29]

Powell remained as chairman for six years. His legislative record was impressive. As early as April 4. 1961, the *Wall Street Journal* reported, "Take a congressman with a record of tax troubles with Uncle Sam, frequent absenteeism from his capital post, uncompromising fixation on a single cause, one-time desertion of his party, and a reputation for play-boy high-jinks, propel this gentleman into a position of high responsibility among his party's legislative leaders, where the White House must count heavily on his ability and willingness to buckle down to hard work as a team player. What's to be expected—statesmanship or sabotage?" The article concluded that "While it's too early to tell just how the drama will turn out, there are signs that a new, more responsible Powell may be replacing the old model, with results pleasing indeed to the New Frontiersmen."[30] The Harlem congressman's involvement with his new job was made evident in the physical changes in his office and the changes in committee procedure which he instituted in his first months as chairman. He had his office repainted, the floor covered with ankle-deep, baby-blue, wall-to-wall carpeting, colorful draperies hung on the windows, and the back wall was decorated with pictures of former committee chairmen. He doubled the size of the staff, the budget, and the number of subcommittees. The new chairman set his subcommittees probing matters ranging from the impartiality of the NLRB to the impact of imports and exports on employment. Powell appointed Negroes to a staff which had hitherto been lily-white, and the first Puerto Rican to have a job on the staff of any congressional committee. He installed an intercommunication system which would enable him to participate in subcommittee meetings from his office. Though a notorious absentee himself, the new committee head made a rule that any subcommittee chairman who missed three consecutive meetings or five meetings during a session without an excuse would be replaced. To prevent filibusters, Powell ruled that in discussing bills no committee member would talk longer than five minutes. He learned how to wield power effectively, how to appear to strip one bill in order to push another, how to play one pressure group off against another, and how to use other means available to a committee chairman in accomplishing his ends. As a potent committee chairman, he was consulted on legislation, briefed on the timetable, and called upon by the White House for help. "Powell kept it [his committee] moving by delegating authority to his subcommittees," wrote Murray Kempton in 1963. "He listens to his chairmen and takes their advice and is a prodigy with the gavel when they need it. His attention span is limited, but he astounds his colleagues by the speed with which he can grasp a bill and the positions on it and then direct a coherent discussion of its merits on no more than a briefing five minutes before a session."[31] The roster of legislation passed by Congress which originated in the House Committee on Education and Labor during Powell's chairmanship includes the $1.25 minimum wage, federal aid to education, trade expansion legislation, and the establishment and maintenance of the antipoverty program. Powell estimated that 40 percent of administration legislation originated in his committee. A lieutenant of House Speaker Sam Rayburn referred to him as one of the dozen most brilliant men in the House. In 1964 Speaker McCormick wrote Powell an unsolicited letter praising "your ability, your progressive outlook, your courage, and outstanding leadership." On March 18, 1965, President Johnson wrote a letter to Powell complimenting him on his "brilliant record of accomplishment." The President went on to say that his chairmanship "represents a successful reporting to the Congress of 49 pieces of bedrock legislation. The passage of every one of these bills attests to your ability to get things done.... I speak for the millions of Americans who benefit from these laws when I say that I'm truly grateful."

An improved social life went along with increased responsibility. One hostess said, "Adam is one of the most delightful men to be around you'll ever meet." Another remarked, "He could charm a band of Ku Klux Klanners."[32] As Powell had frequently made himself the symbol of black protest, so now he became a symbol of their entry into the power structure. Many members of the race held their heads a little higher and walked with a little more dignity, knowing that for the first time in the history of the country one of them had become part of the nation's ruling elite.

With Powell's marriage to Yvette Florés, his interest in Puerto Rico increased. He built a beachfront home on the island. One wit quipped that the Harlem congressman spent so much time in Puerto Rico in order to become brown enough to enable him to pass as a Negro. In 1962 he introduced a resolution permitting Puerto Ricans to vote in presidential elections. The Adam Clayton Powell Foundation was established to help Puerto Ricans in New York. Yet many Puerto Ricans including Governor Luis Munoz Marin were not happy with what they considered Powell's interference in the island's affairs. Puerto Ricans are politically divided into three groups. Some want statehood, others desire to continue the present commonwealth status, while a third group hopes for independence. The Puerto Rican government favored a continuation of the present commonwealth, while Powell allied himself with those who had the closest economic ties to the United States and therefore wanted statehood. The most radical group, those who favored independence, chose Powell as a target, picketing and throwing stones at his house and demanding that he leave the island. He sent a private detective to the island to guard his wife and infant son, and charged that the Independistas were the same nationalists who had fired shots across the floor of the House in 1950 and who had tried to assassinate President Truman, killing a White House guard.

Other Powell activities did not bring him accolades similar to those which he received as a committee chairman. In 1963 he toured Europe, ostensibly to investigate labor conditions, accompanied by two female members of his staff. One, Corrin Hough, had been Miss Ohio and a runner-up in the Miss Universe contest in 1960, while the other, Tamara Wall, was the House Education and Labor Committee's Assistant Counsel. The State Department co-operated, sending ahead to American embassies to secure the theater and concert tickets and to make the travel arrangements which Powell wanted. When the details of the trip were made public, Powell was thunderstruck by the strength of the critical reaction. He cancelled the last two weeks of his trip and flew to Puerto Rico to let the storm subside. The House Administration subcommittee resolved to look into Powell's payroll. A *Times* editorial referred to his trip as "Powell's shameless junket." Laughs and snickers greeted him when he appeared on the floor of the House for the first time after his trip. On the other hand the *Amsterdam News* in a front-page editorial defended Powell: "We do not agree with everything that Congressman Adam Clayton Powell does.... But we do agree that he is entitled to all the privileges and rights that pertain to other congressmen." "Once again," wrote Hickey and Edwin, "the great wagon-train of Negro loyalty to Powell, as a symbol of the most vital and personal aspirations of so many of them, was drawn in a circle around him—to the dismay and bewilderment of white America. Yet the source of his problem was not so much in racism as in the fact that he had cast a strong public light on certain well-guarded congressional privileges."[33] In the year of his trip Powell was reelected to his ninth term in Congress with 70 percent of the vote.

The early 1960's found the civil rights movement in its heyday. The sit-ins of 1960, the Freedom Rides of 1961, and demonstrations in Albany, Georgia, in 1962 and in Birmingham in 1963 were merely the most famous of nationwide efforts of Negroes and white sympathizers to obtain integration and equality. Although Powell had battled for civil rights as far back as the 1930's and had made himself into a symbol of black protest, he marched in no picket lines and engaged in no sit-ins in the early 1960's. He may have felt that the movement was passing him by or that civil rights leaders had not given him adequate support in coping with his personal problems. In any case he appeared with Malcolm X on Seventh Avenue and 125th Street on March 23, 1963. In a speech he called Malcolm X his friend and went on to say that "We Negroes are not going to get anything more in this life except that which we fight for with all our power." He added, "This may sound like black nationalism. If it is, then what is wrong with it? Why is it that racism and nationalism are dirty words only when applied to Negro people? What the white man fears is the coming together of Negroes.... One of the things I am very close to agreeing on almost completely with Malcolm X is his analysis of our present national organizations. Unless we can seize completely the administration and policy-making of our national Negro organizations, then we must say there is no hope for us. And I include the NAACP, Urban League, CORE and SCLC under Martin Luther King." He went on to say that the civil rights struggle would be won only by those groups "that are totally owned, controlled, and maintained by Negro people." These sentiments are widely held by Negroes today, but in 1963 they were held only by black nationalists and disapproved by most participants in the civil rights movement. A. Philip Randolph replied to Powell, "The Negroes can't solve the problem except with the aid of white people committed to its solution morally and spiritually. I was quite shocked that he [Powell] called on Negroes to boycott the civil rights organizations. It's almost incredible. If we didn't have white people committed to the problem, we'd never solve it." Whitney Young of the Urban League felt that "at a time when the whole world is crying for and working toward unity, it comes as a terrible shock to hear the voice of a person of Congressman Powell's stature sowing the seeds of racial discord." Jackie Robinson said, "It is my sincere belief that you have grievously set back the cause of the Negro, let your race down, and failed miserably in the role which our race justly expects you to play as an important national leader of the Negro." Powell made subsequent speeches demanding an all-Negro civil rights group and condemning middle-class Negroes. The brutality of the treatment of Negroes in Birmingham unified the black community. As plans for the March on Washington progressed in the summer of 1963 and Powell was not given a leadership role, his attitude toward the leaders of the civil rights movement changed from one of hostility to one of almost sycophantic respect. He publicly referred to them as "my leaders" and phoned them to offer his services. But no elected officials were permitted to speak at the March, and Powell remained on the periphery of the civil rights movement of the 1960's.[34]

During these years Powell and J. Raymond Jones continued to be the most powerful political figures in Harlem. Their relationship was off again on again. In 1961 they were on opposite sides in the mayoralty primary. When Powell appeared at the rally with Malcolm X and demanded complete control of civil rights organizations by Negroes, Jones showed his disagreement with these sentiments by publicly announcing that he had purchased a life membership in the NAACP for his grandson. In the early stages of Jones's bid for the City Council in 1963, Powell supported Jones, becoming honorary chairman of his campaign. But he and Jones broke, and he, Powell, aided Jones's opponents both for City Council and for district leader. Although Jones had tried to avoid a public break with Powell, they now bitterly denounced each other. Powell described Jones as "a traitor to the black revolution" and termed his campaign "a personal grab for power supported by a flood of white money." Jones responded by hitting the congressman where it hurt: "Powell is no longer considered a national leader of any importance in the civil rights movement. He can't even get into the conference of Negro leaders." Again: "He has nothing but contempt for the Negro masses. In relaxed moments, Powell refers to Negroes as 'my slaves.' ... [He] has had some difficulty in deciding whether he is a Negro or a Puerto Rican."

One of Jones's first acts as Democratic county leader in December 1964 was to go to Washington to see Powell.

Another cause for the split between Powell and Jones was a real estate development which the two along with a builder incorporated in January 1961. The group financed the construction of the Clayton Apartments at Seventh Avenue and 135th Street. As relations between Powell and Jones worsened, front organizations for the two leaders tried to gain control of the project. In October 1963 a consulting firm, one of whose vice-presidents had been Powell's secretary, sued the city, asking for preferential payments and claiming that Jones had, as a director of the project, used confidential information to enable his friends to get control of it. By March 1964 the suit had involved seven supreme court justices, more than a dozen lawyers, and ten defendants, including three city officials besides Jones.

Powell and Jones further disagreed on the naming of the executive director of Haryou-ACT. This organization, the antipoverty unit in Harlem, resulted from a 1964 merger of Harlem Youth Opportunities Unlimited and Associated Community Teams. Haryou had been headed by Professor Kenneth Clark of City College, who with a twenty-five-member staff had produced a study entitled *Youth in the Ghetto,* documenting the effects of powerlessness on the Harlem community. In his report Clark cited facts and figures showing the high rate of unemployment, overcrowding, narcotics addiction, juvenile delinquency, and other effects of ghetto living, and recommending remedial programs which would cost 110 million dollars. ACT had created a miniature domestic peace corps, training sixty young men and women and putting them to work in hospitals, schools, and welfare agencies. In addition, it had set up an adult volunteer service corps to assist community enterprises. From the beginning ACT had been a project supported by Powell. It was headed by Livingston Wingate, formerly assistant counsel of the House Education and Labor Committee. Its office adjoined the Adam Clayton Powell Community Center and the Abyssinian Baptist Church on 137th Street, and its executives had pictures of Powell on the walls. Clark hoped that a professional social worker would be appointed as director of the merged organization, while Powell hoped for Wingate. Since Jones was a member of the Haryou board and a political ally of the Mayor and since former Welfare Commissioner James R. Dumpson was frequently mentioned as the candidate favored by Clark, the dispute was sometimes pictured as a power struggle between Powell and the Wagner Administration. In July 1964, a month after the merged organization began to operate, Clark resigned from the Haryou-ACT board. The board named Wingate director in November. When Wingate had held the job less than a year, Haryou-ACT was the subject of special investigations and audits by the city and Federal governments and of a series of articles in the *Herald-Tribune*. The probes revealed that Wingate had been an inspirational leader and had become one of the most popular figures in Harlem, but that the organization's record keeping had been faulty, some nonsalaried board members had been receiving consultation fees, promotions for staff members and increases in their salaries had sometimes been made with loyalty to Powell and Wingate as a principal criterion. After Wingate had made veiled threats of violence if enough money were not given to Haryou-ACT, he was suspended as executive director in November 1965.

Powell's popularity with his Harlem constituents remained undiminished. In April 1963 Dave Balch gave the *World-Telegram* his impressions of a Powell sermon: "His ministerial robes which bear rich touches of crimson braid brightening the subdued Baptist decor, swirl about his tall, broad-shouldered frame as he strides back and forth on the floor of the church, pleading the cause of salvation.... The voice is rich and marvelously flexible—deep with authority, soft with persuasiveness, warm with welcome. The dark eyes span the congregation ... and the pastor's immaculately manicured hands stretch out to them, offering to lead the way to grace. Most impressive of all, though, is the Powell smile. It is a small smile, curving the ... mouth only slightly and offering only a glimpse of the even white teeth beneath the neat black mustache.

But it is a smile of infinite strength and sweetness, and as he reaches out to caress his flock it appears to suggest that there is room for all in their pastor's heart."[36] On Adam Clayton Powell Day, September 20, 1964, the twentieth anniversary of his first election to Congress, sixty cars and four brass bands paraded up Seventh Avenue. The hero of the day led the parade in a Cadillac convertible. Harry van Arsdale, president of the Central Trades and Labor Council, and Whitney Young, national secretary of the Urban League, headed a list of twenty-three speakers who offered testimonials to Powell's legislative skill. After his congressional victory of 1962 Powell told reporters, "I won without even mailing out a postcard or putting up a campaign poster." At a victory rally that year he told his followers, "I know you are going to vote for me till the day I die. And I do believe that after I'm dead some of you will go to the polls and write my name in." In March 1964, Powell modestly suggested that he would make an ideal vice-president, "The best security measure the nation could take would be to have Adam Clayton Powell as vice-president because then no one would dare shoot the president."[37]

Despite his controversial activities Powell probably would have remained not only a congressman but a powerful congressional committee chairman if he had not become involved in a lawsuit with Mrs. Esther James. On the evening of Sunday, March 6, 1960, the Harlem congressman was asked to appear on a TV interview show called "Between the Lines" after the scheduled guest, Senator Hubert Humphrey, then a contender for the Democratic Presidential nomination, was unable to fly up from Washington because of bad weather. In the course of the show Powell called Mrs. James a bag woman or graft collector for the police department. Mrs. James sued Powell for libel, retaining the services of Raymond Reuben, a lawyer whom she had read about in the newspapers. By January 1967 the case had involved eighty judges, ten courts, four juries, fifteen lawyers, and Congress. The legal papers in the case added up to a stack about twenty feet high. Some of Powell's lawyers had not anticipated Reuben's tenacity in pursuing the case. Reuben said that he had spent more than $30,000 out of his own pocket on expenses, including the cost of having briefs printed, buying stenographic transcripts, investigative expenses, and filing fees. When the suit was first brought, the station and sponsor were named as defendants along with Powell. But they settled with Mrs.

James for $1,500. Mrs. James sued Powell for a million dollars. He offered her $10,000 and a formal apology, but Reuben felt that he could get more. At the trial Mrs. Jones admitted that she was a police informer, but denied that she was a graft collector. She attended the trial while Powell did not, and several jurors later said that they had taken this fact into consideration in arriving at their decision. In April 1963 the jury awarded Mrs. Jones $211,500. Powell appealed to the Appellate Division, which unanimously affirmed the decision, but reduced the judgment to $46,500. The Court of Appeals affirmed the decision, and the Supreme Court of the United States refused to review the case. Collecting the money was another matter. Reuben began serving Powell with subpoenas to force him to pay the $46,500 judgment and to submit to a financial examination as to his ability to pay. Powell would neither pay nor submit to an examination. At least seven subpoenas directed the Harlem congressman to appear in court on specified dates. He did not appear, nor would his lawyers. Reuben then made a motion calling upon Powell to defend himself in court against the charge that he should be held in contempt of court. One of his lawyers attended the proceedings and claimed that the congressman had not received the subpoenas or that they had technical defects and were therefore invalid. The legality of the subpoenas was argued, and twice special referees were appointed to consider the matter. Both referees found that Powell had received proper notification of the order directing him to appear. These findings were accepted by the state judges, but their rulings were appealed to higher courts and took months. On May 8, 1964, Powell was found guilty of civil contempt of court. The court ordered his imprisonment for six months or until the judgment was paid. But the arrest order and two others could not be served while Congress was in session or on Sundays. Mrs. James also filed suit against Powell in Criminal Court, claiming that he had transferred ownership of his home in Puerto Rico to his wife's relatives to avoid having it seized to pay the defamation judgment. She also claimed that he had transferred property in Westchester for the same reason. A Manhattan grand jury began investigating the criminal charges on January 22, 1965. The grand jury found that no crime was committed by Powell in concealing his assets. Mrs. James tried to have him ousted from Congress on the ground that he was not a bona fide resident of New York State, and ninety-two of his constituents went to court to have the arrest order nullified because, they claimed, it kept them from access to their congressman. (The trial jury increased the $46,500 to $575,000, which was cut on appeal to $155,785. Amount with interest: $165,000.) Mrs. James became a virtual recluse in her Harlem apartment. The locks on her doors were changed five times; she installed an unlisted telephone. In June 1966 she went to live in Jamaica. On October 28 of that year Powell was convicted of criminal contempt and ordered jailed for thirty days any time he was found in the state, including Sundays and times when Congress was in session. Legal authorities believed that the Powell case had raised two important constitutional questions. The first involves the major arguments made by Powell in his defense against defamation; he contended that his remarks about Mrs. James were legitimate extensions of remarks he had previously made on the floor of the House, where all congressmen are virtually immune from any type of slander suit. The second point regards the clarification of the rights of congressmen to immunity in civil cases when Congress is in session.[38]

Through all the notoriety which his court case and other activities brought him, Powell remained apparently imperturbable. When criticized for touring Europe at government expense accompanied by two female members of his staff, he asked reporters if he was expected to take along an all-black staff (Tamara Wall was white). Criticized at another time for his lavish expenditure of government money, he responded, "As a member of Congress I have done nothing more than any other member and by the grace of God, I intend to do not one bit less." When questioned about his court case, he described himself as "just a humble parish priest fighting a crazy decision." The story of his life seemed to prove that he could ignore all critics and triumph over all vicissitudes. But by the fall of 1966 the notoriety seemed endless. Moreover, the temper of the American public worked against him. By late 1966 the civil rights movement of the early 1960's and the interracial thrust for integration and equality had been all but spent. In the summers of 1964, 1965, and 1966 major riots had erupted in Harlem, Brooklyn, Watts, Cleveland and other cities. Many white Americans, liberals as well as conservatives on the race issue, reacted to the hostility and violence born of Negro frustration with their own hostility and fear. "White backlash" and "black power," the latter in its context of hostility and separateness, became commonplace American expressions. Powell had become a racial folk hero by cultivating the image of the fearless and outspoken black man. But the temper of white America combined with the impact of his own activities was to prove too much even for Adam Clayton Powell. Congressmen's mail from home expressed dislike for Powell and demanded that action be taken to curb his power. His first setback came in the form of a revolt against his leadership by members of the House Education and Labor Committee. Despite the committee's impressive legislative record, many members resented Powell's absenteeism, his stalling on the antipoverty bill for his own reasons during that session, his arbitrary hiring and firing of staff members, his looseness with committee funds, and his identification with the Black Power movement. Under the leadership of Representative Sam Gibbons of Florida, a moderate on the civil rights issue, the committee voted 27–1 with two abstentions to deprive him of his powers as committee chairman. Henceforth the committee majority would hire and fire staff members and control the pace of legislation.[39]

Powell's problems mounted. An examination of his committee payroll revealed that his wife was receiving a $20,000 annual salary although she lived in Puerto Rico, and the law required that those on the payrolls of congressmen must work either in Washington or in the congressman's district. Moreover, Powell was cashing his wife's checks and depositing them in his bank account in Washington. In December 1966 a subcommittee of the House Administration Committee investigated the use of House Education and Labor Committee funds. The subcommittee was headed by one of Powell's long-time critics, Representative Wayne Hayes of Ohio. After taking 380 pages of testimony, the subcommittee report criticized Powell for payroll padding, for misuse of committee credit cards, for the submission of fraudulently signed vouchers, and for generally loose spending. But its report did not recommend any action against the Harlem congressman.

The Powell question was the first order of serious business facing the 90th Congress, which convened in January 1967. Some congressmen reported that they were receiving more letters about Powell than about the war in Vietnam. On January 9 the Democratic caucus by a vote of 122–88 deprived him of his committee chairmanship. The next day the whole House, by a 305–166 vote, rejected a compromise supported by the leadership which would have permitted him to take his seat during a proposed investigation and adopted by 364–64 a Republican substitute, declaring his seat vacant during the investigation. "I'm a black Dreyfus," he told supporters gathered on the Capitol steps. Referring to the Democrats who had voted against him, he declared, "Jesus had one Judas. I had about 120...I haven't seen anyone as crucified since Jesus Christ." Questioned by reporters about his plans, he responded, "When you've been here twenty-two years and you love Congress and you love the House, you know you want to stay." When asked if he expected to be seated after the investigation, he answered, "I'm always optimistic. To be pessimistic is to die." Asked if he would run for reelection if the House voted not to seat him, he was confident. "Of course, naturally. And I'll win by the biggest majority anyone outside Mississippi ever got."[40]

The reaction of the black community revealed a degree of ambivalence. In their public statements and proposals for action Negroes once more closed ranks in his defense. A few days after his expulsion, A. Philip Randolph proposed a pilgrimage to Washington in his behalf. Roy Wilkins presented a resolution which the NAACP annual meeting adopted unanimously urging Congress to establish guidelines for the conduct of its members. In a public statement Wilkins urged the House to take no action against Powell until such guidelines were established. Manhattan Borough President Percy Sutton termed Powell's ouster "unfortunate" and "distressing" and "a painful reminder of discriminatory practices." Martin Luther King sent a four-page telegram from Atlanta to Powell's office, calling the moves against the Harlem congressman "part of the same old white backlash that has eternally vacillated, hesitated, and practiced hypocrisy concerning Negro rights." Yet blacks took no real action in defense of Powell. Not only the pilgrimage to Washington but proposed demonstrations in various cities failed to develop. At least one congressman publicly expressed surprise at the lack of organized effort by civil rights leaders on behalf of Powell. He went on to say that he did not get one communication except mimeographed material from a civil rights leader or group.[41] The seemingly contradictory reaction of blacks to Powell's ouster reflects their ambivalence toward themselves and their own situation. Members of the race naturally took great pride in the fact that one of their number, one with whom they could identify, had achieved such power and position. Moreover, they could not help but recognize that part of the reason for his ouster was a resentment on the part of many white people not only of Powell's outspokenness but of the very fact that a black man possessed so much power. But if one of the reasons for Powell's ouster was racism, an equally important reason was his conduct, and his conveying the impression that his race would protect him from disciplinary action. This complexity of motivation was reflected in the attitudes of white and black Americans toward the controversial Harlem congressman.

The appointment of a committee of investigation posed a knotty problem for the House leadership. No congressman wanted to be on the committee. Regardless of how he voted, a Southerner could not win. If he favored Powell, he would be in trouble with his constituents at home, while if he opposed the Harlem congressman, he would be accused of racism. Many Northern congressmen also claimed that they would be in trouble with their constituents regardless of which way they voted on the Powell question. Speaker McCormack eventually appointed a committee of nine, with Emanuel Cellar, chairman of the Judiciary Committee, as its head. After taking testimony, the committee recommended that Powell be seated, but that he be censured for gross misconduct, that he be stripped of his seniority, and that he pay $40,000 as a punishment. However, the House disregarded the recommendations of the committee and voted to expel Powell.

By this time Powell had been separated from his wife, Yvette, who continued to live in Puerto Rico. The congressman's favorite haunt was now Bimini, two islands sixty miles off the coast of Florida which he christened "Adam's Eden." With his usual charm and flair for publicity, Powell endeared himself to the inhabitants and put Bimini on the map. American newspaper and magazine readers learned how he had become the first member of his race to be admitted to the Bimini Fishing Club, hitherto restricted to wealthy white vacationers, and how his boat, *Adam's Fancy*, had won trophies in two consecutive years. Readers were also told how he had secured supplies for the inhabitants during Hurricane Betsy in 1966 and how he played dominoes and drank Scotch and milk at the End of the World Bar with the island's black inhabitants who had dubbed him "Mr. Jesus."[42]

Powell did not have to return from Bimini to campaign when after his expulsion from the House he ran in a special election to fill his own unexpired term. At first the Republican leadership persuaded James Meredith, the man who had integrated the University of Mississippi, to run against Powell. But pressure from the black community caused Meredith to withdraw. The nomination then went to a Republican party worker who made one speech during the campaign. The winner of the contest was a foregone conclusion.[43]

Despite his reelection Powell did not attempt to take his seat in the 1967–1968 congressional session. He was again reelected by a wide margin in the fall of 1968. In January 1969 he was permitted to take his seat in the House, but deprived of seniority. The Supreme Court of the United States declared his expulsion unconstitutional in the fall of 1969. Powell paid his debt to Mrs. James with the help of money received from a book of sermons and a record, both of which were entitled "Keep the Faith, Baby." He had first used this phrase in a statement to reporters who questioned him on Bimini as to what advice he might have for his followers when he was about to be expelled from Congress.

During 1969 and 1970 Powell seldom appeared in Harlem, making his permanent home in Bimini. His readmission to the House and the Supreme Court decision denying the validity of his expulsion removed the necessity of his being supported as a symbol of racial unity. Led by Manhattan borough president Percy Sutton and Harlem assemblyman Charles Rangell, Harlem political leaders openly urged his replacement because he seldom appeared in his district. Rangell, who had been one of his strong supporters, opposed him and narrowly defeated him in the 1970 congressional primary.

In the fall of 1971 the Dial Press published his autobiography characteristically entitled *Adam by Adam*.[44] The book detailed the various aspects of his career from his point of view. Reviewers noted that it included interesting descriptive material, but little analytical awareness of the sources of his power and strength.[45]

Powell resigned as pastor of the Abyssinian Baptist Church in November 1971. He died of cancer in Miami on April 5, 1972. A few days before his death, his estranged wife and the woman with whom he was then living went to court in a controversy about who really was his wife. The court decided that he was still married to his former wife, but that his present companion was entitled to his body, and that a will which he had made leaving property to her was valid.[46]

The position of Negroes in America has made the question of leadership one of the race's major preoccupations. Frequently, blacks will get together and discuss the characteristics of a good leader or compare one leader with another. Adam Clayton Powell will undoubtedly be regarded as one of the foremost leaders in the history of the American Negro. Yet in evaluating Powell's role, the potential for leadership which he squandered is as important as that which he used. Hickey and Edwin astutely analyze Powell's ambition, the reason for its nonfulfillment, and his place in the hearts of black people. The Harlem congressman attempted to be a national party leader with his committee chairmanship as the font of his authority. At the same time he tried to be a spokesman for all black Americans, his stated purpose being to show that under proper leadership they could be powerful, "that, individually, they could become 'someone' and, collectively, they could meld with American society and thus win its material and spiritual benefits." Powell's biographers believe that no other contemporary American has held such an opportunity to succeed. Powell had it in his grasp to be a national figure who happened to be black and a black race leader who happened to be a powerful legislator—all at a time when the black revolution, of which he was a prophet, was cresting in the nation, both North and South. White society's demands of a successful Negro combined with Powell's personality to thwart this ambition. "Negroes in America have traditionally been viewed as subhuman, occupying by toleration a subculture inside the affluent and expansive American ambiance. On the other hand, Negroes are expected to be more than human—indeed almost saint-like—to win favor and recognition from business, the arts, the professions, or politics." Powell has become a hero to black people because he has shown how capable, strong, and urbane a member of the race could be. At the same time he maintained that his right to full equality meant the right to be as bad as the worst white man. Regardless of its moral justification, this demand weakened him as a black leader in a white society. His leadership was further weakened by his inability to work with other Negroes of comparable stature. He quarreled with J. Raymond Jones, with the civil rights leaders at the time of the march on Washington, and with Kenneth Clark over Haryou. He did his most effective work when his ego and vanity were satisfied and when he worked alone. Yet Adam Clayton Powell has undoubtedly enshrined himself as a permanent black hero. His greatest contribution is in giving black Americans "a sense of self and self-esteem, of full malehood, of having wombs to give birth to fully male humans. Powell himself was the creature of the black ghetto and of a manner of life designed, enforced, and perpetuated by white men. The fatal dualism in him is, in fact, a symptom of the double moral standard and, ultimately, of the hypocrisy of white America."[47]

J. Raymond Jones

One other New York Negro has possessed as much political power if not the fame of Adam Clayton Powell. The political styles of Powell and of J. Raymond Jones are a study in contrast. Powell made himself a symbol of black aspirations, while Jones's career resembles that of a political leader of a white ethnic group whose members have not yet moved into the middle class. For Jones as for generations of poor white immigrant boys with ability and ambition but without formal education, political leadership has been the road to money, power, and social mobility. Jones's biography is much harder to write than Powell's because until the past few years he has not obtained much publicity. The New York *Post* accurately characterized his role when it titled a feature on him "Political Productions Need Directors as Well as Stars."[1] Beginning in politics in the 1920's, he ran for his first public office in 1963. He has wielded power because of a combination of his astuteness and the increasing importance of the black vote. Although he does not particularly appreciate his nickname, "The Fox," it has been well earned over several decades.

John Raymond Jones was born at St. Thomas in the Virgin Islands, November 19, 1899. His father was a schoolteacher. The boy received a grade-school education at St. Thomas, but was unable to accept a scholarship for further study because of the coming of World War I. He became a seaman at the age of sixteen and sailed for Puerto Rico. In 1918 he landed in New York, knowing no one but having the names of a few family friends in his pocket. He got married the next year. In the early years he made his living as a redcap at Pennsylvania Station, a waiter, a truant officer, the proprietor of a bicycle shop, and an ice man. He obtained the ice concession for the Dunbar Apartments, the first black co-operative. One of Jones's early acquaintances was William "Kid" Banks, the black lieutenant of Martin J. Healy, leader of the 19th A.D. in

144

Harlem. Recognizing the increasing percentage of Negroes in his district, Healy asked Banks to hire some black election inspectors. Although American and foreign-born Negroes were frequently hostile to each other and Americans were in a dominant position at this time, Jones accepted the job. In 1966 he reminisced about what had happened when the polls closed after the 1921 primary: "They told me to take the registration books to the clubhouse and, like a fool, I took them to the Cayuga Club, a beautiful brownstone with a nice brass plate on the front. I was feeling pretty good, and I was promptly told I had come to the wrong place." The Cayuga Club was the white district club, and in those days black people were not permitted there and were expected to stay at their own segregated club.

The racial pattern of the Cayuga Club undoubtedly helped Jones decide to make politics his career. Another and probably more important reason was his realization that as the black community increased in numbers its political power or at least its potential for political power would also increase and that competent and experienced black political leaders could make money and wield power. His ambition for leadership may have influenced him to serve his political apprenticeship in the 22nd rather than in the 19th or 21st A.D. Lying immediately north of 145th Street, the 22nd was close enough to Harlem for Jones to participate in the politics of the area. Yet because in his early years not many black people were in the district, Jones could learn political strategy and rise to leadership as an individual rather than as a member of a racial group. One of Jones's earliest political lessons, which would serve him well in his later career, was the mastery of the rules for preparing nominating petitions. This process has been made deliberately difficult to protect incumbent candidates and entrenched political leaders. Many times insurgents with organizations which have been effective enough in other ways have been partly or wholly kept off the ballot because their petitions were found to be defective. Jones was one of the first Negroes to master this technical aspect of party organization.[2]

John Kelly served as leader of the 22nd A.D. from 1933 to 1941. By the mid-thirties Jones had become one of his chief lieutenants. In 1936 Kelly gave Jones his first full-time political job, that of Deputy U.S. Marshall. His duty was to escort prisoners from one jail to another. Jones held this position until 1938, when he became clerk of the Board of Elections. In the next few years he served briefly as secretary to the Commissioner of Elections and examiner in the office of the Manhattan borough president. Mayor O'Dwyer appointed him Deputy Housing Commissioner in 1947.

Jones's first try for party office came in 1939 when he ran against Harry C. Perry, the white leader of the 19th. Kelly and other leaders of the 22nd supported him. In a district which was overwhelmingly black, members of the race had been trying unsuccessfully for eight years to elect one of their number as leader. Jones did not win, but his campaign forced Perry to resign in favor of Daniel L. Burrows, a black member of his club who was then in the State Assembly. In 1941 Jones made the first of those political maneuvers which have earned him his nickname, enabled him to emerge on the winning side of most political controversies, and to remain a leader of New York politics for a quarter of a century. Besides Jones and Kelly, the two most powerful leaders in the 22nd were Congressman Joseph Gavagan and Assemblyman Daniel Flynn. Gavagan, supported by Jones and Flynn, successfully opposed Kelly in the district leadership contest of 1941. Jones's position in the district organization was further strengthened when Daniel Flynn went into the Navy in World War II and left the black leader in charge of his predominantly Irish following. In 1943 Jones made another foray into Harlem, this time running against Herbert Bruce for the leadership of the 21st, which Bruce had held since becoming the first black Tammany leader in 1935. At this time Tammany Hall had been out of power for ten years, and its leadership was badly divided. The most powerful faction was that of Clarence Neal and Burt Stand. Neal, the leader of a district bordering on Harlem, tried to maintain a party loyal to him in neighboring districts. Bruce and the two leading Negro weeklies, the New York Age and the Amsterdam News, opposed the Neal-Stand group's influence in Harlem, while Jones worked with Neal and Stand. Moreover, Neal, Stand, and Jones supported the Oklahoma-born realtor Fred Dickens in opposition to the incumbent leader Daniel Burrows in the 19th. Dickens defeated Burrows, while Bruce, more intrenched in his district, was able to withstand the challenge of Jones. Yet Bruce emerged from the contest weakened, and Jones's alliance with Neal and Stand quickly brought profitable results. In January 1944 Gavagan resigned both his congressional seat and his district leadership to accept a judgeship on the State Supreme Court. His resignation left Jones in control of the 22nd. At the same time the Tammany leadership itself was being decided. Neal and Stand supported Edward Loughlan against the incumbent, Michael Kennedy. The contest was so close that Jones, who had become Acting Leader of the 22nd a few days before, found himself with the deciding vote. He gave his support to Loughlan, who thereupon became leader. In 1944 assembly districts were reapportioned, and their number was reduced from twenty-three to sixteen. Part of the 22nd was incorporated into the new 13th. The leadership of the 13th was divided. The western half was given to Angelo Simonetti, while the eastern half, which by this time had become predominantly black, was given to Jones.[3]

In 1945 Jones was one of the managers of William O'Dwyer's successful campaign for mayor. Throughout O'Dwyer's years in City Hall Jones was one of the Mayor's closest political allies as well as becoming a personal friend. The Mayor regarded the Harlem leader as the most astute politician in the city, and he said that he would have supported Jones for Tammany leader if he had been white. One of O'Dwyer's first political maneuvers as mayor was to oust Edward Loughlan as leader of Tammany Hall and thus reduce the power of Neal and Stand. Loughlan was replaced by Frank Sampson, a leader who owed his position to the Mayor. Jones was one of O'Dwyer's chief allies in the Mayor's successful bid to dominate the Manhattan organization. In return for his support of the Mayor, Jones received at least three important patronage jobs, two for others and one for himself. In 1946 Vernon Riddick, a lawyer who was president of Jones's Carver Democratic Club, became a magistrate. The same year Daniel Flynn, the assemblyman from the 13th, decided to run for Congress, and Harold Stevens, another lawyer who was a member of Jones's club, secured the nomination for assembly. Stevens's subsequent election meant that four of the sixteen members of the Manhattan delegation to the State Assembly were black between 1946 and 1950. At this time Negroes constituted about 15 percent of the Manhattan population. Moreover, Stevens was elected from a district which was over half white. The Mayor appointed Jones Deputy Housing Commissioner in 1947. This appointment served several purposes. It rewarded Jones for faithful service. He proved to be the only district leader appointed to office by Mayor O'Dwyer. The job given Jones was one of the highest held by a Negro up to this time.

But the Jones appointment was more than merely an honor or a job. It signaled the Mayor's recognition of the increasing number and voting power of the black community. In addition to his duties in the Housing Department, the Mayor expected Jones to act as a liaison between City Hall and Harlem.[4]

Because of the nature of their work professional politicians are especially liable to charges of wrong-doing. During his long career Jones has experienced his share of such charges, though none of them has been proven. The O'Dwyer Administration resulted in a number of scandals. As a city official and a Tammany district leader, Jones was almost sure to be charged with something during these years. The nomination of Francis L. Valente as surrogate in 1948 touched off a public controversy. The office of surrogate in New York is particularly important to politicians because that official has jurisdiction over the probation of wills. In 1948 the ethnic balancers of the New York electoral ticket agreed that the job of surrogate should go to an Italian, but they disagreed as to which Italian. A group of Tammany district leaders headed by Carmine DiSapio favored either General Sessions judge Francis Valente or his uncle, State Supreme Court Justice Louis Valente. The nephew was chosen because his uncle was too near the retirement age. The Mayor, the then Tammany leader Frank Sampson, and another group of district leaders favored Vincent R. Impelleteri, who at this time was president of the City Council. Jones and other Harlem leaders at first supported Impelleteri, but then switched to Valente because DiSapio agreed to support a Negro for the next vacancy in the Court of General Sessions. A rumor was circulated that Jones and other Tammany leaders had been paid $1,000 each for their support of Valente. The charge was made public on June 30, 1948, and Jones immediately resigned his position in the Housing Department. He was replaced by Ruth Whitehead Whaley, a lawyer who had been the first black woman admitted to the New York bar. Manhattan District Attorney Hogan and a grand jury investigated the bribery charge. The grand jury probe revealed the charge to be untrue. In August Jones was restored to his housing job, and Mrs. Whaley became secretary to the Welfare Department, the first Negro to hold a position on this level. As the quid pro quo for the Harlem leader's support of Valente, Carmine DiSapio had promised that he would support a Negro for the next vacancy in the Court of General Sessions. The next vacancy occurred in 1950, and Harold Stevens became the first member of his race to be a General Sessions judge. Later, Stevens became the first Negro to be a member of the State Supreme Court, and to date is the only race member to be a justice of the Appellate Division.[5] A month after his return to the Housing Department, Jones's political position was strengthened when he became chairman of the Tammany Hall Rules Committee. This post gave him a full vote on the Tammany Executive Committee while most other district leaders held fractional votes. In the 1950 mayoralty campaign Jones worked for the Democratic candidate Ferdinand Pecora. In the course of the campaign the Republican candidate Edward Corsi charged him with demanding a $1,000 campaign contribution in exchange for aid to Mt. Morris Hospital. Jones immediately began a $50,000 libel suit against Corsi. The hospital administrator supported the Harlem leader. The charge and the suit were dropped after the election. Vincent R. Impelleteri was elected mayor in 1950. Because Jones had supported Pecora, he resigned from the Housing Department in December.

Throughout his years in politics Jones had looked forward to retirement. Moreover, he did not feel comfortable working with the new Tammany leader, Carmine DiSapio. While Jones had become a citywide figure, he had neglected to keep the political fences mended in his own district. The Truman Democratic Club had arisen under the leadership of Antonio Rasmus to oppose Jones and the Carver Club. In June 1953, Jones resigned the district leadership. Three months later, Rasmus defeated Jones's lieutenant and successor, Lucius Butts.

When Jones retired as a district leader, he took a job as secretary to General Sessions Judge Harold Stevens, whom he had helped to put on the bench. Stevens was elevated to the State Supreme Court in 1955. Since the secretaries to Supreme Court justices must be lawyers, Jones became secretary to General Sessions Judge Gerald Colkin. "That was the only job I ever thoroughly enjoyed," Jones later recalled. "Judge Colkin is an artist. He paints and he loves flowers as I do. We built a roof garden from nothing on the seventeenth floor of the Criminal Courts building, and it's still there."[6]

While Jones was not particularly seeking an opportunity to re-enter the political arena, events made such an opportunity irresistible. By the mid-1940's Jones and Powell were already the best-known Harlem politicians. In their rise to power and eminence they were neither friends and allies nor enemies. Coincidentally, they were both competent and ambitious and in the same community at the same time. Carmine DiSapio's attempt to purge Powell in 1958 brought them together. Jones contributed not only his ability to draw up petitions (Acy Lennon, the member of Powell's staff who usually did this work, sat out the campaign in jail for income tax evasion), but his knowledge of political strategy. From the beginning Jones saw an opportunity to strike at Carmine DiSapio, whom he disliked, while at the same time putting himself back on the Harlem political scene. In Powell's fight for renomination Jones was a tireless organizer and strategist. The Powell victory restored Jones's power in Harlem politics. In 1959 Powell and Jones completed the job which they had begun the previous year. Both men, along with a supporter, Mark Southall, defeated leaders who had supported the Powell purge. Lloyd Dickens, the only Harlem leader who had backed Powell in 1958, won reelection. Only Hulan Jack survived the Powell-Jones landslide. Charting an independent course between DiSapio and the reform Democrats, Powell and Jones dubbed their coalition the United Harlem leadership team.

Powell and Jones became business partners as well as political allies. Together they organized the first Mitchell-Lama limited dividend housing co-operative in Harlem. Their combined efforts brought about the construction of the Clayton Apartments at Seventh Avenue and 135th Street.[7]

The selection of Edward Dudley as borough president of Manhattan completed the break between the Mayor and DiSapio and strengthened Jones's position not only in Harlem but in Manhattan, Dudley had been a member of Jones's Carver Club since it was first organized. DiSapio supported Lloyd Dickens. Dudley was chosen over Dickens largely because of the last-minute switch of Councilman Earl Brown. Although a member of the Carver Club at this time, Jones and Brown disliked each other, and Jones's woman co-leader had threatened to run against Brown in the 1961 primary. In a newspaper interview after Dudley's selection Jones predicted DiSapio's defeat in 1961, a prediction which proved accurate.[8]

The mayoralty campaign of 1961 not only showed Jones at his shrewdest, but transformed him into one of the leading Democrats of the city and state. For two and a half years the Democratic Party had been divided between the followers of County Leader Carmine DiSapio and the reform Democrats. As the mayoralty campaign approached, many New Yorkers were dissatisfied with both Mayor Wagner and DiSapio. The Mayor was felt to be indecisive, to lack a strong will, and to have no program aside from his continuation in public office. Since the Democratic defeat in the election of 1958 and the assumption of the leadership of the reformers by ex-Senator Lehmann, Eleanor Roosevelt, and Thomas K. Finletter, the image of DiSapio as a traditional Tammany boss had been gaining public acceptance. The Mayor's break with the Tammany leader came gradually, and the reformers could not accept him as one of them. Yet by the spring of 1961 his break was final, and the reformers offered and he accepted their support in his bid for a third term. In accepting reform support, the Mayor alienated not only the Manhattan county leader but the leaders of the other four counties which comprise New York City. Jones's inability to work with DiSapio had been one of the causes of his retirement from politics in 1953 and of his wholehearted reentry into the political arena five years later. In June 1961, guessing that dislike of the county leader would prove greater than dissatisfaction with the Mayor, he became the first district leader not a reformer to come out in support of Wagner's reelection. As their candidate against the Mayor, in the primary, the county leaders selected State Comptroller Arthur Levitt, a popular vote-getter and the only Democrat to win statewide office in 1958. Powell and other Harlem leaders supported Levitt. Jones became one of Wagner's campaign managers. In the September primary Harlem proved to be one of the Mayor's banner areas. He carried the district by a 2–1 majority. The process was repeated in the general election. The Mayor defeated the Republican candidate, Attorney General Louis Lefkowitz, this time by a 3–1 majority.[9]

Democratic party rules require that the county leader must also be a district leader. In the 1961 contest Carmine DiSapio lost the leadership of his Greenwich Village district and thus became ineligible to continue as county leader. The followers of DiSapio and the Harlem leaders, the latter group having for the most part remained neutral in the struggle between DiSapio and the Mayor, supported Jones for county leader. Those favoring the Harlemite pointed to his early support of the Mayor and to the majorities for the Mayor which were larger in Harlem than in districts led by reformers. On the other hand the reform Democrats opposed Jones because he had never supported them and had kept his ties with the old-line leaders although supporting the Mayor for reelection. Powell and other Harlem leaders expressed the opinion that the reformers opposed Jones because he was black. Although Jones's race could well have been a reason why he had not been chosen county leader by Mayor O'Dwyer in the later 1940's, politics rather than pigmentation proved the deciding factor in 1961 and 1962. Jones's position was too well known to permit him to be acceptable to the reformers. Although Harlem had furnished the Mayor with large majorities, the reform leaders had been his earliest supporters. In the face of the opposition Jones expressed his willingness to step aside in favor of Edward Costikyan. Costikyan considered himself a member of the reform group, but many of the reform leaders did not agree because Costikyan had frequently remained neutral in factional disputes and had not joined the Committee for Democratic Voters, the central reform organization. In March 1962 Costikyan was chosen county leader. Jones became vice-chairman of the New York County Executive Committee and liaison between the Mayor and the five county leaders.[10]

As the result of the election of 1963 Jones became the most powerful Democrat in the city. In June Herbert Evans, the city councilman from Harlem, accepted an appointment as a member of the City Housing and Redevelopment Board. Jones replaced Evans on the City Council. The new councilman was required to run for election in the fall. In the September primary he faced opposition for both his newly acquired council seat and for the district leadership. The majority of the Harlem leaders supported Jones's opponents, while he possessed the backing of the Mayor and of reform leaders. Powell at first supported Jones, but then changed his mind and backed his opponents. Powell and Jones, whose rivalry for the Harlem political leadership was aggravated· by disagreements about business affairs, engaged in a public controversy. Jones accused Powell of being ineffective as a civil rights leader, while Powell charged Jones with attempting to become boss of Harlem with the aid of money and workers from outside the district. When the votes were counted, Jones retained both his council seat and his district leadership. The race for council was closer than that for district leader, and Jones, opposed by blacks for both positions, received a larger percentage of votes in white districts than in Harlem, but he did receive an overall majority.[11] Costikyan resigned as Democratic county leader in November 1964. Relations between regulars and reformers had improved during his tenure as leader. At the time of Costikyan's resignation the reformers controlled six and five-sixths votes out of sixteen on the Democratic County Executive Committee. On December 3 the majority with the support of the Mayor chose Jones as county leader. The black leader had become so powerful that the only reference to his race was the mention that he was the first black county leader in the state and perhaps the only one in the nation. On the day of his selection he told reporters that as a Negro he was proud of the honor conferred upon him: "I will work harder than I normally would to prove to all the people of the county that they can have confidence in us." The next day he expressed the opinion that his race would have no effect upon his leadership: "It's been a long time since I've stopped worrying about being a Negro or thinking about being a Negro. I've always been able to work with people.... I've never been concerned about any difference between us and I'm not going to assume there is any now."[12]

Jones's rise to prominence naturally caused him to become the subject of newspaper and magazine features. As early as May 1960, the journalist Theodore H. White described him as a "master political technician." Although World War I had interrupted Jones's education before he could attend high school, White in the same article discusses the Harlem leader's reading habits: "He is the only Tammany leader in the private rooms of whose clubhouse rest a copy of Toynbee, a collection of books on Africa, a study of American sociology. At home... his library runs from the complete Balzac and the complete Shakespeare to the memoirs of Harry Truman embedded in a vast collection of books on economics and science." Descriptions of his physical appearance were sometimes combined with comments upon his air of dignity. White described him as "tall and oak-limbed, dark brown and handsome; his silver-gray hair and pencil thin mustache establishing an air of aristocratic dignity," while a writer in the New York *Post* in 1961 characterized him as "a large, quiet, self-educated grandfather. He talks and moves with the ease that comes from sitting habitually at head tables." In February 1967, shortly before Jones resigned as county leader, Anthony Hiss wrote a feature on him for the *New York*

Times Magazine. He described Jones as "a man of somewhat more than middle height, well filled out, with a fine, big head. His skin is deep ginger-bread color, and his hair, which he keeps short, is fleecy white. He sports a small and elegant mustache; its upper part is white; and its nether part gray. Jones's voice has pleasantly modulated West Indian vowels and the rest of his diction is upper-class nineteenth-century English—he drops terminal Gs and uses plural verbs with singular subjects. When he talks, he likes to cock his head to one side and close his eyes almost all the way. This gives him his habitual expression, which is somehow both sardonic and serene." Though nothing has ever been proved against Jones, he has been accused of irregularity or wrong-doing a number of times. Perhaps such accusations are inevitable in that portion of the political arena in which he has operated throughout his career. In any case they have frequently been made against leaders of Tammany Hall. "He is commonly suspected of having engaged in all sorts of political intrigue," wrote Hiss. "There are whispers that he has been involved in middle-income housing projects in Harlem and murmurs that he is senior partner in an elaborate brokerage of judgeships. . . . Similar suspicions have attached to all Tammany leaders, and Jones is a firm believer in the importance of keeping up traditions. As the spiritual heir of William Marcy Tweed, Carmine DiSapio, and Charles F. Murphy, he is inclined to look upon these suspicions as subsidiary titles to the office—in the same way the Queen of England is also styled 'Defender of the Faith.'" Hiss quoted Jones's favorite political maxims as "'Never say never in politics'" and "'Nobody ever does anything for nothing!'" Various writers have commented on the political astuteness which has earned him the nickname of "The Fox." "I don't make a fuss about it," Jones once told a reporter, "but that nickname, 'the Fox,' is not the sort of thing I want or need." Anthony Hiss quoted an estimate of Jones's operating procedure with evident agreement "'Ray will never tell you a lie, but he will often omit bits of the truth.'" Among a group for whom chances of recognition and distinction are still comparatively rare, the elevation of Jones to the county leadership made him something of a race hero. Hiss found that some Harlemites felt that he was not getting sufficient material rewards: "Ray hasn't been given enough scratch," one man was heard to comment. "He deserves better of the city. They ought to give him something commensurate with his talents."[13]

Jones served as county leader from December 1964 to March 1967. During the first weeks in his new position he and Queens county leader Moses Weinstein acted as negotiators for the Mayor in the organization of the State Legislature. The Johnson landslide of 1964 had brought with it Democratic control of both houses of the State Legislature for the first time in thirty years. But factional disputes within the Democratic Party delayed the start of the legislative session for over a month. The Mayor supported Anthony Travia of Brooklyn for Speaker, while his opponents backed Stanley Steingut of the same borough. Several candidates for the senate leadership were considered by both sides. In 1964 Robert Kennedy had been elected United States Senator from New York. Although Kennedy and Wagner never publicly opposed each other and the former remained neutral in the struggle to organize the legislature, observers viewed the Senator and the Mayor as vying for party control. This feeling was given added impetus because several of the county leaders who had been early supporters of Kennedy opposed the legislative choices of the Mayor. Jones became the center of a controversy when on January 18 the Mayor accused State Chairman William McKeon, one of his opponents, of offering a judgeship to Travia and chairmanships of Senate committees with increased expense accounts to two state senators who were supporters of the Mayor if they switched their vote. The offer was allegedly made to Jones at a meeting at which six leaders were present. Jones was the only one to back up the Mayor's accusations. The State Investigation Commission held hearings, while Jones and McKeon publicly called each other liars. In the end nothing was proved, the Mayor admitted that nothing was illegal about the offer if it had been made, and the State Committee gave McKeon a vote of confidence. Democratic leaders of the legislature who were supporters of the Mayor were finally chosen. Travia became Speaker of the Assembly, while Joseph Zaretzky became Senate majority leader.[14]

Jones's next problem was the selection of a Manhattan borough president. Edward Dudley, the incumbent, was nominated and elected to a Supreme Court judgeship in 1964. Earl Brown, the former city councilman who at this time was Deputy Borough President, was acceptable to the Mayor and to most of the Harlem leaders, but not to Jones. Although Jones and Brown had never liked each other, Brown had been a member of Jones's club until he had supported the leader's opponent for City Council in the 1963 primary. After Jones's victory newspapers carried a story that Brown had been expelled from the Carver Club and had joined another Harlem Democratic club. Before becoming county leader, Jones had characterized Brown's candidacy for the borough presidency as "personally obnoxious." To block the election of Brown, Jones gave his support to State Senator Constance Baker Motley. Mrs. Motley's work as director of the NAACP Legal Defense Fund had made her a national Negro figure. But she had played no part in politics until February 1964, when she was elected to the State Senate to succeed James Watson, who had become a civil court judge. She was reelected to the State Senate in the fall of 1964. Most Harlem leaders opposed her selection as borough president because they felt that she had not been politically active for a long enough time. Jones may have shared this opinion, but he preferred her selection to that of Brown. In 1964 the Manhattan councilmanic delegation consisted of six Democrats and two Republicans. Jones called a closed caucus of the Democratic councilmen in the Mayor's office. Five of the six Democrats attended. Jones persuaded the caucus to abide by the will of the majority. Of the five councilmen who attended the caucus, Jones and two others supported Mrs. Motley, while two voted for Brown. In this way Jones secured five votes for Mrs. Motley, which gave her a majority.[15]

From the time of his first political campaign Jones's tenure of the office of county chairman seemed ill-starred. Part of the problem lay beyond his control. Although Jones by the force of his personality wielded more power than either his predecessor or his successor, the power of the leader of Tammany Hall had been in a continuous decline for at least thirty years. Since the coming of the New Deal the Federal government had assumed many functions formerly performed by local politicians, thus causing most urban political machines to lose much of their power. Manhattan, which had once been the most populous of the five boroughs, was fourth in population at the time Jones became county leader; only Staten Island was smaller. Moreover, the political situation posed difficulties not only for Jones but for the other Democratic leaders whose counties make up New York City. In 1964 the Democrats had been out of power in the state for six years. The party in the city was divided between regulars and reformers, with only the vote-getting ability of Mayor Wagner to hold it together. And he had had to engage in bitter primary battles two of the three times he had run for office. In June 1965 the Mayor announced that he would not run for a fourth term, without devising a means of preventing a scramble for the nomination. Four candidates, including the two leading officeholders of the Wagner Administration, president of the City Council Paul Screvane and Comptroller Abraham Beame, as well as Congressman William Fitzryan and Councilman-at-large Paul O'Dwyer, ran in the primary. Jones supported Screvane, as did Mayor Wagner. Beame won. In the general election Lindsay, the Fusion candidate, carried Manhattan. While the Democrats did carry Harlem, dissatisfaction with the Wagner Administration, Lindsay's wooing of minority groups, and Beame's comparative indifference to them caused reduced Democratic majorities in the black area.

Jones suffered another setback in the 1966 primary contest for Manhattan surrogate. Although the office of surrogate is important to politicians because its occupant controls millions of dollars' worth of patronage every year, the selection usually attracts little public attention. Over the objections of the reformers but with a comfortable majority, the New York County Democratic Committee nominated State Supreme Court Justice Arthur Klein for surrogate in May 1966. The Republican County Committee unanimously endorsed him. Although judges of other courts frequently receive bipartisan nominations, the post of surrogate had always been contested. When the Republicans endorsed Justice Klein, reform Democrats accused Jones of making a deal with the Republican County Chairman, although they never made clear exactly what Jones had promised in return. For the first time since his entry into New York politics Senator Robert Kennedy participated in an intraparty struggle. Joining with the reform Democrats and the Liberal Party, he endorsed State Supreme Court Justice Samuel Silverman in a primary fight against Klein. Although Klein's political and personal ties were with old guard leaders, the question of the honest administration of the office of surrogate did not enter into the contest. With the support of Jones, Klein announced that he would make public the names of the lawyers he appointed along with their fees. He further promised that he would not make appointments on a political basis. Neither Klein nor Silverman was widely known to the public before his nomination, nor did either of them make much of an impression during the campaign. Kennedy and Jones became the principal symbols of the struggle. The Silverman campaign was conducted by a group of veterans of previous Kennedy campaigns, headed by the Senator's brother-in-law Steven Smith. Although black people participated in the campaign on both sides, Harlem district leaders and officeholders rallied around Jones and tried to raise a race issue. Eighteen of them, with the principal aide of Adam Clayton Powell as spokesman, issued a statement that while they could not definitely accuse anyone of being antiblack, there was "an aura of suspicion toward those who support Silverman." A group of five, four of them black, expressed more specific grievances. Psychologist Kenneth Clark, State Senator Basil Patterson, civil liberties lawyer Morris Ernst, ex-Welfare Commissioner James R. Dumpson, and ex-Civil Service Commissioner Thomas B. Dyett issued a joint statement: "The issue of the selection of a surrogate was not made a major inter- or intraparty fight until a Negro became chairman of the New York County Democratic Committee and played a crucial role in the selection process. Only then were questions of 'good government,' 'corruption,' 'ideals' and 'the integrity of the Judiciary' raised in spite of the fact and ignoring the fact that the present chairman was responsible for instituting unprecedented safeguards in the selection process.... This struggle could be interpreted even by moderates as an attempt to constrict the power and prerogatives of any political office or as a desire to control or remove a Negro who seeks to exercise the usual authority of any office." On the other hand James Farmer, formerly national director of CORE, issued a statement denying that Jones was the issue and pointing to the Kennedy record on civil rights. Benjamin McLauren, of the Brotherhood of Sleeping-Car Porters, and James Meredith, the first Negro to enter the University of Mississippi, also issued statements in support of Silverman, while Andrew Hatcher, who had been assistant press secretary to President John F. Kennedy, served as one of the managers of the Silverman campaign.

On election night the result was known about an hour after the polls closed. Silverman won by 21,000 votes, or a 3–2 majority. The *Times* thus analyzed the cause of the victory: "The Kennedy campaign for Justice Silverman was characteristically well-organized, thorough, and intense. Overshadowing the usual newspaper ads, radio spots, and telephone recordings, however, were the Senator's street-corner appearances with his candidate, all over Manhattan, all day, all night. Everywhere the Senator was the main attraction, forcing the Justice to remark just before primary day, 'I wish somebody would ask once, "Who is that man walking with Judge Silverman?" ' "[16]

After the defeat of Justice Klein, Jones's days as county leader were numbered. His continuation in office for ten additional months bears testimony to his strength as a leader. Public attacks upon him by reform Democrats and his differences with Senator Kennedy continued. His position was further weakened by the Democratic defeat in the election of 1966 and by Governor Rockefeller carrying Manhattan. Jones resigned the county leadership in March 1967, giving lack of support by Senator Kennedy as the reason for his resignation. The Senator admitted that Jones was not his favorite lieutenant: "Ray Jones may have had his own reasons for resigning. In any event, our success in New York County has not been exactly spectacular. For all of us in the Democratic Party, the main point now is to get together with all elements of the party, to build a strong organization, to work for all the people of New York."[17] Jones quit as a district leader at the same time as he resigned as county chairman. His term as city councilman ended in December 1969. His career in active politics has probably ended. In 1961 his wife became Collector of Customs for his native Virgin Islands. The Joneses have a house in St. Thomas, and he hopes to enjoy his retirement there.

Jones's career was caused by a combination of his political astuteness and the increasing power of the black vote. From his first campaign for a district leadership in 1939 to his simultaneous campaigns for district leader and for the City Council twenty-four years later, he displayed an almost uncanny knack for correctly judging the political situation. His appointment by Mayor Wagner as liaison with the county leaders and his selection as Democratic leader of New York County were less tokens of racial recognition than recognition of an individual who was a talented political strategist. On the other hand the difference in the recognition given to Jones by Mayors O'Dwyer and Wagner illustrate the relationship of his career to the strength of the vote of his racial group. O'Dwyer had as great a respect for Jones's talents as did Wagner, yet in 1947 he could only become the Mayor's man in Harlem, while in 1964 he could become Manhattan county leader. Jones recognized and publicly acknowledged his dependence on the black vote existing as a bloc. When the American Civil Liberties Union tried to have the federal census drop all racial identification, Jones vigorously opposed the idea. "Silliest damn thing I ever heard of," he told reporters. "How am I going to bargain for the Negroes if I can't prove where they are? I'm losing too many as it is, with all this crossing of the color line." In a feature on the Harlem leader Harry Ashmoor concludes, "Ray Jones ... is perhaps an inevitable part of the shifting patterns of urban life. ... He exists and performs in the old manner, simply because Negroes in fact make up the last real bloc vote left in the land."

Notwithstanding Jones's personal abilities and accomplishments, his career is important primarily because it symbolizes the increasing power of the black vote and through it the increasing role played by Negroes in the political life of New York.[18]

CHAPTER 8

The Negro Immigrants

New York is the only American city with a large number of Negroes
who are first- or second-generation immigrants. They have played
leadership roles in politics and in other phases of New York Negro
life far out of proportion to their numbers. In their book *Beyond
the Melting Pot* Daniel P. Moynihan and Nathan Glazer estimate
that from one fifth to one fourth of New York Negroes are foreign-
born or children of foreign-born parents. In the late 1930's Ira
D. A. Reid in the only published study of the subject estimated
that one third of the black professionals were foreign-born. The
Negro immigrants in New York City are usually referred to by
the term West Indians.[1] The majority of them did come from
the islands of the British West Indies, although some came from
British Guiana, the Virgin Islands, and from French Caribbean
possessions.

The reasons for their migration and the extent and limitations
of their contribution to New York Negro political life can be under-
stood by reviewing the history and class structure of the islands.
The West Indies were first discovered by Columbus, and they
remained under Spanish rule until the seventeenth century. The
British occupied the first of the West Indian islands in 1623,
Jamaica in 1655, Trinidad in 1699, and British Guiana after the
Napoleonic wars. In the eighteenth century the British and French
West Indies were economically more important than the mainland
colonies. Most wars of the seventeenth and eighteenth centuries
were reflected in heavy fighting in the Caribbean, and every peace
treaty included transfers of West Indian territory. In 1763, after
the British had defeated the French in the French and Indian War,
a large minority of the members of the British Parliament favored
returning Canada to France and keeping the French islands of
Martinique and Guadeloupe. The West Indian islands were important mainly because they provided the world with its chief

161

source of sugar. Indigo and cacao were also raised on some islands. Jamaica became the chief slave market of the world. Many shiploads of slaves were brought from Africa to Jamaica and then sold. Both the slave trade and the sugar trade contributed to making the British West Indies largely black. When Columbus came to the islands, they were inhabited by primitive Arawak Indians. The Indians died off quickly from disease, starvation, and forced labor. Sugar and indigo production required large plantations, and black slaves became the chief source of labor. Small landholders disappeared, and slaves greatly outnumbered the small group of planters, overseers, merchants, and professional men who remained. Daniel G. Smith, a sociologist working at the University of the West Indies in Jamaica, has recently published an analysis of the class structure of the islands in 1820. In significant ways West Indian society both resembled and differed from that of the antebellum Southern United States. Slavery played a vital role in the economics of both regions. Both on the islands and on the Southern mainland slaves worked on plantations producing staple crops. Both Southern and West Indian bondsmen who had the closest personal ties to the masters frequently received special treatment and were encouraged to feel superior to other slaves. Free blacks lived in considerable numbers both in the South and in the West Indies. Although they suffered from legal and political disabilities in both societies, individuals among them became prosperous, and some free Negroes owned slaves themselves. Racism ran rampant both in the South and in the West Indies. Ruling white upper classes forced their institutions and values upon their social inferiors. But West Indian racism varied from its Southern counterpart in several important respects. Lightness of skin color could prove an advantage in both the West Indies and the South, but whether slave or free, being lightskinned on the islands automatically put a Negro in a superior social position. New Orleans and Charleston were the only parts of the United States which resembled the West Indies in this regard, as well as in the position of concubinage. The number of light-skinned American Negroes is living proof that sexual relations between white men and black women were widespread throughout the South, but in the West Indies concubinage was an established institution. "The refusal of sexual intercourse with a white overseer was equivalent to mutiny," wrote Eric Williams. "It was no uncommon thing for a planter to line up his slave girls before his guest who was invited to take his choice for the night."[2] White men of the highest social class who lived with their white wives and children frequently acknowledged their relationships to their colored mistresses. In the Southern United States white men could do as they pleased with the children which resulted from their liaisons wih black women. The social code of the islands required that gentlemen free their mulatto children and give them an education equivalent to that given their white offspring. Southern mores required white women to feign ignorance of the extramarital affairs of white men with slave women. In the West Indies white women, while themselves being forbidden to engage in extramarital relations with men of any color or class, were expected by their male relatives and friends to recognize their colored concubines and to receive them socially on various occasions. "Free colored women," wrote Smith, "sought, as a major goal of their life, to form concubinage or 'keeper' relationships with white men, and hence avoided marriage to free colored men. Frequently, also, a colored concubine would ask her white protector's kinswomen to stand as godmothers to her children by him." The prevalence of concubinage naturally caused the whole society to be disorganized. Colored fathers considered it a paternal obligation to secure as large a financial and property settlement as possible for their daughters who were about to enter into concubinage relationships. Black men's possible marriage partners were confined to women darker than themselves or to white men's cast-off mistresses. Concubinage among Negroes was as widespread as between white men and black women.

The institution of concubinage and the responsibility for their mulatto children which the society placed upon upper-class white men brought into existence a group of light-skinned and comparatively well-educated free Negroes. In 1820 they were prohibited from voting or holding office, managing estates, inheriting property of more than a certain value, and giving evidence in court against white men. Some owned small plantations or bossed gangs of slaves working in towns. Others became lawyers, businessmen, journalists, printers, or clerical workers. In a letter to the home government in 1833 the governor of Barbados described them as a "sober, energetic, and loyal race." After the slaves were freed and disabilities were removed, this group formed the West Indian middle and upper classes.

The economic prosperity of the West Indies did not long survive the end of the eighteenth century. Sugar production in other parts of the world led to a decline in the price. The abolition of the African slave trade in 1807 ended that source of wealth. The anti-slavery movement in England increased in the 1820's and the early 1830's. Slave revolts erupted on several islands. In the largest of these 50,000 slaves rebelled in northwest Jamaica in the week after Christmas, 1831. Ten white men and four hundred slaves were killed in the fighting, while one hundred of the ringleaders were executed, and an equal number were severely flogged. Yet the planters were willing to grant equal rights to free blacks. By Orders in Council in 1828 the British government abolished all legal disabilities based on color, while the Jamaican legislature in 1830 and those of the other islands shortly afterward followed suit. According to the Emancipation Act which Parliament passed in 1833, masters were to be compensated and final freedom was to be preceded by a period of apprenticeship. This period was limited to a maximum of six years for field laborers and four years for all others. Apprentices were to be paid no wages, but were to be supplied with food and clothing and were required to work no more than forty-five hours a week. Colonial legislatures could and sometimes did shorten the period of apprenticeship or dispense with it altogether. On July 31, 1834, about 668,000 slaves in the British West Indies became free. The ex-bondsmen showed restraint and no general refusal to work. Most of them became small landowners and laborers. In 1846 the British government ended its special protection of West Indian sugar. This move had the direct effect of impoverishing the already overburdened planters and the indirect effect of making the islands still more predominantly black, since many of the white planters left.[3]

After the repeal of the political restrictions, most but not all high government officials were white. Many black men did become members of the legislatures of the islands. In the late nineteenth century Sir Conrad Reeves, a mulatto who had been a poor boy, became Chief Justice of Barbados. Another member of the race served as Solicitor General and Attorney General of the Leeward Islands between 1881 and 1886. Others became doctors, lawyers, theologians, and educators. On some islands they monopolized the professions and the lower ranks of the civil service. By the early years of the twentieth century the laws of the islands forbade racial discrimination. For example, the Jamaican constitution which was in effect in 1926 prohibited the governor from giving his assent to "any bill whereby persons not of European birth or descent may be subjected or made liable to any disabilities to which persons of European birth or descent are not also subjected or liable."[4]

Individual West Indians migrated to the United States and played prominent roles in American history as early as the beginning of the nineteenth century. Prince Hall, the founder of the first lodge of black Masons, and Peter Ogden, the founder of the first lodge of black Odd Fellows, were natives of the islands, as was Denmark Vesey, the free carpenter of Charleston who led a widespread slave revolt in 1820 which was second only to that of Nat Turner ten years later in its impact on the South. John B. Russwurm, a Jamaican by birth, became the first member of his race to graduate from an American college. In 1828 Russwurm founded *Freedom's Journal,* the first black newspaper in the country.

Most of the West Indian islands suffered economically in the last half of the nineteenth and the early years of the twentieth centuries. Jobs were scarce, the standard of living remained low, and many natives of the islands sought work elsewhere. "Few vocational avenues were open to the ambitious youth of the Bahamas," one immigrant recalled. "Fishing and farming brought meager financial returns and offered a scanty livelihood.... The trades were equally discouraging. I could be employed by the government as a schoolteacher or policeman...or get a job as a clerk in a store in the city of Nassau.... Home-returning pilgrims told exaggerated tales of their fame and fortune in the 'promised land.' As convincing evidence of their claims, they dressed flashily and spent American dollars lavishly and prodigally. Those American dollars had a bewitching charm to a country lad who worked for wages ranging from $.36 to $.50 a day. Moreover, the splendid appearance of those boys from the states stood out in striking contrast to us ill-fashionably clad country lads."[5] In 1881 the governor of Jamaica reported that workers were leaving the islands at the rate of 1,000 a month.[6] Many went to Panama where the French company which had built the Suez Canal was attempting to construct a canal across the Isthmus of Panama. Other West Indians migrated to Central America to work on railroads and banana plantations. When the French abandoned the canal project and the Americans renewed it twenty years later, many West Indians were again among the laborers. Some sailed the seas. "I became the breadwinner of the family at ten, . . . earning fifty cents a week as an errand boy," a native of British Honduras who later came to the United States remembered. "At twelve, I succumbed to the lure of the sea and became a deckhand on a sailing vessel plying between Belize and Yucatan, Mexico, at three dollars per week." With many islanders migrating and no immigration quotas in the United States, some naturally came North. One immigrant later described his preparations for settlement: "Out of my meager salaries I subscribed to American Negro newspapers and magazines, read everything I could find on American life and customs and traditions, and familiarized myself with the philosophies of Dr. Booker T. Washington, Dr. W. E. B. Dubois . . . and other native-born leaders and educators. . . . I worked on several ships which touched at American ports, getting a perspective of the country, studying its cultural and economic advantages." The bulk of the West Indian migration to the United States occurred between 1899 and congressional passage of immigration quotas in 1924. After 1924 a few West Indians did enter the country under the British quota, but their number was very limited.

Year	Number of Black Immigrants	Year	Number of Black Immigrants
1899	412	1916	4,576
1900	714	1917	7,971
1901	594	1918	5,706
1902	832	1919	5,823
1903	2,174	1920	8,174
1904	2,386	1921	9,873
1905	3,598	1922	5,248
1906	3,776	1923	7,554
1907	5,633	1924	12,243
1908	4,626	1925	791
1909	4,307	1926	894
1910	4,966	1927	955
1911	6,721	1928	956
1912	6,759	1929	1,254
1913	6,634	1930	1,806
1914	8,447	1931	884
1915	5,660	1932	183[7]

Like European immigrants, those from the West Indies found many American ways different from those to which they were accustomed. Most of those who came were poor, and they sought ways to improve their economic status. They found jobs, but the kind of jobs were limited, not by class as in the islands, but by race prejudice. This problem particularly affected immigrants who had held white-collar jobs on the islands, where they were regarded as a badge of middle-class status. Most of the newcomers had to accept unskilled jobs, although some took great pains to hide the fact from the people back home. One immigrant contrasted the racial attitudes of Americans and Europeans, "The European is more polite, painfully polite, and superbly hypercritical—he succeeds in almost making the native believe he is merciful, so skillfully (*sic*) is he in dismembering and subjugating racial entities. The white American, in his relations with the Negro, is nervously blunt, apologetic, and pathetically undiplomatic when thrown on the defensive."[8] Again like Europeans, many came because they heard that in America one could obtain a free education. In the islands there were few free schools beyond the elementary grades and few scholarships.

The immigrants also had to adjust to a different set of racial relations. Those who were dark-skinned found their position within the black community improved. Shades of color remained important on the islands. "A white skin ... is an indication of social status and the best passport to political influence," wrote Eric Williams. "The nearer one is to the coveted white skin, the more likely is one to be accepted in society. If one is not fortunate enough to have a white skin, the next best thing is a marriage partner with a white skin." "Where so many classes and colors meet and mingle," wrote Ira D. A. Reid, a native of Trinidad, in 1939, "the shades are naturally difficult to determine and the resulting confusion is immense. There are the nearly white hanging on tooth and nail to the fringes of white society, and these, as is easy to understand, hate contact with the dark-skinned far more than some of the broader-minded whites. Then there are the browns, the intermediates, who cannot by any stretch of the imagination pass as white, but who will not go one inch toward mixing with people darker than themselves. . . . There have been heated arguments in committees as to whether such-and-such a person was fair enough to have him or her admitted, without lowering the tone of the institution. Clubs have been known to accept the daughter and mother who were fair, but to refuse the father who is black. A dark-skinned brother in a fair-skinned family is sometimes the subject of jeers and insults and open intimations that his presence is not required at the family social functions. Fair-skinned girls who marry dark men are often ostracized by their families and given up as lost." In America where one drop of Negro blood makes a person black, such distinctions have no basis in reality and quickly disappear. Yet, one of the mistakes of Marcus Garvey was to assume that the same color distinction existed in the United States as in the West Indies. By attacking light-skinned Negroes, he assured himself of the opposition of most of the leadership of the American black community.

In early years American and West Indian Negroes frequently seemed strange to each other, and this strangeness sometimes expressed itself in hostility. Because West Indians came from a region where discrimination based wholly on race was unknown, many white and black Americans saw them as being too resentful of United States racial patterns. The Pullman Company and some railroads refused to employ them as porters because they lacked a subservient manner. Some American Negroes feared that their militancy would arouse the hostility of the whites and thus threaten what little status and power Negroes did possess. "Often," wrote Roi Ottley and William Weatherby in their history of the Negro in New York, "the newly arrived West Indian's clash with the American color line developed in him an exaggeratedly pro-British attitude. If there were discriminations or insults from white Americans, the British consul could be visited and a complaint registered. When the West Indian immigrant became naturalized, it was often citizenship with reservations, for one foot remained on British soil." American Negroes resented the West Indian's foreignness and devised such derogatory names as "Monkey-chaser," "ringtail," and "King Mon." A derisive statement of the early days accused West Indians of coming to the United States "to teach, or open a church, or start trouble." The strong, often exaggerated British accent of many West Indians was distorted by American Negroes into a comic dialect. Sometimes the derision expressed itself in rhyme:

> When I get on the other side
> I'll buy myself a lizzie,
> Climb up in a coconut tree

And knock those monkeys dizzy.
When you eat split peas and rice
You think you're eatin somethin
But man you ain't taste nothing yet
Till you eat monkey-hips with dumplin.
When a monkey-chaser dies,
Don't need no undertaker
Just trow him in de Harlem River
He'll float back to Jamaica.
When I get on the other side
I'll buy myself a mango
Grab myself a monkey gal
And do the monkey tango.

"The island's tropical clothes were ridiculed," wrote Ottley and Weatherby. "Frequently, the white suit and cane brought a shower of stones from Harlem street urchins." Reid summarized the sometimes contradictory stereotypes of the West Indians: He is more intelligent than other Negroes. He is craftier than the Jew and is not to be trusted in financial matters. The West Indian is oversensitive, quick to defend his dignity, hot-tempered, so British or so French that he does not have time to be himself, either too proud or too lazy to work, feels superior to the native-born Negro, and is overbearing in demonstrating his superiority. All West Indians are alike. A West Indian always looks out for himself first, is a troublemaker with white people, is always seeking to make an impression on someone, lacks race pride, is too race-conscious, and talks incessantly.[9]

Immigrants from the West Indies like those from Europe formed societies and clubs which served various functions. In 1939 Reid had discovered thirty benevolent associations and mutual aid societies organized by immigrants from Anguila, Antigua, British Guiana, Dominica, Granada, Jamaica, Monserrat, St. Lucia, Trinidad, and the Virgin Islands. These societies frequently afforded their members the opportunity to purchase inexpensive burial and other insurance. Some still exist today, but their membership consists largely of first-generation immigrants, and they become less active as members of the first generation die. In addition, the immigrants form social, literary, and athletic clubs. Social clubs served the same functions as among European groups, while athletic associations gave their members an opportunity to participate in such games as cricket and tennis. Cricket was brought to the islands from England, while American Negroes had not played much tennis, a game for middle- and upper-class whites. Bertram L. Baker, a native of the island of Nevis who became the first black assemblyman and district leader in Brooklyn, served for many years as executive secretary of a national Negro tennis association. Other organizations included the Afro-American Voters Coalition, to foster naturalization and political participation; Utilités d'Haiti, to promote the sale of Haitian products; Caribbean Fisheries, to foster the development of commerce and trade in sea foods; several Virgin Island societies to promote the civic, political, economic, and social welfare of the Virgin Islands and their people, whether at home or abroad; and the West Indies Communities Development League, to encourage colonization of British Guiana. In March 1933 the West Indies Federation of America was established "to advocate self-government for the West Indies, to stimulate an interest in West Indian affairs among British West Indians in America, and to foster industrial and commercial enterprises." All of these organizations remained small, and none made an impact in its field of endeavor. West Indian organizations did not become really important for two reasons. The immigrant's loyalty was frequently to the island of origin rather than to the West Indies as a whole, and the number of people from each island was small and their resources limited.[10] Moreover, most West Indians, despite the antagonism of portions of the black community, quickly perceived themselves as a part of that community rather than as a separate entity. In 1926 W. A. Domingo, a native of the islands who was a businessman in Harlem and a leader in many West Indian causes, could write: "By virtue of the presence of thousands of West Indians in the United States, a bond is being forged between them and American Negroes. Gradually, they are realizing that their problems are in the main similar, and that their ultimate successful solution will depend on the intelligent co-operation of the two branches of Anglo-Saxonized Negroes."[11] The West Indians never had a newspaper of their own. Although the *Amsterdam News,* the leading black weekly in New York, and the Boston *Chronicle* are owned by West Indians, this fact could not be discovered by reading them. Despite some hostility the West Indians found entry into the American black community comparatively easy because they spoke English and also because they contributed an element of aggressiveness to a group whose past experiences had forced them to develop traditions of subservience. In New York City West Indians not only formed a percentage of black professionals far out of proportion to their numbers, but also became labor leaders and businessmen. Yet the role of the West Indians has been largely limited to that of leadership within the black caste. They have become doctors, lawyers, labor leaders, politicians, and businessmen within the black ghetto; few have held executive positions with advertising agencies, insurance companies, public utilities, industrial corporations, or have been businessmen outside the ghetto. Race prejudice has limited them as it has limited American Negroes. They have played leadership roles within the black community, but in general have not held jobs which have not also been held by native-born members of the race. Finally, the structure of the black community of New York with much of its leadership being West Indian does not vary markedly from that of other black communities.

The traditions and experiences which the immigrants brought with them from the islands caused their entry into politics to be foreseeable. Most islanders could not vote until comparatively recent years, yet even the peasantry frequently discussed and debated public questions. Unlike most American blacks, residents of the islands were accustomed to seeing Negroes assuming responsibility as lawyers, politicians, and civil servants. Although the West Indian class structure was rigid, it was not closed. Occasionally poor boys, even poor boys with dark skins, could rise from poverty to hold comparatively responsible positions. In the early years some immigrants hesitated to become American citizens, feeling that they could appeal to the British consul when confronted with racial discrimination. But the unwillingness and inability of the British government to interfere with American racial patterns and the increased opportunities available to American citizens soon caused this attitude to change. During the early 1930's many West Indians became naturalized because they feared that as aliens they could not receive relief payments. In 1937 the *Amsterdam News* carried a boxed statement: "Become a citizen. Prepare to vote. The Negro's strength in affairs which concern his very existence is gauged by his ballot. If you are not a citizen, become one."[12] By the time these words were written, one of the first two elected black judges and the first Tammany district leader were men of West

Indian birth, and the political prominence of these immigrants undoubtedly encouraged others to be naturalized.

In the 1880's William B. Derrick, a New York Negro minister born in Antigua, was a member of the Republican State Committee. But it was not until the 1920's that young immigrants began entering politics in noticeable numbers. Although Harold C. Burton and William Cornelius, two long-time Harlem Republican leaders, were natives of the islands, many immigrants joined the Democratic Party at a time when most members of the race were still supporting the party of Lincoln. Lincoln's Emancipation Proclamation was not part of the West Indian tradition, but the immigrants did notice that the Democrats held power in the city and state. Moreover, most immigrants joined or at least tried to join regular district organizations rather than the United Colored Democracy. They did so both because the United Colored Democracy was controlled by antagonistic native-born race members and because the concept of a political organization based on color was unknown to their experience on the islands. At least two immigrants who later became prominent received their political baptism by innocently going to a white district club and finding that they were expected to join a segregated black organization. By refusing to accept segregation, both men eventually became members of regular organizations. In this way the young West Indians helped to undermine the power of the United Colored Democracy and to integrate the Tammany clubs in the Harlem districts.[13]

James S. Watson was the first foreign-born Negro to obtain elective office. Born in Jamaica in 1882, the son of a government employee, Watson came to New York in 1905. One of the first black immigrants to be admitted to the bar, he obtained a job in the Corporation Counsel's office in the middle 1920's. When the State Legislature created a new municipal court district in Harlem in 1930, West Indian voters proved numerous enough for Watson to obtain one of the two judicial nominations. He probably would have found more difficulty in getting the nomination if the Democrats had expected to win. But the results of the 1930 elections in Harlem proved an upset, and the Jamaica immigrant became one of the first two members of his race to be a judge in New York City.

As a boy, Herbert L. Bruce was brought from his native Barbados by a widowed mother. After holding various jobs which included redcapping at Grand Central Station and owning a Harlem cabaret, Bruce became active in the Beaver Democratic Club, an insurgent club dedicated to achieving black leadership, in 1933. Two years later, he was chosen the first black Tammany district leader in the history of the city.[14]

During these years native- and foreign-born Negroes sometimes vied for political power. West Indians held the balance of power in a number of Harlem precincts. In 1936 a foreign-born leader wrote: "The position is getting worse and worse daily. It is known that several public offices of honor, note, and dignity have been recently allowed to get out of the hands of colored people because of mutual intraracial jealousies. It has occurred that political offices which could have been won at election if there was united action were lost to the whites because there was a common understanding that rather than allow it to go to a member of one or the other faction or group it would be preferable in their own blindness that the whites should win." In the 1937 mayoralty primary Herbert L. Bruce was accused of ousting his woman co-leader because she was native-born and, it was alleged, he wanted a West Indian co-leader. Bruce's opponents issued a handbill which openly fanned the antagonism: "IS THIS FAIR? BRUCE OUSTS MRS. ELIZABETH ROSS HAYNES so he can have a West Indian woman for co-leader. IS THIS FAIR? Leader Bruce is a West Indian, the State Committee-man, Thomas B. Dyett, is a West Indian. The majority of his Negro jobholders are West Indians." Fortunately for the New York black community, this type of antagonism was short-lived, as native- and foreign-born Negroes peacefully shared political jobs.[15] By 1945 one of the most powerful Tammany district leaders was J. Raymond Jones, a native of the Virgin Islands, who was the son of a schoolteacher. Another schoolteacher's son, this one from Nevis, migrated to Brooklyn. In the middle 1930's Bertram L. Baker organized the United Action Democratic Club in the Kings County assembly district with the largest black population. After two un-successful attempts to gain a seat on the City Council, Baker in 1948 became the first Negro to be elected to the Assembly from Brook-lyn. Five years later, he became the first black man to be a Brooklyn Democratic district leader. The next Brooklyn Democratic district leader, Thomas R. Jones, was the son of immigrants. Shirley Chis-holm, the first Negro elected to Congress from Brooklyn and the first black woman elected to Congress in American history, was the daughter of Barbadian immigrants, her father working as an un-skilled laborer and her mother as a domestic. Hulan E. Jack, the first black man to be elected borough president of Manhattan, and Walter Gladwin, the first to be elected to the Assembly from the Bronx, were natives of British Guiana. When Gladwin became a judge, he was replaced in the Assembly by a second-generation West Indian, Ivan Warner. Today Edward Stevenson, a native of Jamaica, represents a Bronx district in the Assembly. The first Negro to be a district leader in Queens was J. Foster Phillips, a native of the islands.

In political office West Indians as a group have acted no dif-ferently from American Negroes as a group. In politics as in other fields they are important because they provide so much of the leadership of the New York black community. Moynihan and Glazer correctly analyze the cause: "Likely the fact that they came from islands which were almost completely Negro and in which therefore Negroes held all positions in the society except the highest, inhibited the rise of a feeling of inadequacy and inferiority, and gave them the experiences and self-confidence that Southern Negroes on the whole lacked."[16]

CHAPTER 9

The Negro in Civil Service

As with European immigrants, the number of black people in civil service jobs has multiplied with increasing political power. As members of a group become politically active, they become familiar with governmental structure and with the available job opportunities. As the group's voting power increases and some of its members are elected to office, those who are politically active possess leverage necessary to help members of the racial or ethnic community obtain positions. Civil service has been particularly important for those groups whose members are largely unskilled. For Negroes perhaps even more than for Irish or Italians, civil service positions have provided a vehicle for moving into the middle class. While Irish political leaders controlled New York City government in the late nineteenth and early twentieth centuries, other immigrants from Erin entered the police and fire departments in such large numbers that their presence became proverbial. The careers of Thomas McEvoy, who upon his retirement as a police captain became a powerful Tammany district leader; Mayor John F. Hylan, who studied law while working as a subway motorman; and William O'Dwyer, who pursued his legal studies while a policeman and later was elected Kings County District Attorney and Mayor, illustrate the link between Irish political power and their presence in civil service jobs. First entrenching themselves in the Sanitation Department, Italians have entered civil service in large numbers while at the same time prospering politically.

A representative of the New York City Department of Personnel estimates that today approximately one fourth of New York City employees are black.[1] Most Negroes either hold top-level positions or unskilled jobs. They are underrepresented in what might be termed middle management and in technical and professional categories. The upper-level positions are political appointments of recent

175

origin and are often highly visible to the public. Negroes are found in the largest numbers in departments such as the Transit Authority, the Human Resources Administration, the Post Office, and the Department of Hospitals which employ large numbers of unskilled or semiskilled workers.

Negroes have never been prohibited by law from holding civil service positions in New York. In the late nineteenth century many middle- and upper-class blacks lived in the city of Brooklyn before it became a part of Greater New York. A member of the race became a Brooklyn policeman in 1891,[2] and about the same time at least two held jobs as clerks in the city's Department of Public Works. Although some Negroes attended integrated schools as early as the 1880's, segregation remained on the statute books until the turn of the century. Negro schools were staffed by Negro teachers. When segregation was abolished, black teachers retained their jobs in integrated schools. Before the creation of the United Colored Democracy in 1898 virtually no blacks held jobs in Manhattan, because the vast majority of the members of the race voted Republican and Tammany Hall usually controlled the city. Increased patronage is a goal of every individual and group in politics. When Andrew M. Robinson and Dr. E. P. Roberts offered their support to the Democrats in the 1897 mayoralty campaign, they made clear that their objective was "jobs just like white men, and not all cuspidor-cleaners." The next year when Tammany leader Richard Croker created a black auxiliary, he specifically stated its purpose as being the distribution of jobs. The creation of the United Colored Democracy gave Negroes a place in the dominant political organization of the city, which opened many jobs to them. Tammany jobs ranged from Assistant Corporation Counsel to janitors and elevator operators in public buildings and street sweepers. During the first year of the existence of the United Colored Democracy ten Negroes secured employment in the Dock Department, while forty members of the race found jobs as laborers and inspectors in the Street Cleaning Department. The patronage distributed through the United Colored Democracy helped make inroads into traditional black Republicanism on a local level more than a decade before the race transferred its allegiance to the Democratic Party nationally. In 1911 Mary White Ovington counted 511 black city employees, which constituted nine-tenths of one percent of the New York City work force. She mentions a dozen clerks scattered through city departments, and laborers employed by the Departments of Docks, Parks, Street Cleaning, and Water Supply.[3]

Yet the first black men in the police and fire departments experienced difficulties in getting accepted and hostility from some of their co-workers, which the departments for a long time did little or nothing to suppress. Although Negro difficulties frequently took the form of race prejudice, the problem really arose because the police and fire departments for several generations had been regarded by the Irish almost as their private clubs. Some Irish policemen and firemen used the departments as stepping-stones into the professions, while other Irish families had several members or several generations employed. The Irish had an antiblack tradition which extended back before the Civil War when the two groups competed for unskilled jobs. Moreover, the Irish, who are frequently conservative and tradition-bound, sought to preserve their accustomed ways. Although their white skin enabled early Italian and Jewish policemen and firemen to escape many of the difficulties of the Negroes, they, too, were often looked upon by the Irish as interlopers.

In 1911 Samuel J. Battle became the first member of his race to join the police force of greater New York. Battle was born in Newburn, N.C., in 1883, the son of former slaves. His great-grandfather had fought beside his master in the American Revolution. Coming to New York, Battle secured a job which has served as the training ground and sustenance for many black men: he became a redcap at Grand Central Station. Eventually, he rose to be assistant chief of redcaps. He first took the police examination in 1910, but his appointment was delayed for a year on the pretext that he had a heart condition. After the nationally known black political leader Charles W. Anderson intervened on his behalf, he received his appointment. Battle was assigned to the West 68th Street station, where most of the other patrolmen ostracized him. In 1918 he decided to study for the sergeant's examination and applied to the Delahanty School, where classes were being given. The black man was told that the other policemen studying there would have to vote on his admission. Between the time he applied and the time the vote was taken, Battle rescued another officer from a Negro mob. The Delahanty students voted unanimously to admit him. Although he passed the sergeant's examination high on the list, he had to wait until 1926 to become the first race member to hold the rank. He became the first black lieutenant in 1931 and the first Negro captain four years later. Mayor LaGuardia appointed him Parole Commissioner in 1941, a job which he held for ten years. He died in 1966. The Redding family contributed two pioneer Negro policemen. Wesley and George came to New York from Atlanta, where their father worked in a bank and engaged in real estate and their mother was a teacher. The older brother, Wesley, became the first Negro detective, while George became the first member of the race in every rank from captain to Deputy Chief Inspector.[4]

Although another black man preceded Wesley Williams in the Fire Department, Williams is regarded as the pioneer Negro fireman. He was the first black man to actually fight fires. Wesley Williams was born in New York City on August 27, 1897. His father, a redcap at Grand Central Station for forty-eight years, ended his career as chief of redcaps. When the son decided to become a fireman, many celebrities, including an ex-president of the United States, signed character references. Young Williams, an amateur weight-lifter and boxer, was the second man in the history of the department with a 100 percent physical rating. He became a fireman on January 10, 1919. In 1927 he became the first black lieutenant, and eight years later the first race member to be a captain. Perhaps because they do such hazardous work, firemen frequently have a strong sense of group unity. This feeling did not extend to Negroes. As late as 1937 only four members of the race were firemen. Although this number had jumped to fifty by 1940, Negroes were frequently given a hard time. "Many white firemen considered the presence of a Negro in the company a social stigma," Wesley Williams later remembered. In an historical sketch of Negroes in the Fire Department Clifford Goldstein wrote: "In 1940 they were assigned menial jobs in the fire house, they were not assigned the tasks of driving or operating the tiller or ladder trucks; they were given beds next to the toilet, solely for their use; they were ostracized at the dinner table and if they turned their backs, salt or some foreign substance was often dumped into their food." In some cities black firemen were assigned to segregated fire houses, and the New York City Fire Department formulated plans by which this procedure could be followed. Wesley Williams became a battalion chief in 1938. Two years later, he risked his own security in order to organize black firemen. During the next few years he frequently headed protest delegations to various levels of the department from individual fire houses to the operating chief of the department and the

Commissioner. In 1944 the Vulcans, the organization of black firemen, secured hearings before the City Council. Leaders of the department lined up on one side of the room and the Negroes on the other and the black firemen told of their difficulties, and the officials of the department defended themselves. Conditions began to improve, but Negroes did not really secure equal treatment until William O'Dwyer became mayor in 1946. Mayor O'Dwyer's Commissioner chose chauffeur aides from all ethnic organizations, gave each organization direct access to the Commissioner, and removed some of the old-line officers.[5]

The names and careers of pioneer Negroes in other city departments are not as well known as those of Battle and Williams. Tammany Leader Charles F. Murphy undoubtedly recognized the importance of city jobs to Negroes when in 1922 he appointed his friend, the black lawyer Ferdinand Q. Morton, as one of three members of the Municipal Civil Service Commission. Morton served on the Commission for twenty-five years, and one of the commissioners has been black ever since. Estimates of Morton's effectiveness vary. Those who were his friends point to members of the race for whom he secured jobs. On the other hand, Warren Moscow in his book *What Have You Done for Me Lately?* states that his presence on the Commission made no real difference, and Morton is known to have asked another Commissioner to make decisions in cases involving Negroes.[6] Mayor LaGuardia helped pave the way for increased black jobs in civil service by insisting that regulations be strictly enforced, thus reducing the possibility of discrimination. Yet no significant number of Negroes obtained city jobs until the late 1930's, and the really big increase did not come until after World War II.

The New York transportation system was one of the earliest city departments to employ a large number of Negroes. The Independent Subway was completed by the city in 1932, while the city took over the IRT and BMT from independent companies in 1940. The IRT and BMT had never employed blacks except as porters. At the time the city assumed control of the lines, a shortage of motormen and conductors existed. Therefore, the Municipal Civil Service Commission permitted dining car and Pullman porter work to be counted as prerequisite job experience needed to take the examinations. In 1940 a committee headed by Adam Clayton Powell and another Harlem minister organized a boycott of the bus lines of the New York Omnibus Company and threatened to march on the company's downtown offices. As a result, 210 Negro drivers and eight mechanics were hired.[7]

Organizations of workers in most city departments represent racial, religious, and ethnic groups. For example, the Police Department recognizes organizations of Negroes, Puerto Ricans, Jews, Irish, Italians, Poles, Germans, Catholics, and Protestants. All of these groups give social affairs at which funds are raised. A city employee may join as many of these organizations as are represented in his or her background and origins. Undoubtedly the major justification for the existence of these divisions is that they strive for group recognition. They can exercise political pressure, and sometimes they make financial contributions to political campaigns. "I . . . learned a good deal about ethnic warfare in the city," wrote Anna Arnold Hedgman of the early 1950's when as an assistant to Mayor Wagner she was the first Negro to hold a cabinet-level post in the city government. "The Irish and the Italians carried on a subtle power battle, with the Irish usually on the winning side. Both groups found some unity in the war with what they called the over-aggressive Jews. The Negro simply didn't count."[8]

Negroes justify the existence of their organizations of city employees both because other groups have them and because of the role which their members feel they play in fighting discrimination. Twenty-one groups representing black employees in various departments are affiliated with the Federation of Negro Civil Service Organizations. They vary widely in size, effectiveness, the outlook of their leadership, and the percentage of their workers in the particular department who are members or who are active. The Federation claims to represent 55,000 employees, which makes it of about average size compared with other ethnic organizations. The oldest group, that of the black sanitation workers, was organized in 1935. Nineteen years later, Mayor Wagner issued an executive order permitting organizations of city employees to negotiate with the city. The next year four Negro groups joined to form the Federation. They represented firemen, sanitation workers, employees of the United States Treasury Department and of the Transit Authority. The then Manhattan Borough President, Hulan Jack, and Anna Arnold Hedgman, who was serving as an assistant to Mayor Wagner, helped the group obtain its charter, which was presented to it by the Mayor. In its early years the Federation aimed at nonpartisanship by choosing co-chairmen, one of whom was a Republican and the other a Democrat. It has in general served as an umbrella organization, facilitating communication among its component groups. At times the Federation has investigated complaints of alleged discrimination and channeled the complaints to the proper authorities. It has also aided political leaders who in the opinion of the Federation leadership symbolize racial advancement. For example, a founder and former president told the writer that the Federation had taken a stand in support of J. Raymond Jones for the New York County Democratic leadership and had aided Hulan Jack in retaining his city pension when he was in danger of losing it because he was forced to resign as borough president. The organization has also lobbied for legislation such as a law giving preference to city residents on civil service examinations. In 1967 the Federation testified at a hearing called by the Governor on the lack of minority employees in state departments. For blacks a civil service job has frequently been a badge of middle-class status. In a group which has always been plagued by unemployment and underemployment, the civil service worker has enjoyed a steady and comparatively well-paying job protected by tenure. Several leaders of the Federation expressed the opinion that the organization had been too middle-class in its outlook and that it had not become sufficiently involved in the life of the community aside from its concern about the job problems of its members.[9]

Of the organizations which compose the Federation, the strongest and most effective are those which have arisen from a need for fighting discrimination or at least for gaining group recognition. The Vulcans, the organization of Negro firemen, offer a prime illustration of this idea. Formed to combat hostility to black firemen, the Vulcans have made their presence felt both in the Fire Department and in the black community. Although most Vulcan activities are typical of those of Negro civil service groups, they are unusual because of their variety and because the firemen have kept a written record of what they have done. In 1945 the Vulcans became the first civil service organization to purchase a life membership in the NAACP. In the 1950's the firemen inaugurated a program which conferred meritorious service awards and honorary memberships in the Society on "citizens of the community who have made significant contributions to the cause of social justice." The Federation began giving similar awards in 1961. The first two recipients were firemen. The Vulcans conduct annual Christmas parties for shut-in children at Harlem Hospital. The organization also awards death benefits to beneficiaries of members and scholarships to their children. According to an official history compiled for their twenty-fifth anniversary in 1965, they had contributed $25,000 to the NAACP, Urban League, and YMCA. The influence of the Vulcans within the Fire Department is shown by the fact that at this writing Robert Lowery and Arthur Williams, two black career firemen, hold the positions of Fire Commissioner and Deputy Fire Commissioner respectively.[10]

The activities of the Guardians, the organization of Negro policemen, and their position in the black community, have been influenced as much by police-community relations within the ghetto as by the structure of the Police Department. Although discrimination within the Police Department was not as obvious as within the Fire Department, black policemen, as well as firemen, had to contend with an Irish group determined to maintain its traditional control of the department. An organization of Irish policemen was not formed until the 1950's because previously such a large percentage of the police force had been Irish that an organization had proved unnecessary. Negroes believe that until recent years they were automatically limited to 5 percent of the police force, and that at times their promotions were deliberately blocked. Although one of the Deputy Police Commissioners has been black since the early 1950's, he has not usually been a former policeman. Outwardly the activities of the Guardians have resembled those of the Vulcans. Both groups have given scholarships and awards for meritorious service and contributions to charitable causes. The unique position of the Guardians arises from the image of the policeman in the black community which is different from that of other civil servants not only in New York but throughout the country. The vast majority of policemen in Negro neighborhoods have been white, and many have been prejudiced. By the very nature of their jobs they possess power and authority. A veteran black policeman told the writer that unconsciously people even feared their relatives and friends who were on the police force because of their power. Moreover, Negroes of all classes have been suspected and questioned by the police more often than whites. At times their color leads to cases of mistaken identity, particularly by prejudiced policemen. Consequently, white policemen in black neighborhoods have often been regarded as possessors of hostile power.

Until the middle 1960's no Negro had commanded a police precinct in Harlem. One of the results of the riots in Harlem and Brooklyn in the summer of 1964 was the appointment in August of that year of Lloyd Sealy as commander of the 28th precinct in Harlem. Sealy, a native of Brooklyn whose parents had come from Barbados, had been a policeman for twenty-five years. He is also a lawyer, and he was the first Negro sent by the police department to the FBI school. In February 1965, when he had commanded the precinct for seven months, he told a New York *Post* reporter what in his opinion was the most important result of having a black man in command of a precinct: "The initial effect of my transfer here was an opening of communications between the police and the people in the community.... The people felt that they were getting a fairer shake and they come in here now, alone and in small groups, and they talk about their problems.... The residents feel that action is forthcoming on their complaints.... They're beginning to understand that police work isn't a form of retaliation. The improvement in communications between the police and the people is the biggest gain." In 1965 Sealy was promoted and moved to Brooklyn, and another black man, Éldredge Waith, was given command of one of the other Harlem precincts.

The question of an independent civilian complaint review board illustrates the conflicting loyalties which being a policeman can pose for Negroes. In the middle 1960's civil rights groups took the lead in demanding a board composed of nonpolicemen and chosen independently of the department to hear and decide upon complaints of alleged police brutality. Such a board existed in Philadelphia, Rochester, and a few other cities. Negroes naturally took a special interest in the question because a large percentage of the victims of the misuse of police power had always been black. On the other hand policemen and their organizations contended that an independent civilian complaint review board would hinder the police in the performance of their rightful duties. Mayor Wagner straddled the issue. A Harlem assemblyman introduced a bill for the creation of such a board in the 1965 session of the legislature, but the bill did not pass. In his successful 1965 mayoralty campaign John Lindsay advocated the creation of a civilian review board. After his election he brought one into being by executive order, although a police commissioner resigned when he did so.

The Patrolmen's Benevolent Association spearheaded the opposition to an independent civilian complaint review board. The group succeeded in getting the question on the ballot in the 1966 election. This referendum raised a dilemma for black policemen. Most of them were members of the Patrolmen's Benevolent Association, although no black men were among its leaders. Moreover, every ethnic organization in the department opposed the board. On the other hand, the black community was united in its demand for the board's retention. After much discussion and soul-searching the Guardians decided to oppose the Patrolmen's Benevolent Association and come out in support of the review board. "As Negroes, we and our families are inextricably bound up in the civil rights movement," William Johnson, president of the Guardians, told reporters, "but as police officers we must uphold the law. We insist that it be upheld for everyone and without either favoritism or prejudice." The Association set aside a fund of a million and a half dollars to defeat the civilian review board. The Negro group started a lawsuit designed to obtain an accounting of its finances by the PBA and to get the organization to call a new election of officers and delegates. By conducting a scare campaign featuring threats of violence if the civilian review board were retained, the PBA defeated it. Nevertheless, Police Commissioner Howard Leary created a civilian review board within the department. This action and other policies have considerably reduced the antagonism between the department and the black community which had reached its peak during the last years of the Wagner Administration. The lawsuit brought by the Guardians against the PBA was settled out of court. The ethnic, racial, and religious organizations in city departments give social events to which they invite the officers of other organizations in their department. In retaliation for the Negro group's opposition to the PBA and for the lawsuit, several of the ethnic organizations refused to invite the Guardians to their functions and in return refused to attend Guardian functions in 1967 and 1968. Nevertheless, the president of the Guardians told the writer that probably as a result of the Negro lawsuit, the structure of the PBA has been changed so as to permit delegates to be elected more democratically.[11]

The Negro Benevolent Association, the organization of black

sanitation workers, is the oldest Negro civil service group and one whose duties bear a special relationship to black communities. Moreover, 1,300 of the 1,400 Negro sanitation workers are members, an extraordinarily high percentage. The president told the writer that a reason for such a large percentage of members was that the men had "a common bond, the collection truck." Probably a more important reason is that the Sanitation Department was the first city department which Italians entered in large numbers. Consequently, the organization of black sanitation workers, from the time of its formation in 1935, had to contend with Italian middle-class aspirations. Also, the position of Negroes in the Sanitation Workers Union causes an organization of black workers to serve more of a purpose than in some other departments. Such unions as the Transport Workers, the State, County, and Municipal Workers, and, despite a recent and bitter conflict with most of the black community, the United Federation of Teachers, have been integrated on all levels, have contributed manpower and money to the civil rights movement, and have made racial equality one of their prime objectives. On the other hand the Sanitation Workers Union has not been a conspicuous advocate of civil rights, and in 1969 two business agents were the only black officials.

Negroes, like other people who are poor and whose neighborhoods are crowded, engage in a constant and often losing battle to keep their streets, sidewalks, and empty lots clean. In 1962 members of the Brooklyn chapter of CORE dumped garbage from the streets of Bedford-Stuyvesant on the steps of Borough Hall because, ironically, garbage in that neighborhood was being collected three times a week while it was being picked up five times a week in other parts of the city. The cleaning of Harlem streets has become so much a part of that neighborhood's culture that a song from the musical "Golden Boy" refers to endless clean-up campaigns. Therefore, it is not surprising that the president of the black sanitation workers group feels himself to be an intermediary between the department and the community. He offered a program of cooperation between sanitation workers and local residents, and he advocates decentralization of the Sanitation Department to meet local needs for the same reasons that have made Negroes leading advocates of decentralization of schools.[12]

The organization of workers in the Welfare Department is one of the newest and fastest-growing and, more than most organizations of civil service workers, it attempts to reflect the black militancy of the late 1960's. The constitutions of most other organizations of Negro civil service employees allow anyone working in the department regardless of race to join, and the Associated Transit Guild has had white members. On the other hand the Chama Society, the organization in the Welfare Department, emphasizes that it is for blacks. Moreover, it takes the name "Chama" from the Swahili word for "union, guild, or togetherness." Founded in 1966, the Society now has 2,000 members, one third of the black employees in the Welfare Department. Every black employee regardless of the level of his or her job is eligible for membership. Another reason for the militant tone of the organization is that most of the administrators in the Welfare Department are Jewish, and the Negroes are reacting to what they consider to be a symbol of white liberalism. In an interview with the writer the group's president predicted a power struggle between Negroes and Jews in the Welfare Department as well as in the Board of Education. Despite its militant style the Chama Society engages in most of the same activities as the more traditional civil service organizations. It processes cases of alleged discrimination, gives courses in the preparation and taking of examinations, helps black students enter schools of social work, and awards partial scholarships. Its leaders hope to found chapters in other cities. The union recognized by the Welfare Department is the strong and integrated Union of State, County, and Municipal Workers. In 1965 this union and an independent union of civil service employees called a strike of welfare investigators. The strike resulted in higher wages, lighter caseloads, and the right of the unions to negotiate issues which hitherto had been within the scope of civil service regulations. Since then, the two unions have merged. The president of the Chama Society, a former vice-president of the independent civil service workers union who had gone to jail during the 1965 strike, claims that the organization of black workers handles racial matters which are not the function of the union. The future of the black group depends upon the general civil rights climate as well as the way in which the Chama Society and the union meet the needs of black workers in the Welfare Department.[13]

A detailed description of the recent controversies surrounding the New York school system and the Negro part in these controversies is beyond the scope of this chapter. Membership on boards of education has frequently been one of the earliest demands made by Negroes and one of the earliest forms of recognition given to them. Naturally, the effectiveness of black board of education members varies widely; often their presence is no more than a token of recognition. Three successive Negro members served on the Brooklyn Board of Education when that borough was an independent city. In 1917, when the New York City Board of Education consisted of forty-six unpaid members, Mayor John Purroy Mitchel appointed Dr. Eugene P. Roberts, a Negro physician, for a three-year term. A Negro has been a member of the New York City Board of Education since the late 1940's, although until 1968 there had been only one member at a time. A Negro Deputy Superintendent of Schools, John B. King, served for a time as Acting Superintendent. Nevertheless, the number of black school administrators has been negligible. Although more than 50 percent of the school population and 27 percent of the city's population is black and Puerto Rican, Martin Mayer in February 1969 reported that fewer than 10 percent of the teachers were black. This percentage is very low when compared with other cities which have large nonwhite populations. Most New York City teachers are graduates of the city colleges, which until recently have accepted students from the upper ranks of their high school classes. As late as February 1969 only about 3 percent of the students at the city colleges were black. In New York as elsewhere, children who are members of minority groups have been receiving vastly inferior educations. The average gap between black and Puerto Rican children and white children at the age of twelve has been estimated at two years. New York Negroes have been prime advocates of decentralization and community control of schools, maintaining that the individual community knows the needs of the children best. The American Federation of Teachers and its New York local, the United Federation of Teachers, have a long tradition of interest in and support of civil rights. Teachers with the blessing of the union have participated in civil rights demonstrations, and Albert Shanker, president of the UFT, joined the March on Selma in 1965. Moreover, Shanker maintained that a partnership between the union and minority group parents would bring about integrated quality education. The executive board of the UFT voted to support an independent civilian review board, and the union formulated plans to set up machinery to hear and act upon complaints of parents against the school system. Nevertheless, the union entered into a bitter conflict with most of the black community in 1968. The controversy arose when the local governing board of a Brooklyn district which had been established as an experiment in community control dismissed eighteen teachers who were members of the union. Other union teachers in the district went on strike in 1968, and in the fall the union called three successive work stoppages, which kept virtually all the schools of the city closed for the first two months of the semester. The demonstration district, that of Ocean Hill–Brownsville, hired nonunion teachers and kept its schools open. The issue began over the restoration of the teachers to their jobs. After the first and second strikes, the teachers tried to return to their schools but community sentiment, encouraged by the governing board, prevented them from teaching. As a result of the strike, the Ocean Hill–Brownsville district was taken over by a state trustee, but continued to operate as a demonstration district with nonunion teachers. The State Legislature passed a modified plan for decentralization in 1969. It provides for the election of five of a seven-member Board of Education, instead of all members being appointed. The new plan divides the school system into thirty-three districts, with some power to hire and fire teachers and to plan curriculum. Many Negroes object to the plan because it retains the Board of Examiners as the agency for licensing teachers and because it does not give districts the power to hire unlicensed teachers. Ocean Hill–Brownsville and two other demonstration districts will probably either be constituted as districts themselves or incorporated into districts. Despite the resentment of the union by Negroes during the strikes of 1968, most black teachers will undoubtedly retain their union membership. On the other hand resentment of the union by organizations of minority-group parents will probably prevent them from working with the union in the near future.[14]

The problems of getting minority group members into civil service jobs and getting them promoted exist in most departments. Today the City Department of Personnel as well as black civil service organizations are actively seeking minority group members. Despite the often strained relations between blacks and the police, the number of black policemen never until recently exceeded five percent. Today the Police Department is seeking to raise the percentage. In the spring of 1969 a police officer told the writer that 100 of the 525 graduates in a class of the Police Academy were black. Three patrol cars distribute literature in Negro and Puerto Rican neighborhoods and in such areas as the garment district, where many black and Spanish people are underemployed but motivated to work. A radio advertisement includes a speech by a patrolman who identifies himself as black and goes on to say that great opportunities for promotion exist in the Police Department for people of all backgrounds. Lloyd Sealy, who until his retirement in 1969 was the highest-ranking Negro in the Police Department, says a few words in the same ad. Under the Manpower Development and Training Act a program has been funded in which high-school drop-outs simultaneously study for their equivalency diplomas and study at the Police Academy to prepare to pass the patrolman's examination. Several of the Negro civil service groups including those of the Police, Firemen, and Transit Authority employees hold classes which prepare potential jobholders for entrance examinations.

Negroes in many departments are concerned with getting more members of the race promoted. In departments with large numbers of blacks such as the Transit Authority and the Welfare Department, the number of Negroes in supervisory positions is very small. Although about one third of the employees of the Transit Authority are black, less than 300 of the 4,000 supervisory employees are Negro, as are the holders of only four of the 74 noncompetitive positions and one of the seventeen exempt positions. Six thousand of the 21,000 employees and two of the four deputy commissioners of the Welfare Department are Negro, yet according to the president of the Chama Society one bureau head and one assistant bureau head out of a dozen of each in the department are members of the race. Negroes usually ascribe their lack of promotion to discrimination or to the inapplicability of examination questions to their experience. Some express the fear that in a mysterious way their records are kept differently from those of white employees. Unquestionably race prejudice has played a role in preventing Negro promotions. Perhaps a more important factor has been a lack of power of the Negro community. Although jobs requiring civil service examinations are theoretically divorced from politics, the level as well as the number of jobs held by a group inevitably multiplies as its political power increases. Moreover, the requirements and examination questions necessary to obtain city jobs and to get promoted have frequently been geared to the thought patterns

and to the experience of the group which has traditionally been
dominant in the department. The Union of State, County, and
Municipal Workers, which in New York City is about 35
percent black and Puerto Rican, has, along with foundation grants,
helped to finance a study which resulted in a plan designed to
attract more members of minority groups to civil service jobs and
to increase the number of those promoted. Formulated by Sumner
Rosen, formerly Education Director of District 37 of the union,
the plan aims at structuring examinations, promotion ladders, and
training in such a way as to equalize the chances of those with
natural ability but without formal education or previous experience.
An effort would be made to eliminate "dead-end" jobs, defined as
jobs where "there is no opportunity for promotion, or a restricted
promotional ladder, a promotional line which peters out after two
or three steps, or a gap in the promotional line too steep for most
people to cross." Promotional ladders are also restricted when clerical employees cannot qualify for administrative positions or when
workers serving as assistants to those with technical skills cannot
hope to get appointed to technical jobs themselves. "Dead-end"
jobs can be eliminated or at least greatly reduced in number both
by restructuring job categories and by permitting on-the-job training
or experience to substitute for formal education or outside experience. Many examinations would be rewritten to increase the appli-
cability of the questions to the duties performed on the job. Moreover, the plan calls for the establishment of a Civil Service Academy
as part of the City University of New York. Performance in class
would be one criterion taken into consideration in determining
eligibility for promotion. Although it has as yet gone largely
unimplemented, the plan has been approved in theory by the
New York City Department of Personnel. It has also received the
approval of the Committee on Labor, Civil Service, and Public
Pensions of the New York State Constitutional Convention of 1967.
The committee reported, "The various civil service commissions
at the state and city levels, government administrators and employers, and most organizations of the employees, all seem to be
more or less wedded to the traditional conservative mode of operation
of civil service, with its undue emphasis on written 'objective'
examinations and formal educational achievements, with its highly
refined compartmentalization, and with apparent reluctance to
inaugurate or agree to imaginative and innovative use of recruiting

and upgrading techniques.... Thus, many persons who are uniquely equipped to work in certain areas by reason of their background and experience therein, may be precluded because their backgrounds have not been conducive to excelling in written competitive examinations. This result is not only unfair to the applicants, it also deprives government of willing, capable employees that are badly needed."[15]

Innovations such as these are essential if opportunities for Negroes in civil service are to be equalized in New York City and State and in other cities and states and in the Federal Government as well. The number of black people in government jobs will undoubtedly increase in the foreseeable future both because of increased black political power and because a job in civil service brings about instant middle-class status. This latter consideration is particularly important to a group whose members have suffered from continuous discrimination, unemployment, and underemployment. In addition, their position in government service is, at least at the present time, more crucial to Negroes than to any of the ethnic immigrant groups as a means of social mobility because black people have not owned businesses in large numbers, and because until recent years comparatively few members of the race have been employed at white-collar jobs in the private sector of the economy. Efforts must aim both at equalizing chances for Negroes within civil service and diversifying the opportunities for entry into the middle class other than through government employment.

In their book *Beyond the Melting Pot* Moynihan and Glazer point to the strength of ethnic survivals in New York City. Organizations of city employees based on race, religion, and ethnic origin show no signs of disappearing. While other groups maintain such organizations, Negroes will undoubtedly maintain theirs. The effectiveness of black civil service organizations will vary inversely with the strength of unions of public employees, their degree of integration, and their attention to Negro grievances. Strong unions can exercise power more effectively than small groups of workers based on race, religion, or ethnic origin. Unions which represent workers regardless of background have opportunities for developing dignity, self-respect, and a healthy and constructive atmosphere of human relations. Yet the presence of black civil service organizations possesses a symbolic significance. In civil service as in politics, members of the race are becoming of increasing importance in the life of the city.

CHAPTER 10

The Shape of the Future

The role of Negroes in the future political life of New York City will depend upon the racial climate of both the city and the nation. Its course will help to determine the importance which the black community places upon politics as a remedy for its grievances and as a means of achieving money, power, and status. Moreover, the political clout of the black community in the city as elsewhere will depend upon the political alignments of the city, state, and nation. The speed of the rise of the black middle class will influence both the degree and character of black political participation. Finally, the character of black political leadership and the force of personality of individual leaders will not only help to decide how high and how soon Negroes rise in the political hierarchy, but will be an additional factor in shaping the role of blacks in the city's political makeup.

In the past, Negroes in New York as in other cities have frequently regarded politics with cynicism and suspicion. Although suspicion of politicians has sometimes characterized Americans generally, blacks have had specific reasons for this feeling. The most important factor has undoubtedly been their sense of powerlessness. Groups which are powerless feel themselves as being acted upon rather than acting, as tools or victims of those who do have power. Blacks have frequently felt that political candidates and issues were irrelevant to their needs. Their suspicions about politics have been directed at political leaders of both races. Whites have been accused of being unresponsive to black needs and demands, while black leaders have been charged with subservience to white domination and with opportunism. Not only have blacks shared a suspicion of politics and government with other powerless groups, but their particular experience in America until recent years has done much to reenforce the idea of political power as a white man's tool. Blacks were partially or completely disfranchised in most Northern states, including New York, until the Republican Party for its own political reasons granted equal suffrage to blacks by the adoption of the Fifteenth Amendment in 1870. During the Reconstruction period Negroes made impressive political advances in the South, including the election of two United States Senators, several lieutenant governors, more than a dozen congressmen, and many local officials. However, Reconstruction was followed by the virtually complete disfranchisement of blacks in the South. Wherever they may live today, most Negroes have their cultural roots in the South. Political attitudes have naturally reflected this background. The West Indians are the one group within the black community who do have a tradition of political participation. They have settled mainly in New York, where they have risen to political leadership out of proportion to their numbers.

Although distrust of politics persists as part of the black cultural heritage, Negroes, like immigrants of the past, and Latin Americans today, discovered the importance of political participation as a means of gaining leverage in American society. In striving for political power, blacks have resembled other groups and yet have faced problems peculiar to their own situation and experience. Like members of ethnic groups, they have received recognition as their numbers have increased. But recognition has frequently come more slowly and hesitantly because of race prejudice, because of the feeling of powerlessness which has sometimes caused blacks to be reluctant to register and vote and because the majority of Negroes have been poor and therefore have had only votes and not much money to contribute to the political party coffers.

Since the adoption of the Fifteenth Amendment, black participation in the politics of northern cities has accelerated. The passage of the voting rights act of 1964 and the intraparty battle waged by the Mississippi Freedom Democratic Party with the regular party delegation at the 1964 Democratic convention in Atlantic City have opened the South to widespread voting and officeholding. Today black members sit in every Southern state legislature. A member of the race is vice-mayor of Atlanta, and 1972 saw a Negro congressman elected from Houston, the first from the South since George White of North Carolina, the last of the Reconstruction congressmen, bade farewell to the House in 1901. In 1971 Charles Evers received the second-largest number of votes in the Mississippi

Democratic primary for governor. Although he was defeated, his showing is nevertheless symbolic of the future role which the black community will undoubtedly play not only in the political life but in all aspects of society in the state which is the symbol of black oppression.

Black political activity in New York is important for the same reasons which make New York political activity important nationally. As has frequently been true of other groups, more Negroes live in New York City than in any other city in the world. Although the 1970 census reveals that the black population of Harlem has been surpassed by that of Brooklyn, the uptown area of Manhattan remains the symbol of black America. New York City contains the national headquarters of the leading civil rights organizations. It has provided the stimulus for two of black America's most important culture heroes, Marcus Garvey and Malcolm X, and it has produced black America's best known political leader, Adam Clayton Powell. The size of New York City and its cosmopolitan atmosphere have frequently provided more opportunities for blacks in New York than in other parts of the country. The large Jewish population of New York has undoubtedly promoted equality for blacks and other groups. As long ago as 1911, a civil rights act was passed, largely at the behest of Jewish groups. The national offices of Jewish civil rights organizations such as the Anti-Defamation League, the American Jewish Congress, and the American Jewish Committee are in New York. These organizations were instrumental in causing the Empire State to be the first to establish a state commission against discrimination in 1945. Despite recent outbreaks of hostility among elements of the Jewish and black communities, history will undoubtedly document the vital role played by Jewish individuals and organizations in the passage of civil rights legislation and in the establishment of the cosmopolitan atmosphere of the city.

While the role of Negroes in the political life of New York City is increasing and will continue to increase, it will never be as great as in some smaller cities. The 1970 census revealed that Negroes made up about 19 percent of New York City's population. New York's size prevents the numbers of any group from beginning to approach the percentage of the population which is black in such cities as Newark and Washington. No Negro has been a serious contender for the mayoralty, and at this time none seems prominent enough to be one in the near future. A Negro could be elected mayor of New York, and the cosmopolitan atmosphere of the city might make race a less important factor than in other cities. Yet a Negro running for mayor could not base his campaign wholly or even primarily upon the black community, although the combined support of blacks and Latin Americans would constitute a significant base. The comparatively small percentage of blacks in New York probably accounts for the fact that no Negro running for President of the City Council or Comptroller has survived the Democratic primary, although State Senator Basil Patterson was the Democratic candidate for lieutenant-governor in 1970.

Except for the fact that Negroes began voting Democratic in state and local elections earlier in New York than in other cities, the voting patterns of black New Yorkers have resembled those of members of the race in other areas. The last black non-Democrat was elected to public office in 1933. Since the 1930's Negro neighborhoods have constantly produced large majorities for the Democratic Party. The percentages have been larger in low-income than in middle- or high-income areas and larger at some times than at others. Negroes gave Mayor LaGuardia large numbers of votes in 1937 and 1941. Members of the race gave Governor Stevenson reduced majorities in 1956, and the decrease in votes in New York was about average in the nation. Blacks also gave Nelson Rockefeller a sizable percentage of votes in 1958. John Lindsay gained large numbers of black votes in his first campaign for mayor, and a majority of black votes in his second. In his first campaign in 1965 dissatisfaction with the performance of Mayor Wagner and Lindsay's concentrated efforts to obtain the votes of minority groups enabled him to garner about one third, while in 1969 he was the liberal candidate running against two avowed conservatives, who made no effort to appeal to black voters. The increasing conservatism of the Rockefeller Administration and the adherence of Mayor Lindsay to the Democratic Party have insured black Democratic majorities in the foreseeable future.

Blacks have frequently profited by divisions within the Democratic Party. Such divisions have resulted in judgeships as well as in the election of the first black state senator and a black borough president of Manhattan. Negroes will probably find more difficulty in taking advantage of party divisions in a citywide constituency than on a local level. When a Negro gets elected to citywide office, it will probably be largely because of the force of his or her individual personality, as was the case of Senator Brooke of Massachusetts.

The changing style of black political leadership in New York as elsewhere reflects now, and will continue to reflect, changing patterns of race relations and the increased number of blacks in the middle class. Perhaps the most important as well as the most obvious change in the character of black leadership in and out of politics is its increased militancy. The civil rights successes of the past two decades and, what is probably more important, the increased visibility of the black community have enabled racial spokesmen of all shades of opinion to say things which have heretofore gone unsaid. This is true both because in the past there were fears of reprisals and because increased visibility has made blacks aware that, whether whites react with sympathy or antagonism, they listen.

The two leading Harlem politicians, J. Raymond Jones and Adam Clayton Powell, possessed a wide variety of skills. Powell's performance as a congressional committee chairman and Jones's success as a political strategist transcend time and ethnic or racial background. The racial aspects of their careers are important primarily because they represent a stage in the historical development of the black community of New York and, in Powell's case, of the nation. Both men's roles would be somewhat different if they were on the scene today.

Jones entered politics and eventually rose to party leadership because he was one of a very few Negroes who had systematically mastered the technical aspects of party organization and the running of political campaigns. As an individual and as a citizen, Jones was always deeply concerned with racial progress. Yet his power was based not on positions taken on issues but on his knowledge of political organization, his ability to distribute patronage, and his almost uncanny knack of guessing who would win in party controversies. His style resembled that of ethnic leaders of the late nineteenth and early twentieth centuries whose constituents had not yet moved into the middle class in large numbers. Today, more Negroes have moved into the middle class, but whether accepting or rejecting middle-class values, Negroes are demanding that their leaders take positions on issues and not merely be party functionaries or intermediaries between the party and the community.

On the other hand Adam Clayton Powell's contribution to American race relations came as a protest leader. In the 1930's he led demonstrators to Harlem Hospital and helped to secure jobs for members of the race. As the first black New York City councilman and for more than a decade as one of only two black members of the House of Representatives, Powell was virtually a voice crying in the wilderness as he kept issues of civil rights and racial discrimination before the public. In Congress his protests ranged from advice to his staff members to use facilities used by other congressmen to the introduction of antisegregation amendments to appropriations bills. Today a dozen black congressmen sit in the House of Representatives. They have formed a caucus to voice black grievances and to articulate black demands. Groups of black political leaders in New York and other states have formed similar caucuses. No single political leader today can stand as a symbol of black protest as Powell did in the 1940's and 1950's. Paradoxically, Powell's most effective years were spent working alone; his power though not his prestige declined when in the 1960's he had to share his protest leadership with civil rights leaders.

In the foreseeable future municipal, state, and federal civil service will continue to provide a major source of middle-class employment for Negroes in New York City as elsewhere. The percentage of black servants may well increase as members of immigrant groups move into what are often more lucrative jobs in private employment. The opportunities for blacks in civil service should tend to increase along with their percentage. Black civil service employees today cluster in top-level, highly visible positions that reflect political influence and muscle and in jobs on the lowest levels. Few are in middle-level positions. The dynamics of social change will influence this state of affairs. Civil service jobs are theoretically nonpolitical, but in practice increased political power and recognition will continue to mean more civil service jobs for blacks just as it has for other minority groups seeking their place in the social, economic, and political sun. Moreover, such efforts are being exerted both by groups of black civil service employees and by integrated unions of government workers. These efforts are aimed at recruiting more minority group members and at increasing the opportunities for their promotion. There is an insistent demand that examination questions be geared to life styles and experiences different from those of the white middle class, and that promotion ladders be modified to give members of minority groups more opportunities to qualify. Increased educational opportunities and a higher level of aspirations will enable more Negroes to acquire the necessary skills.

The general racial climate will undoubtedly be the most important factor determining the shape of Negro political activity and its effectiveness in New York and throughout the nation. Color prejudice is the basis of the Negro's unique position throughout American history. Consequently, blacks will continue to think of political issues in racial terms. Disillusionment with white America and a feeling that separation or migration is the only answer is not a modern phenomenon; it goes back at least a century and a half. In the early 1800's Paul Cuffe, a wealthy black shipowner, transported a boatload of blacks to Africa. "...One can describe Negro social thought as ranging along a continuum of ideologies from assimilation to nationalism," wrote August Meier and Elliott Rudwick.

At one end of this continuum have been the advocates of complete biological amalgamation and cultural assimilation with members of the dominant society, and the complete disappearance of Negroes as a racial group. At the other end have been those who advocated complete withdrawal from American society and the creation of independent Negro states. Between these two extremes have been a great variety of philosophies recognizing the Negro as an American citizen, yet recognizing his distinctiveness as an ethnic group.[1]

Thirty years ago, in his monumental work *An American Dilemma,* Gunnar Myrdahl wrote that "Negroes seem to be held in a state of preparedness for a great number of contradictory opinions—ready to accept one type or another depending on how they are driven by pressures or where they see an opportunity."[2] During the 1960's the national spotlight focused on the civil rights question more than at any other time since Reconstruction, and substantial changes resulted in particular areas of race relations. The efforts to obtain these changes and the reactions to them have ranged from demands for integration to assertions of separateness. Yet one strategy never precluded the other. The rise of the black Muslims coincided with the period of the sit-ins and freedom rides, and Malcolm X was given a respectful hearing and recognized, even by some of the staunchest integrationists, as having earned credentials placing him within the tradition of black protest. Yet the desire for acceptance within American society remained strong in the late 1960's, even

Notes and References

Chapter 1: *Overview*

1. James Q. Wilson, *Negro Politics and the Search for Leadership* (Glen Cove, N.Y.: Free Press of Glen Cove, 1960); Allan Spear, *Black Chicago* (Chicago: University of Chicago Press, 1960); Horace Cayton, St. Clair Drake, *Black Metropolis* (New York: Harcourt, 1945); Harold F. Gosnell, *Negro Politicians* (Chicago: University of Chicago Press, 1935).

2. Samuel Lubell, *The Future of American Politics* (New York: Harper & Row, 1965), p. 81.

3. Quoted in George Furniss, "The Political Assimilation of Negroes in New York City," unpublished Ph.D. dissertation, Columbia University, 1969, p. 195.

Chapter 2: *Slavery and Disfranchisement*

1. For accounts of the arrival and early history of Negroes in New York, see William Renwick Riddell, "The Slave in Early New York," *Journal of Negro History*, XIII (January 1928), p. 53; Leo H. Hirsch, Jr., "The Negro and New York, 1783–1865," *Journal of Negro History*, XVI (October 1931), p. 386; I. N. Phelps Stokes, *The Iconography of Manhattan Island 1485 to 1909* (New York: Dodd Co., 1915–1928 and Arno Press, 1967), six volumes, VI, p. 501; James Weldon Johnson, *Black Manhattan* (New York: Alfred A. Knopf, Inc., 1930), p. 3; and Roi Ottley and William Weatherby, eds., *The Negro in New York* (New York: New York Public Library, 1967), p. 1.

2. The slave revolts of 1712 and 1741 are described in Riddell, pp. 70–76; Aaron Hamlett Payne, "The Negro in New York Prior to 1861," *Howard Review*, I (June 1923), pp. 13–19; Johnson, *Black Manhattan*, pp. 3–8; Mary White Ovington, *Half a Man* (New York: Longman's, Green, and Co., 1911), p. 6; Ottley and Weatherby, pp. 27–28, and Edgar J. McManus, *A History of Negro Slavery in New York* (Syracuse, New York: Syracuse University Press, 1966), pp. 121–141.

3. Quoted in Dixon Ryan Fox, "The Negro Vote in Old New York," *American Political Science Quarterly*, XXXII (June 1917), p. 253.

4. The most comprehensive account of the abolition of slavery in New York is found in McManus, pp. 161–181.

5. Fox, pp. 255–256.

6. Joseph Sidney, "An Oration Commemorative of the Abolition of the Slave Trade in the United States Delivered before the Wilberforce Philanthropic Association in the City of New York on 2 January, 1809." A copy is at the Schomberg Collection, New York Public Library.

7. "Extracts from the Minutes of the Electors of the People of Color of the Fifth Ward at a Meeting to Express their Congratulations to His Excellency, June 15, 1820." DeWitt Clinton Papers, New York Public Library.

8. For a description of the legislation designed to restrict Negro suffrage, see Fox, pp. 256–258; Emil Olbrich, *The Development of Sentiment on Negro Suffrage to 1860* (Madison: University of Wisconsin Press, 1912–1914), p. 29; and Charles H. Wesley, "Negro Suffrage in the Period of Constitution-Making," *Journal of Negro History*, XXXII (April 1947), pp. 56–58.

9. For the debates on Negro suffrage, see Fox, pp. 259–262; Hirsch, pp. 401–402; C. Z. Lincoln, *The Constitutional History of New York from the Beginning of the Colonial Period to 1905* (Rochester, New York: Lawyers Co-operative Publishing Co., 1906), five volumes, I, pp. 252–261, and Mary M. Joyce, "History of the Suffrage in New York to 1821," unpublished M.A. thesis, 1914, Columbia University, pp. 14–28.

10. Filmore L. Groissier, "The Free Negro in New York, 1850–1860," unpublished M.A. thesis, Columbia University, 1939, p. 17.

11. Howard H. Bell, "A Survey of the Negro Convention Movement, 1830–1860," unpublished Ph.D. dissertation at Northwestern University, 1953.

12. *Ibid.*, pp. 10–37, 55–65. See also Charles H. Wesley, "The Negroes of New York and the Emancipation Movement," *Journal of Negro History*, XXIII (January 1939), p. 92; Herbert Aptheker, ed., *A Documentary History of the Negro People of the United States* (New York: Citadel Press, 1951), two volumes, I, pp. 198–205.

13. See, for example, *Colored American*, December 16, 1837, March 3 and 12, April 12 and 19, July 14 and September 8, 1838. Howard H. Bell has examined the Gerritt Smith Miller Papers at the Syracuse University Library and has made the results of his research available to me.

14. For the economic conditions of Negroes before the Civil War, see Hirsch, pp. 437–438; Arnett G. Lindsay, "The Economic Conditions of Negroes in New York City Prior to 1861," *Journal of Negro History*, VI (April 1921), pp. 190–199; Leon F. Litwack, *North of Slavery*,

the *Negro in the Free States, 1790–1860* (Chicago: University of Chicago Press, 1961), pp. 163–165; *New York World,* March 16, 1867.

15. Litwack, pp. 87, 159. For the attitude of the Irish toward slavery, see Florence E. Gibson, *The Attitude of the New York Irish toward State and National Affairs, 1848–1892* (New York: Columbia University Press, 1951), pp. 86–111, and Carl Wittke, *The Irish in America* (Baton Rouge: Louisiana State University Press, 1956), pp. 125–135.

16. *New York Tribune,* April 28, 1845; Charles Wesley, "The Negroes of New York in the Emancipation Movement," *Journal of Negro History,* XXIV (January 1939), pp. 65–103; H. P. Hastings, "An Essay on Constitutional Reform," New York, 1848. Cited in Fox, "The Negro Vote in Old New York," p. 267.

17. For accounts of Negro suffrage at the convention, see Fox, pp. 268–270; Olbrich, p. 73; Lincoln, II, pp. 118–123; and Hirsch, p. 422.

18. Olbrich, p. 77, and Hirsch, p. 423.

19. Bell, pp. 188–189; and Benjamin Quarles, *Frederick Douglass* (Washington: Associated Publishers, 1947), pp. 146–147.

20. Olbrich, p. 126; Litwack, p. 271; Fox. p. 273.

21. For efforts of Negroes to gain equal suffrage between 1865 and 1870, see Bernice C. Williams, "The Negro in Politics in New York, 1777–1900," unpublished M.A. thesis, New York University, 1937, p. 75; Leslie H. Fishel, Jr., "Northern Prejudice and Negro Suffrage, 1865–1870," *Journal of Negro History,* XXXIX (January 1954), pp. 13, 20; Lincoln, II, pp. 314–315; and *Nation,* V (October 1867), p. 247.

Chapter 3: *Working toward Elective Office*

1. *New York Times,* January 10, 1880.

2. See, for example, *New York Times* and New York *Sun,* July 4 and August 22, 1895.

3. New York *Post,* October 26, 1903.

4. New York *Globe,* April 5, June 7, and July 5, 1884.

5. Elting Morrison, *The Letters of Theodore Roosevelt* (Cambridge: Harvard University Press, 1951–1954).

6. *New York Times,* November 3, 1876 and October 27, 1880, and New York *Age,* September 8 and 15, 1888.

7. *New York Times,* July 25, 1895.

8. *Ibid.,* January 19 and May 28, 1880, June 10, August 30, and October 12, 1883; New York *Sun,* July 8 and 11 and September 29, 1873, and New York *Freeman,* January 6, 1883, and January 19, 1884.

9. New York *Age,* September 28, 1905, August 23 and September 6, 1906, and October 8, 1908. Charles W. Anderson to Booker T.

Washington, January 23, 1908, and Anderson to Emmett Scott, April 16, 1908. Booker T. Washington Papers, Library of Congress.

10. James Weldon Johnson, *Along This Way* (New York: Viking Press, 1933), p. 128.

11. Washington to Roosevelt, February 20, 1904, and Roosevelt Memorandum, February 23, 1904. Theodore Roosevelt Papers, Library of Congress, and Washington to Anderson, December 20, 1904. Booker T. Washington Papers, Library of Congress. See also Leslie H. Fishel, Jr., "The Negro in Northern Politics, 1870–1900," *Mississippi Valley Historical Review,* XLII (December, 1955), p. 487.

12. Anderson to Washington, January 23, 1908. Washington Papers. *Pittsburgh Courier,* July 24, 1928.

13. *New York World,* April 4, 1915.

14. Interview by the writer with Alan Dingle, March 1956. Gilbert Osofsky, *Harlem—the Making of a Ghetto* (New York: Harper and Row, 1963), pp. 165–166.

15. New York *Sun,* July 8, 1873; *New York Times,* January 10, 1880; August 18, 1888, and October 11, 1891; New York *Globe,* January 6, February 3, and March 3, 1883; and March 29, 1884; New York *Freeman,* May 16, 1885; and Leslie H. Fishel, Jr., "The Negro in Northern Politics, 1870–1900," p. 481.

16. *New York Times* and New York *Herald,* January 8, 1898. Edgar J. Levy, "An Election in New York," *North American Review,* CXLV (December 1887), p. 681. Interview by the writer with William Singleton, December 1955.

17. *New York Times,* October 23, 1897, July 31, 1920. See also "History of the Tammany Hall United Colored Democracy, Jubilee Program of Exercises Commemorating the Founding of the Tammany Hall United Colored Democracy," June 1923. Interview by the writer with Andrew M. Robinson, December 1955.

18. New York *Herald,* January 8, 1898. See also Claude McKay, *Harlem—Negro Metropolis* (New York: E. P. Dutton and Co., 1940), p. 122; Roi Ottley, *New World A-Comin'* (Boston: Houghton Mifflin Co., 1944), p. 210; Henry Lee Moon, *Balance of Power—the Negro Vote* (Garden City, N.Y.: Doubleday, 1948), p. 88; John A. Morsell, "The Political Behavior of Negroes in New York City," unpublished Ph.D. dissertation, Columbia University, 1955, p. 27. Also see Wesley Cutright, "Political Activities and Organizations," and Waring Cuney, "The United Colored Democracy," in "The Negro in New York," unpublished ms. of WPA Project, Schomberg Collection, New York Public Library.

19. John E. Bruce, "The Democratic Party and the Negro," leaflet

issued November 4, 1905. John E. Bruce Papers, Schomberg Collection, New York Public Library.

20. Interview by the writer with Andrew M. Robinson, December 1955; interview by the writer with William Singleton, December 1955; interview by the writer with R. W. Griffin, January 1956. The race riot of 1900 is described in Osofsky, pp. 46–52 and Seth Scheiner, *Negro Mecca, a History of the Negro in New York, 1865–1920* (New York: New York University Press, 1965), pp. 121–128.

21. New York *Evening Post,* May 12, 1900; Mary White Ovington, *Half a Man* (New York: Longman's, Green, and Co., 1911), pp. 204–206.

22. See New York *Tribune,* August 8, 1902; New York *Age,* October 26, 1907, December 16, 1909, March 16, September 21, October 5 and 26, 1911, January 4, 11, and 25, February 8 and 22, March 14, April 4 and 25, and May 2, 1912, May 22 and June 12, 1913. See also M. Rothman, " 'Chief' Lee," and Harry Robinson, "Biography of Edward E. 'Chief' Lee," in "The Negro in New York," Federal Writers Project, Schomberg Collection, New York Public Library. Charles W. Anderson to Booker T. Washington, November 11, 1910. Booker T. Washington Papers. Interview by the writer with L. S. Alexander Gumby, November 1955; interview by the writer with Andrew M. Robinson, December 1955; interview by the writer with Oscar Waters, February 1956.

23. George Furniss, "The Political Assimilation of Negroes in New York City, 1890–1960," unpublished Ph.D. dissertation, Columbia University, 1969, p. 171.

24. Osofsky, pp. 11–12.

25. *Ibid.*

26. Ottley, p. 28.

27. Osofsky, pp. 71–72.

28. *Ibid.,* pp. 96–104; Johnson, *Black Manhattan,* pp. 147–149.

29. New York *Herald,* August 20, 1905.

30. Osofsky, pp. 106–110; *Pease and Elliman's Real Estate Indicator,* December 22, 1912, and Harlem *Home News,* July 28, 1911.

31. Osofsky, pp. 115–117.

32. New York *Age,* May 11, 1911, February 12, 19, and 26, 1914.

33. Johnson, *Black Manhattan,* pp. 147–149.

34 Furniss, p. 220. The campaign of Royall is described in the issues of the New York *Age* of September and October, 1913. See also *New York Times,* September 17, 1918. Charles W. Anderson to Booker T. Washington, October 16 and November 14, 1913. Washington Papers. Interview by the writer with Alan Dingle, March 1956.

35. Harlem *Home News,* October 10, 1917; New York *Age,* November 8 and 15, 1917. Furniss, p. 228.

Chapter 4: *The Recognition of Harlem*

1. *New York Times,* October 29, 1967.
2. Furniss, p. 202.
3. James Q. Wilson, *Negro Politics and the Search for Leadership* (Glencoe, Ill.: Free Press of Glencoe, 1960), pp. 98–99, 107, 151.
4. New York *Age,* November 9, 1918, November 15, 1919, November 6, 1920, November 12, 1921.
5. *New York Times,* October 29, 1926; New York *Age,* November 12, 1921; November 11, 1922.
6. Lester A. Walton, "The Negro in Politics," *Outlook,* LXXXVII (July 23, 1924), pp. 472–473.
7. See, for example, *New York Times,* October 2 and November 5, 1921, October 29, 1924.
8. New York *Age,* May 3, 1924.
9. New York *Age,* November 29, 1924; Warren Moscow, *What Have You Done for Me Lately?* (Englewood Cliffs, N.J.: Prentice-Hall, Inc., 1967), p. 134. Interview by the writer with Collis Crocker, February 1956; interview by the writer with Oswald C. Newton, February 1956.
10. Quoted in Walton, *op. cit.*
11. *New York Times,* 1930; New York *Age,* April 18, 1925; interview by the writer with Collis Crocker, February 1956.
12. New York *Age,* March 16, 1918; November 8, 1924, November 10, 1928, and November 9, 1929. "Memoirs of Joseph P. Gavagan," COHP, p. 26.
13. *New York Times,* July 7, 1921; New York *Age,* March 29, 1924.
14. New York *Age,* April 5, 1924; *New York Times,* December 4, 1964; interview by George Furniss with Henri W. Shields; interview by George Furniss with Darwin W. Telesford.
15. New York *Age,* June 27, July 25, August 1, and September 25, 1925; January 9, July 24, and 31, August 7, September 4, and 11, 1926; and August 10, 1929.
16. *New York Times,* January 23, 27, and 28, February 1, 2, and 7, 1926; New York *Age,* January 30, February 6 and 13, 1926; June 25, 1927.
17. New York *Age,* June 25 and November 12, 1927. Interview by the writer with David B. Costuma, March 1956. DePriest's speech is quoted in *New York Times,* August 22, 1929 and New York *Age,* August 31, 1929. The successful campaign for Negro leadership of the

19th A.D. can be followed in the pages of the New York *Age* from February 25, 1928 to September 28, 1929.

18. New York *Age*, January 9, March 20, and April 10, 1926; February 26, March 26, and April 2, 1927; March 29, April 12, May 3 and 31, June 28, July 5 and 19, and November 15, 1930. *New York Times,* June 30, 1930. Interview by George Furniss with Francis E. Rivers.

19. See various issues of the New York *Age* and the *Amsterdam News* between 1932 and 1935; New York *Herald-Tribune,* August 11, 1935; New York *Post,* August 9, 1935; *New York Times,* October 17, 1935. Ottley, *op. cit.,* pp. 214–215, and McKay, *op. cit.,* p. 128. Interviews by George Furniss with Herbert L. Bruce and Henri W. Shields and interview by the writer with Charles Horowitz, March 1956. For editorial comment on the Bruce victory in the Negro press, see *Amsterdam News,* October 19, 1935, and New York *Age,* October 26, 1935.

20. *New York Times,* March 20 and 24, 1935; Allan Nevins, *Herbert Lehmann and His Era* (New York: Charles Scribner's Sons, 1963), p. 165.

21. These events are naturally covered in the pages of the New York *Age* and *Amsterdam News.* See also *New York Times,* March 10, April 5 and 21, September 19 and October 1, 1935; February 3, 4, and 9, 1936; April 21, September 12, 24, and 28, 1937; March 1, June 27, and October 5, 1939. New York *Post,* June 23, 1937; New York *Sun,* February 4, 1936 and March 17, 1939. Interview by the writer with Daniel Burrows, December 1955.

22. Interview by George Furniss with Herbert L. Bruce; interview by the writer with Collis Crocker, December 1955; interview by the writer with Oscar Waters, December 1955.

23. *New York Times,* September 2 and 3, 1936; July 23, 1939; September 14 and 15, 1943; New York *Age,* September 12, 1936, January 6 and 20, 1940; August 8, 1942, and September 18 and November 6, 1943.

24. New York *Age,* August 1 and November 14, 1942.

25. Among the accounts of the early life of Adam Clayton Powell are those in New York *Post,* March 27, 1956; Dan Wakefield, "Adam Clayton Powell, the Angry Voice of Harlem," *Esquire,* LII (November 1959), p. 119, and Neal Hickey and Ed Edwin, *Adam Clayton Powell and the Politics of Race* (New York: Fleet Publishing Corp., 1964), pp. 1–69.

26. New York *Post,* February 2, 1961; *New York Times,* December 3, 1964.

27. *New York Times,* February 2, 1946; March 4, 1947; New York

Herald-Tribune, November 7 and December 31, 1946 and January 2, 1947; New York *Age,* August 31, 1946, and January 11, 1947.
28. *New York Times,* July 8 and 9, 1949; Abner W. Berry, "All-American Councilman," *New Masses,* LVII (October 9, 1945), p. 4; *Daily Worker,* August 30, 1964.
29. Berry, *op. cit.; New York Times,* November 10, 1943; *Daily Worker,* November 24, 1943.
30. New York *Age,* May 6 and 13, 1944; May 12, 1945; *New Masses, op. cit.; Daily Worker,* May 7 and June 27, 1945; New York *Post,* July 20, 21, and 27, 1945; New York *Daily News,* July 21, 25, and 26, 1945.
31. *New York Times,* March 9, October 17 and 19, November 4, 5, 9, and 29, 1949; August 24, 1964; New York *Post,* November 9, 1949; "Harlem Homecoming," *Time,* LIV (November 14, 1949), p. 26; Boston *Post,* November 10, 1949; Boston *Herald,* November 14, 1949. Interview by the writer with Collis Crocker, December 1955; interview by the writer with Earl Brown, March 1956.

Chapter 5: *To the Present*

1. Ralph Foster Weld, *Brooklyn Is America* (New York: Columbia University Press, 1950), p. 154. See also Brooklyn *Tablet,* December 1, 1966.
2. New York *Age,* March 14 and April 4, 1891; Furniss, p. 179.
3. Brooklyn *Eagle,* October 6, 1918 and June 1, 1919.
4. Brooklyn *Eagle,* July 27, 1954, and New York *Herald-Tribune,* July 25, 1965; Nicholas Marlowe, "Bedford Stuyvesant-Place Names," unpublished master's thesis, Brooklyn College, 1963.
5. Brooklyn *Eagle,* August 3, 1930.
6. *New York Times* and New York *Herald-Tribune,* October 24, 1946; Interview with Mrs. George E. Wibecan and other members of the Wibecan family, January and February, 1955; scrapbooks in the possession of Mr. and Mrs. Jerry Foster of Brooklyn and Martha's Vineyard.
7. New York *Herald-Tribune,* November 4, 1948; Brooklyn *Eagle,* January 18 and 20, 1945; October 13, 1948; January 9, 1949; February 19, 1954; New York *Age,* January 25, 1936; *Amsterdam News,* April 24, 1948; July 4 and 18 and September 19, 1953; July 3 and September 18, 1954, and August 6, 1955. Interview with Bertram L. Baker, February 1956 and interview with Wesley Holder, March 1956.
8. New York *Herald-Tribune,* June 29, July 1 and 2, 1949; *New York Times,* July 6, 1950; interview by the writer with J. Raymond Jones, March 1956.

9. *New York Times,* August 20 and 21 and November 8, 1952; *Amsterdam News,* April 26, August 23, and September 20, 1952.

10. *Amsterdam News,* July 27 and August 10, 1946, and April 18, 1959. Interview with Walter Gladwin, February 1956.

11. Interview by the writer with Ewart Guinier, February 1956; interview by the writer with Carl Lawrence, October 1955; interview by the writer with Hulan Jack, March 1956. In the summer of 1953 numerous articles appeared on the selection of the Negro candidates for borough president in all the daily papers as well as in the Negro press.

12. New York *Daily Mirror,* February 28, 1954; New York *Post,* December 18 and 20, 1959.

13. Naturally, the press gave extensive coverage to Powell's support of Eisenhower and to DiSapio's attempts to purge him. See, for example, *New York Times,* October 12, 13, and 26, 1956; May 16, 17, and 18 and August 13, 1958; *Amsterdam News,* October 13, 20, and 27, 1956; May 24 and 31 and August 16, 1958; Hickey and Edwin, pp. 134–153.

14. *New York Times,* May 18, June 24, July 15, August 3 and 12, September 7, 9, and 16, 1959; January 12, 1960; *Amsterdam News,* July 4, September 19 and 26, 1959; Hickey and Edwin, pp. 155–166.

15. See, for example, *New York Times,* December 15, 18, 19, and 22, 1959; *Amsterdam News,* November 21 and 28, December 12, 19, and 26, 1959; New York *Post,* December 16, 18, and 20, 1959.

16. *New York Times,* January 10, March 15, April 15, 22, 23, June 10 to July 7, November 14 to December 7, 1960; January 17, 1961; April 4, 1962; New York *Post,* June 26 and July 10, 1960; April 3, 1962.

17. *New York Times,* January 19, December 12, 19, and 24, 1960; January 2, 5, 6, 9, 20, and 31, 1961; New York *Herald-Tribune,* December 9, 18, 29, and 31, 1960; January 6, 9, 23, and February 1, 1961; *Amsterdam News,* December 10, 1960, January 7 and 28 and February 11, 1961; New York *Post,* February 2, 1961.

18. *New York Times,* June 7 and 16, July 11, August 5, September 8, and November 8, 1961; New York *Herald-Tribune,* June 26, July 11 and 20, 1961; Hickey and Edwin, p. 194.

19. *New York Times,* November 16, December 6, 10, and 17, 1961; January 8, February 9, and March 3, 1962; *Amsterdam News,* November 25, 1961, February 24 and April 7, 1962; New York *Post,* December 11, 1961 and March 29, 1962; New York *Herald-Tribune,* November 12 and 17 and December 17, 1961; February 25 and March 30, 1962; New York *World-Telegram,* January 8, 1962; Hickey and Edwin, p. 202.

20. *New York Times,* September 9 and November 8, 1962; *Amsterdam News,* September 15 and November 10, 1962; New York *Post,* September 9 and 19, 1962.

21. *Amsterdam News,* October 28, 1961.

22. *New York Times,* July 3, August 14, September 2, 3, and 4, 1963; New York *Herald-Tribune,* May 15, September 2 and 3, 1963; New York *World-Telegram,* June 26, 1963; Moscow, *What Have You Done For Me Lately?* p. 137.

23. *New York Times,* February 5, 1964; New York *Herald-Tribune,* January 17, 23, and 24, 1964; *Amsterdam News,* January 18 and 25, February 1 and 8, 1964; Edward I. Costikyan, *Behind Closed Doors* (New York: Harcourt Brace and World, 1966), pp. 110–132.

24. *New York Times,* July 30 and September 14, 1964; New York *Herald-Tribune,* July 30, October 1 and 8, 1964; New York *Post,* July 21, 1964; *Amsterdam News,* August 7, September 12, October 3 and 10, and November 8, 1964.

25. *New York Times,* December 3 and 4, 1964; New York *World-Telegram,* December 3, 1964; New York *Journal-American,* December 4, 1964; *Amsterdam News,* December 12, 1964; New York *Post,* December 6 and 7, 1964.

26. New York *Herald-Tribune,* December 8, 1964; February 9, 1965; New York *Daily News,* February 22, 1965; *Amsterdam News,* December 26, 1964, January 16, February 3 and 20, 1965.

27. For two summaries of the role of Negroes in the mayoralty campaign of 1965 and of the reasons for Lindsay's strong showing in Negro communities, see New York *Post,* October 29, 1965 and New York *Herald-Tribune,* January 2, 1966.

28. See, for example, *New York Times,* June 5, 6, 8, 10, 13, and 29, 1966; March 11 and 14, 1967; New York *Herald-Tribune,* March 11 and 12, 1967; *Amsterdam News,* May 28, June 11, and July 2, 1966.

29. See, for example, *New York Times,* January 9 and 10 and March 2, 1967, and January 4, 1969; *Newsweek,* LXVIII (October 3, 1966), pp. 29–30, and LXIX (January 16, 1967), pp. 28–29; Hickey and Edwin, pp. 167–176, 211–219.

30. *New York Times,* March 18, September 13 and 22, 1966; New York *Herald-Tribune,* April 17, 1964; January 26 and February 25, 1966; New York *World-Journal-Tribune,* August 21, 1966; New York *Post,* September 13, 1966; New York *Daily News,* September 14, 1966.

31. *New York Times,* July 31, 1963, December 29, 1964, September 5, 1965, December 26, 1956; New York *Herald-Tribune,* June 19, 1964, January 7, July 20, August 3, September 8 and 16, and December 14, 1965; New York *Post,* June 24, 1962, August 27, 1965; *Amsterdam News,* July 20 and December 28, 1957, January 11, 1958,

June 6, 1964, July 31 and August 7, 1965, April 16 and August 3, 1966. Institute of Urban Studies, Fordham University, *A Profile of the Bronx Economy,* New York, 1967. Interview with Edward Stevenson, August 1969. Interview with J. William Dunkin, September 1969. Interview with Andrew C. Parks, January 1970.

32. *Daily Worker,* July 3, 11 and 13, 1952, September 5, 1954, July 2, 1957; New York *Age-Defender,* September 12, 1953; *Daily Compass,* June 30, 1952; *Sunday Worker,* May 13, 1956; *Amsterdam News,* July 5, 1952, April 7 and May 12, 1956, May 20 and June 15, 1957, January 4 and May 17, 1958, October 28, 1961; *New York Times,* December 27, 1957, September 29, 1963; *Queens Voice,* April 1966; *Long Island Star Journal,* August 3, 1937; *Long Island Press,* June 13, 1947. Interview with Charles Rochester, February 1969. Interview with Guy Brewer, December 1969.

33. *Amsterdam News,* October 31, 1959, November 11, 1961, June 23 and August 11, September 15, 1962, November 9, 1963, March 14, June 6 and 13, July 18, 1964; New York *Post,* August 2, 1964.

35. Shirley Chisholm has been the subject of numerous feature articles. See, for example, *New York Times,* February 2, 1969, and "New Faces in Congress," *Ebony,* Vol. 44, February 1969, p. 56.

34. *Life* LXIV (March 8, 1968), p. 83.

Chapter 6: *Adam Clayton Powell*

1. Hickey and Edwin, p. 1.

2. *Ibid.,* pp. 15–22, 58–59; New York *Post,* March 27, 1956; Dan Wakefield, "Adam Clayton Powell, Jr., the Angry Voice of Harlem," *Esquire,* LII (November 1959), p. 119. Adam Clayton Powell, Sr., *Against the Tide* (New York: R. R. Smith, 1938).

3. Hickey and Edwin, pp. 24–27.

4. Wakefield, *op. cit.*

5. Hickey and Edwin, pp. 56–58.

6. *Ibid.,* pp. 60–61.

7. New York *Herald-Tribune,* November 2 and 8, 1941; *P.M.,* November 4, 1941; Hickey and Edwin, pp. 67–69; Ottley, *New World A-Comin',* pp. 233–234.

8. Hickey, pp. 73–74; Ottley, *op. cit.*; New York *Herald-Tribune,* June 8, 1943. Several letters and other documents relating to the controversy over Negro faculty members at the city colleges can be found in the Stanley M. Isaacs Papers, New York Public Library.

9. There is a complete file of the *People's Voice* in the Schomberg Collection, New York Public Library.

10. *New York Times,* July 2, 1943; March 24, April 9, 13, 19, 30,

and May 13, 1944; *People's Voice,* July 17, 1943; April 1, June 24, August 5, and November 11, 1944; New York *Herald-Tribune,* July 2, 1943; March 24, April 19, and November 8, 1944.

11. Wakefield, p. 120; Hickey and Edwin, p. 90; Adam Clayton Powell, Jr., *Marching Blacks* (New York: Dial Press, 1945).

12. Hickey, pp. 89–109.

13. New York *Herald-Tribune,* October 26, 1948.

14. See, for example, *New York Times,* May 9, 1950; New York *Herald-Tribune,* October 7, 1943; New York *Daily Mirror,* September 1, 1948; *Christian Science Monitor,* January 31, 1961; *People's Voice,* August 7, 1943, and January 15, 1944.

15. The Bandung Conference and Powell's role in it are naturally described in detail in the New York papers. See, for example, *New York Times,* March 7, 16, 19, and 23, 1955; New York *Herald-Tribune,* April 18, 1955, and New York *Daily Mirror,* May 20, 1955.

16. *New York Times,* July 4, 1956.

17. *New York Times,* October 3, 12, 13, 14, 15, and 26, and November 7, 1956; *Amsterdam News,* October 13, 20, 27, and November 10, 1956; *Daily Worker,* October 23, 1956; Hickey and Edwin, pp. 186–187.

18. Quoted in Hickey and Edwin, pp. 137–138.

19. *Ibid.,* p. 134.

20. Wakefield, p. 122.

21. *New York Times,* May 17, 1958.

22. *Ibid.,* May 18, 1958.

23. Hickey and Edwin, p. 143.

24. *Ibid.,* p. 147.

25. *New York Times,* May 19, 1958; James Q. Wilson, "Two Negro Politicians, an Interpretation," in Harry A. Bailey, Jr., ed., *Negro Politics in America* (Columbus, Ohio: Merrill Books, Inc., 1967), p. 147.

26. *New York Times,* May 29, July 25, August 4, 10, 12, and 13, 1958; New York *Herald-Tribune,* August 11, 1958; New York *Post,* August 11, 1958; Hickey and Edwin, pp. 145–154, *Amsterdam News,* August 9, 1958.

27. *New York Times,* October 8, 9, 21, 22, and 23, 1958; September 7 and 16, 1959; *Amsterdam News,* October 25, 1958, and September 19, 1959.

28. *New York Times,* March 8 and 9 and April 23, 1960; New York *Post,* March 30 and April 22, 1960; D. Pearson and N. Ritter, "Dark Enigma of Congress," *Saturday Evening Post,* CCXXXVII (March 28, 1964), p. 76.

29. *New York Times,* January 23 and 26, 1960; January 30, 1961.

30. *Wall Street Journal,* April 4, 1961.

31. New York *Herald-Tribune*, March 12, 1961; July 17, 1962, and April 2, 1963; New York *World-Journal-Tribune*, February 23, 1967; Pearson and Ritter, p. 77; Murray Kempton, "Adam Powell, the Ocelot of the House of Representatives," *New Republic*, XIV (May 25, 1963), p. 12.

32. New York *Post*, January 9, 1967; Hickey and Edwin, pp. 188–189.

33. *Ibid.*, pp. 211–219; Pearson and Ritter, p. 78.

34. There is a detailed account of his appearance at the Rally with Malcolm X and of the reactions of Negro leaders in Hickey and Edwin, pp. 236–240.

35. See, for example, *New York Times*, March 19, June 8, 11, 14, 19, and 21, and July 25, 1964; and New York *Herald-Tribune*, June 19 and November 25, 1964, March 11, April 15 and 24, May 10, 11, and 23, June 6, July 21, October 3, 10, 14, and 18, November 2, December 7, 13, and 30, 1965.

36. New York *World-Telegram*, April 1, 1963.

37. *Amsterdam News*, November 7, 1964; *Newsweek*, LXIX (January 2, 1967), p. 149; Pearson and Ritter, p. 75.

38. Powell's court case is summarized and analyzed in New York *World-Journal-Tribune*, January 15, 1967.

39. *Newsweek*, LXVIII (October 3, 1966), pp. 29–30; LXIX (January 2, 1966), p. 149.

40. *New York Times* and *New York Tribune*, January 9 and 10, 1967; *Newsweek*, LXIX (January 23, 1967), pp. 28–29.

41. *New York Times*, January 6 and 13, 1967; New York *World-Journal-Tribune*, January 10, 11, and 12, 1967.

42. *New York Times*, January 30, 1967; Simeon Booker, "The Man Behind the Controversy," *Ebony*, XXII (March, 1967), p. 30.

43. See, for example, *New York Times*, January 4, 6, and 13, and March 1, 1967; New York *World-Journal-Tribune*, January 10, 11, and 12 and April 12, 1967.

44. Adam Clayton Powell, *Adam by Adam: The Autobiography of Adam Clayton Powell* (New York: Dial Press, 1971).

45. *Book Review Digest*, 1971 Compilation, p. 1092; *New York Times*, November 4, 1971.

46. *New York Times*, April 5, 1972.

47. Hickey and Edwin, p. 297.

Chapter 7: *J. Raymond Jones*

1. New York *Post*, February 2, 1961.

2. *Ibid.* See also *New York Times*, February 9, 1967; Interview by the writer with Collis Crocker, January 1969.

3. See, for example, *New York Times,* October 6, 1939, January 10 and August 11, 1943; New York *World-Telegram* and New York *Post,* October 6, 1939; New York *Herald-Tribune,* March 1, 1939, April 21, July 8 and 11, 1943, March 24 and May 11, 1944, January 1 and December 31, 1946; *Amsterdam News,* June 10, 1939, January 20 and 27 and February 3, 1945; New York *Age,* September 16, 1939, May 1, June 5, August 7 and 23, 1943, January 8, 1944. Interview by the writer with J. Raymond Jones, February 1956.

4. *New York Times,* February 2, 1946, January 8 and 15, 1947; New York *Herald-Tribune,* October 1, 1945, October 15 and 17, November 7 and December 31, 1946, January 2, 3, and 10, 1947.

5. *Daily Compass,* December 13, 1950; New York *Herald-Tribune,* June 29, July 1, 2, and 10, August 11, and September 3, 1947, October 10 and 27, November 9, December 10 and 13, 1950.

6. *Amsterdam News,* June 13, July 4 and 11, 1953; New York *Post,* February 2, 1961; Interview by the writer with Collis Crocker, November 1955.

7. *New York Times,* January 4, 1962; interview by the writer with Collis Crocker, March 1969.

8. New York *Post,* February 2, 1961.

9. See, for example, *New York Times,* June 7 and 16, July 11, August 5, September 8, and November 8, 1961; New York *Herald-Tribune,* June 26, July 11 and 20, 1961.

10. *New York Times,* November 16, December 6, 10, and 17, 1961; January 8, February 9, and March 3, 1962; New York *Herald-Tribune,* November 12 and 17 and December 17, 1961, February 25 and 28 and March 30, 1962; New York *World-Telegram,* January 8, 1962; New York *Post,* December 11, 1961, March 29, 1962; *Amsterdam News,* November 25, 1961, February 24 and April 7, 1962.

11. *New York Times,* July 3, August 14, September 2, 3, and 4, 1963; New York *Herald-Tribune,* May 15, September 2 and 3, 1963; New York *World-Telegram,* June 26, 1963; Moscow, *What Have You Done for Me Lately?,* p. 137.

12. Jones's election as county leader is described in the New York papers of December 3 and 4, 1964. See also *Amsterdam News,* December 12, 1964.

13. Theodore H. White, "Perspective 1960," *Saturday Review* (May 14, 1960), pp. 4–5; New York *Post,* February 2, 1961; *New York Times,* February 9, 1967.

14. The controversy over the organization of the legislature is described in the New York papers of January 1965.

15. *New York Times,* September 12 and October 22, 1963, December 8, 1964; New York *Herald-Tribune,* December 8, 1964, February

9, 1965; New York *Daily News,* February 22, 1965; *Amsterdam News,* December 26, 1964, January 16, February 13 and 20, 1965.

16. See, for example, *New York Times,* May 7, 14, 24, June 3, 5, 10, 14, 17, 18, 20, and 29, and July 3, 1966; *Amsterdam News,* May 28, and June 25, 1966.

17. New York papers of March 11 and 12, 1967.

18. New York *Herald-Tribune,* May 10, 1960.

Chapter 8: *The Negro Immigrants*

1. Nathan Glazer and Daniel Patrick Moynihan, *Beyond the Melting Pot, the Negroes, Puerto Ricans, Jews, Italians, and Irish of New York City* (Cambridge: MIT and Harvard University Press, 1964), pp. 34–36; Ira D. A. Reid, *The Negro Immigrants* (New York: Columbia University Press, 1939), p. 41.

2. Michael G. Smith, *The Plural Society of the British West Indies* (Cambridge and Berkeley: Cambridge University Press and University of California Press, 1965), pp. 92–115, and Eric Williams, *The Negro in the Caribbean* (New York: Negro Universities Press, 1969), p. 57.

3. Smith, *op. cit.* See also Philip M. Sherlock, *The West Indies* (London: Thames and Hudson, 1966), pp. 56–57 and Sir Alan Burns, *A History of the British West Indies* (London: George Allen and Unwin, Ltd., 1954), pp. 613–640.

4. W. A. Domingo, "The West Indies," *Opportunity,* IV (November 1926), p. 341.

5. Reid, p. 184.

6. Sherlock, p. 108.

7. Reid, pp. 185–186.

8. *Ibid.,* p. 193.

9. *Ibid.,* pp. 106–112. Ottley and Weatherby, *op. cit.,* pp. 192–194.

10. Reid, pp. 176–177.

11. Domingo, p. 342.

12. Quoted in Reid, p. 165.

13. *New York Times,* December 4, 1964. Interview by George Furniss with Darwin W. Telesford.

14. *Amsterdam News,* May 17, 1952; Interview by George Furniss with Herbert L. Bruce.

15. Reid, p. 166.

16. Moynihan and Glazer, *op. cit.*

Chapter 9: *The Negro in Civil Service*

1. Interview by the writer with Arnold DeMille, May 1969.

2. Furniss, p. 61.

3. See Chapter III, note 22.

4. *New York Times,* August 30, 1961 and August 7, 1966; "Reminiscences of Samuel J. Battle," Columbia Oral History Project.

5. Clifford H. Goldstein, "History of the Negro in the New York City Fire Department," in "Vulcan Society, Testimonial Dance and Dinner, Twenty-fifth Anniversary, September 29, 1965"; Walter Thomas, "The Integration of the Negro in the New York City Fire Department," unpublished term paper for a course at the City College of New York. Copies of this material were given to the writer by Deputy Fire Commissioner Arthur Williams.

6. Moscow, *op. cit.*

7. Report of Conference on Job Training sponsored by the Associated Transit Guild. Unpublished and lent to the writer by Julian Garfield.

8. Interview by the writer with William Johnson, March 1969; Anna Arnold Hedgman, *The Trumpet Sounds: A Memoir of Negro Leadership* (New York: Holt, Rinehart, and Winston, 1964), p. 120.

9. Interview by the writer with Hillel J. Valentine, February 1969; interview by the writer with Norman Saunders, March 1969; interview by the writer with William J. Hart, March 1969.

10. Goldstein and Thomas, *op. cit.*

11. *New York Times,* August 15 and 17, 1964, October 4, 1966; New York *Post,* February 12 and July 1, 1965; New York *World-Journal-Tribune,* November 6, 1966; Interview by the writer with William Johnson, March 1969.

12. Interview by the writer with Wittie McNeil, March 1969; interview by the writer with William J. Hart, March 1969.

13. Interview by the writer with Ishmael Lahab, March 1969; interview by the writer with Sumner Rosen, April 1969.

14. The relationship of the black community to the New York school system is naturally a constant topic of discussion in the New York papers. The events surrounding the 1968 strike are described in a way favorable to the United Federation of Teachers in Martin Meyer, *Teachers Strike, New York, 1968* (New York: Harper and Row, 1969).

15. Interview by the writer with Police Lieutenant James Francis, March 1969; interview by the writer with Sumner Rosen, March 1969; interview by the writer with Arnold DeMille, May 1969; Report of Conference on Job Training sponsored by the Associated Transit Guild, *op. cit.;* "Civil Service Training Programs," reprint from the report of the Committee on Labor, Civil Service, and Public Pensions of the New York State Constitutional Convention of 1967.

Chapter 10: *The Shape of the Future*

1. August Meier and Elliot Rudwick, *From Plantation to Ghetto* (New York: Hill and Wang, 1966), p.102.
2. *Ibid.,* p. 103.

Selected Bibliography

I   *Manuscripts and Pamphlets*

"Reminiscences of Martin C. Ansorge," Columbia Oral History Project.
Associated Transit Guild. "Report of Conference on Job Training."
"Reminiscences of Samuel J. Battle," Columbia Oral History Project.
John E. Bruce Papers, Schomberg Collection, New York Public Library.
DeWitt Clinton Papers, New York Public Library.
"Reminiscences of Joseph P. Gavagan," Columbia Oral History Project.
Goldstein, Clifford H. "History of the Negro in the New York City Fire Department," in "Vulcan Society, Twenty-fifth Anniversary, September 29, 1965."
Stanley M. Isaacs Papers, New York Public Library.
Theodore Roosevelt Papers, Library of Congress.
Sidney, Joseph. "An Oration Commemorative of the Abolition of the Slave Trade in the United States Delivered before the Wilberforce Philanthropic Association in the City of New York on 29 January, 1809." Schomberg Collection, New York Public Library.
United Colored Democracy. "History of the Tammany Hall United Colored Democracy, Jubilee Program of Exercises Commemorating the Founding of the Tammany Hall United Colored Democracy," June 1923.
Booker T. Washington Papers, Library of Congress.
WPA. "The Negro in New York," Schomberg Collection, New York Public Library.

II. *Personal Interviews*

In preparing this book, the writer has interviewed the following:

Bertram L. Baker	Alan Dingle
Guy Brewer	J. William Duncan
Earl Brown	Mrs. Genevieve Eason
Joseph Brown	Police Lieutenant James Francis
Daniel L. Burrows	Oscar Fulcher
David B. Costuma	Julian Garfield
Collis Crocker	Walter Gladwin
Jean Cropper	Abraham Grenthal
Arnold DeMille	Dr. R. W. Griffin

Ewart Guinier
L. S. Alexander Gumby
William J. Hart
John C. Hawkins
Wesley Holder
Charles Horowitz
Hulan Jack
William Johnson
J. Raymond Jones
Ishmael Lahab
Carl D. Lawrence
Wilfred Lewin
Mrs. Fanny Meirowitz

Oswald C. Newton
Andrew C. Parks
Lloyd Peterson
Andrew M. Robinson
Charles Rochester
Sumner Rosen
Norman Saunders
William Singleton
Edward Stevenson
Oswald Thompson
James C. Thomas
Hillel J. Valentine
Oscar Waters

In addition, the writer has used information from the following interviews held by George Furniss:

Bertram L. Baker
Daniel L. Burrows
Herbert L. Bruce

Francis E. Rivers
Darwin W. Telesford

III Newspapers

Amsterdam News
Boston Post
Brooklyn Eagle
Brooklyn Tablet
Colored American
Christian Science Monitor
Daily Worker
Harlem Home News
New York Age
New York Daily Compass
New York Daily Mirror
New York Daily News
New York Evening Post
New York Freeman
New York Globe

New York Herald
New York Herald-Tribune
New York Journal-American
New York Post
New York Sun
New York Times
New York Tribune
New York World
New York World-Journal-Tribune
New York World-Telegram and Sun
Pease and Elliman's Real Estate Indicator
People's Voice
P.M.
Pittsburgh Courier
Wall Street Journal

IV Unpublished Dissertations

BELL, HOWARD H. "A Survey of the Negro Convention Movement, 1830-1860," Ph.D. dissertation, Northwestern University, 1953.

FURNISS, GEORGE. "The Political Assimilation of Negroes in New York City, 1790-1860," Ph.D. dissertation, Columbia University, 1969.

GROISSIER, FILMORE L. "The Free Negro in New York, 1850-1860," M. A. thesis, Columbia University, 1939.

JOYCE, MARY M. "History of the Suffrage in New York to 1821," M.A. thesis, Columbia University, 1914.

MARLOW, NICHOLAS. "Bedford-Stuyvesant Place Names," M.A. thesis, Brooklyn College, 1963.

MORSELL, JOHN A. "The Political Behavior of Negroes in New York City," Ph.D. dissertation, Columbia University, 1951.

WILLIAMS, BERNICE C. "The Negro in Politics in New York, 1777-1900," M.A. thesis, New York University, 1937.

V *Periodicals*

"Adam Cast Out," *Newsweek*, LXIX (January 23, 1967), p. 28.

"Adam's Fall," *Newsweek*, LXVIII (October 3, 1966), p. 29.

BERRY, ABNER W. "All-American Councilman," *New Masses*, LVII (October 9, 1945), p. 4.

BOOKER, SIMEON. "Adam Clayton Powell, the Man Behind the Controversy," *Ebony*, XXII (March 1967), p. 227.

BRESLIN, JIMMY. "Plantation Days in South Jamaica," *New York*, IV (February 8, 1971), p. 6.

DOMINGO, W. A. "The West Indies," *Opportunity*, IV (October 1926), p. 141.

FISHEL, LESLIE H. "Northern Prejudice and Negro Suffrage, 1865-1870," *Journal of Negro History*, XXXIX (January 1954), p. 13.

—————. "The Negro in Northern Politics," 1870-1900, *Mississippi Valley Historical Review*, XLII (December 1955), p. 487.

FOX, DIXON RYAN. "The Negro Vote in Old New York," *American Political Science Quarterly*, XXXII (June 1917), p. 255.

—————. "Harlem Home-Coming," *Time*, LIV (November 14, 1949), p. 26.

HIRSCH, LEO H., JR. "The Negro and New York, 1783-1835," *Journal of Negro History*, XVI (October 1931), p. 386.

KEMPTON, MURRAY. "Adam Powell, the Ocelot of the House of Representatives," *New Republic*, XIV (May 25, 1963), p. 10.

LEVY, EDGAR J. "An Election in New York," *North American Review*, CXLV (December 1887), p. 681.

LINDSAY, ARNETT G. "The Economic Conditions of Negroes in New York City Prior to 1861," *Journal of Negro History*, VI (April 1921), p. 190.

Nation, V (October 1867), p. 247.

PAYNE, AARON HAMLETT. "The Negro in New York Prior to 1861," *Howard Review*, I (June 1923), p. 13.

PEARSON, DREW, and RITTER, N. "Dark Enigma of Congress," *Saturday Evening Post*, CCXXXVII (March 28, 1964), p. 75.

RIDDELL, WILLIAM RENWICK. "The Slave in Early New York," *Journal of Negro History*, XIII (January 1928), p. 53.

WALTON, LESTER A. "The Negro in Politics," *Outlook*, LXXXVII (July 23, 1924), p. 472.

WAKEFIELD, DAN. "Adam Clayton Powell, Jr., the Angry Voice of Harlem," *Esquire*, LII (November 1959), p. 119.

WESLEY, CHARLES H. "Negro Suffrage in the Period of Constitution-making," *Journal of Negro History*, XXXII (April 1947), p. 43.

————. "The Negroes of New York and the Emancipation Movement," *Journal of Negro History*, XXIII (April 1938), p. 155.

WHITE, THEODORE H. "Perspective 1960," *Saturday Review*, XLIII (March 14, 1960), p. 4.

VI *Books*

APTHEKER, HERBERT. *A Documentary History of the Negro People of the United States*, two volumes, New York, Citadel Press, 1951.

BAILEY, HARRY A., JR., ed. *Negro Politics in America*, Columbus, Ohio, Merrill Books, 1967.

BURNS, SIR ALAN. *A History of the British West Indies*, London, George Allen and Unwin Ltd., 1954.

CLARK, KENNETH. *Dark Ghetto*, New York, Harper & Row, 1965.

COSTIKYAN, EDWARD I. *Behind Closed Doors; Politics in the Public Interest*, New York, Harcourt, Brace & World, 1966.

FLYNN, EDWARD J. *You're the Boss*, Clifton, N. J., Augustus M. Kelley, 1954.

GIBSON, FLORENCE E. *The Attitude of the New York Irish toward State and National Affairs, 1848-1892*, New York, Columbia University Press, 1951.

HEDGMAN, ANNA ARNOLD. *The Trumpet Sounds: A Memoir of Negro Leadership*, New York, Holt, Rinehart, and Winston, 1964.

HICKEY, NEAL and EDWIN, Ed. *Adam Clayton Powell and the Politics of Race*, New York, Fleet Publishing Co., 1965.

Institute of Urban Studies of Fordham University, *A Profile of the Bronx Economy*, New York, 1967.

JOHNSON, JAMES WELDON. *Along This Way*, New York, Viking Press, 1933.

————. *Black Manhattan*, New York, Alfred A. Knopf, Inc., 1930.

LINCOLN, C. Z. *The Constitutional History of New York from the Beginning of the Colonial Period to 1905*, five volumes, Lawyers Co-operative Publishing Co., 1905-1906.

LITWAK, LEON. *North of Slavery, the Negro in the Free States, 1790-1860*, Chicago, University of Chicago Press, 1961.

McKAY, CLAUDE. *Harlem—Negro Metropolis*, New York, E. P. Dutton and Co., 1940.

McMANUS, EDGAR J. *A History of Negro Slavery in New York*, Syracuse, Syracuse University Press, 1966.

MEYER, MARTIN. *Teachers Strike: New York, 1968*, New York, Harper & Row, 1969.

MOON, HENRY LEE. *Balance of Power—the Negro Vote*, Garden City, N. Y., Doubleday, 1948.

MORRISON, ELTING. *The Letters of Theodore Roosevelt*, Cambridge, Harvard University Press, 1951-1954.

MOSCOW, WARREN. *What Have You Done for Me Lately?* Englewood Cliffs, N. J., Prentice-Hall, 1968.

MOYNIHAN, DANIEL P. and GLAZER, NATHAN. *Beyond the Melting Pot, the Negroes, Puerto Ricans, Jews, Italians, and Irish of New York City*, Cambridge, MIT and Harvard University Press, 1964.

NEVINS, ALAN. *Herbert Lehmann and His Era*, New York, Charles Scribner's Sons, 1963.

OLBRICH, EMIL. *The Development of Sentiment on Negro Suffrage to 1860*, Madison, University of Wisconsin Press, 1912-1914.

OSOFSKY, GILBERT. *Harlem, the Making of a Ghetto*, New York, Harper & Row, 1963.

OTTLEY, ROI. *New World A-Comin*, Boston, Houghton Mifflin Co., 1944.

––––––, and WEATHERBY, WILLIAM, eds. *The Negro in New York*, New York, New York Public Library, 1967.

OVINGTON, MARY WHITE. *Half a Man*, New York, Longman's, Green, and Co., 1911.

POWELL, ADAM CLAYTON, SR. *Against the Tide*, New York, R. R. Smith, 1938.

POWELL, ADAM CLAYTON, JR. *Marching Blacks*, New York, Dial Press, 1945.

––––––. *Adam by Adam: The Autobiography of Adam Clayton Powell*, New York, Dial Press, 1971.

QUARLES, BENJAMIN. *Frederick Douglass*, Washington, Associated Publishers, 1948.

REID, IRA D. A. *The Negro Immigrants*, New York, Columbia University Press, 1939.

SCHEINER, SETH. *Negro Mecca, a History of the Negro in New York, 1865-1920*, New York, New York University Press, 1965.

SHERLOCK, PHILIP M. *The West Indies*, London, Thames and Hudson, 1966.

SMITH, MICHAEL G. *The Plural Society in the British West Indies*, Cambridge, England, and Berkeley, California, Cambridge University Press and the University of California Press, 1965.

WELD, RALPH FOSTER. *Brooklyn Is America*, New York, Columbia University Press, 1950.

WILLIAMS, ERIC. *The Negro in the Caribbean*, Washington, Associated Publishers, 1942.

WILSON, JAMES Q. *Negro Politics and the Search for Leadership*, Glencoe, Free Press of Glencoe, 1960.

WITTKE, CARL. *The Irish in America*. Baton Rouge, Louisiana State University Press, 1956.

Index

227